YACHT DESIGNS

YACHT DESIGNS

by WILLIAM GARDEN

International Marine Publishing Company
Camden, Maine

CONTENTS

PREFACE

Once upon a time before the term exponential growth was coined and before the miracle of the production of fiberglass yachts was made practical by our runaway market for luxuries, there weren't so many small yachts afloat and, of those on the waters, all seemed to be of varied form and rig. This was probably the result of nearly total confusion regarding optimum proportions for efficiency in going up wind or down, but the boats then seemed much more interesting than today's vast fleets of triangular me-toos.

To be sure, for the pile of material involved, today's small stock yachts afford more comfort and greater all-around ability under sail than the fleets of the past did. But they are uninspiring fare to many boatmen, while the versatile fore triangle with its half dozen headsail choices lacks appeal. So the aesthetic interest of the so-called "character" or period boat continues to attract many. "Caricature" boat unfortunately typifies many, but the reasonably well proportioned ones that we see afloat appear to give their owners a real escape. This book of boats seems to lean toward these varied boat types, rather than those boats that reach their ultimate efficiency only when they are sailed under one or another of the current racing rules.

Today's normal stock boat is usually a good, practical, off-the-shelf item and can be seen by the thousands in every marina and boat show and on the pages of boating periodicals. With many of the sailing yachts described herein, we are concerned with what would seem to be impractical sailing boats when scrutinized by an around-the-buoys sailor. The boats in this book have more of a connection with tradition, or perhaps have more boat-like qualities, which are qualities that satisfy the interests of those sailors who not only enjoy a boat that will sail well but also lean toward boats of a more interesting, timeless form. Several of the boats outlined in our pages are of this more traditional shape or theme and some are more contemporary. Of the powerboats shown, there is a variation of types from heavy commercial boats to modern — by today's measure — motor cruisers. Visually, the modern motor cruisers will age more rapidly than the more traditional power and sailing boats. These latter seem to be of a lasting form, a form that is buoyed up perhaps by the more tangible historical or period appeal. But every type has its following and the more we know about each the broader our general understanding and outlook becomes.

The chapters accompanying each design have been compiled as time has allowed, so there has been no particular attempt at continuity other than to select boats that might be of interest to the cruising boatman. The text centers more on the background of each boat rather than on a technical study; the latter I feel would be of interest mainly to the technician, so illustrations and generalities prevail.

Whether they are sail or power, we must remember that our yachts are toy boats — all yachts are the glint on a lovely brief bubble of time, a time of leisure and affluence for the middle class. A boat's importance as an escape from reality, as a change of pace, as a theme for reflection, and as an art form gives it worth or value. In forming a small yacht, we achieve an entity that is almost completely within the imagination, manual dexterity, and technical ability of one man. One man can select and cut the timber, form the model, set up the molds, frame, plank, work up the spars, and finally slide her into the sea and set sail. Perhaps this is about as close as one man can come to the nearly complete creation of something with a personality and life.

Should any particular boat in this book catch your fancy, a plans list indicating scale of drawings, number of sheets per boat, and cost is available by writing the author at Box 2395, Sidney, British Columbia, Canada. You won't need study plans, since the boats are well outlined in this book. Should you write, let the letter rest on your desk for a week before mailing it to see if the mood doesn't pass. If it does, you will save me a stamp and a reply. Correspondence is probably the life blood, but often the bane, of the poor old boat designer's existence. Each day's mail brings in some notes from people wanting to build, buy, cruise, or just talk about boats. Along with the good letters are some that just waste stamps in answering, such as requests for ferro-cement catamarans.

For about 30 years, I've replied to each letter as a courtesy, but finally I gave up due to the lack of a staff and time. Now I only reply to those people who need information or help. I've noticed that in the years since the new policy went into effect that none of those jettisoned repeat their request. Over the years, about six million dollars in stamps, give or take a few million, have gone down the drain. And the poor old postman, the steps he has wasted.

Only last week I had a nice letter from a man who seemed to be all fired up to build a 40-foot cruising ketch in his backyard, and today another letter from him wanting the plans for a 50-foot steamboat to build simultaneously. I almost answered number one. Thank God for small mercies. On the other hand, yesterday a nice letter came in from New Zealand outlining the cruising travels of a little Spice Island cutter, which tips the balance and makes it all worthwhile:

> Russell
> New Zealand
> January 14, 1975
> Cutter *Puffin*

Here we are 8,000 miles later resting and working for more cruising money in good old New Zealand.

We took a thrashing during the last 1,000 miles between here and Kandavu. 50 knots, 25-foot seas and the *Puffin* came through like a little veteran. We took some damage, broken bobstay (electrolysis in the bolts) but got her to safety anyway. I have since replaced bolts with type 316 S.S. 3/8" stock and I'm now carrying spare bolts.

I wish the previous owner had not converted to marconi main, many miles of light going were more suitable for the large gaff main and topsail. Maybe I'll change her back when we get to the Northwest. We still managed four knots average for the entire trip. This seems to be right up there with the big cruising yachts. Everyone does around 100 n.m. per day.

Our route has been as follows: San Diego through Mexico, Puerto Vallarta to Nuku Hiva Marquesas, 28 days: Nuku Hiva to Ahe Tuamotus 465 n.m. 3½ days, Ahe to Papeete, Tahiti — Papeete through Moorea, Huahine, Riataa, Tahaa, Bora Bora, Roratonga, Nive, Tonga Vavou group, Fiji and Kandavu group then New Zealand. Next April who knows.

> Sincerely,
> G. Taylor

I'll leave you to go through the plans, and I hope that they will give you some measure of the interest and enjoyment that I've had in their development.

William Garden
Toad's Landing

YACHT DESIGNS

Part One

SAILBOATS

1 *Eel*, a Canoe Yawl

LOA — 18' 6"
LWL — 14' 10"
Beam — 6' 0"
Draft — 10"
Sail Area — 201 square feet
Displacement — 1,000 pounds nominal

The term "canoe yawl" evokes a nostalgia in many of us who were brought up on what were, then, not-so-long-ago accounts of some happy do-or-die Englishman working up an improbable ditch or estuary in his little canoe-turned-cruiser, only to be eventually enmeshed in an enormous brush pile at the headwaters or camped out on a sand bank awaiting the tide. Albert Strange seemed to be one of the principals in the gradual development of these craft from the sailing canoe or original canoe, rigged out for cruising, through the canoe-yacht stage, to the eventual canoe-sterned cruising yacht. We remember him mainly for his small cruising yacht designs and for his wonderful paintings of small yacht cruising.

By the late 1890s the British canoe yawls were listed as light displacement yawls, medium displacement yawls, and canoe yachts—the latter having the proportions of today's small sailing yacht. George F. Holmes was another developer and canoe yawl fancier and was referred to in the 1890s as the father of the canoe yawl to that stage of development. His canoe yawl *Eel* is illustrated in Uffa Fox's *Sailing, Seamanship and Yacht Construction*.

One of the best known voyages in the original tiny ships was made by John MacGregor, who wrote of his travels in *A Thousand Miles in the Rob Roy Canoe, Rob Roy on the Baltic,* and *The Voyage Alone in the Yawl Rob Roy.* Terrors of the sea were interspersed with runaway dray horses on land. One wonderful illustration shows his canoe flying through the air in the wake of a galloping horse and a smashed cart, an example of the perils of cruising. MacGregor seemed to think nothing of lighting his cigar from a low lighthouse tower or using the lighthouse lamp for warmth and a reading light. My copy of 1867 has a text full of interesting adventures and some wonderful illustrations.

The *Rob Roy* meandered for hours up one canal or another into out-of-the-way places where never a foreigner was seen. "Sometimes I went into tunnels—but of course without any notion of where they might lead to; and so there suddenly appeared in some lonely but busy farmyard an Englishman in a canoe, grey as to his dress, and beaming with smiles."

Much data can be found in way-back issues of the boating publications, which show an oc-

1

This painting by Albert Strange evokes the mood of canoe-yawl cruising.

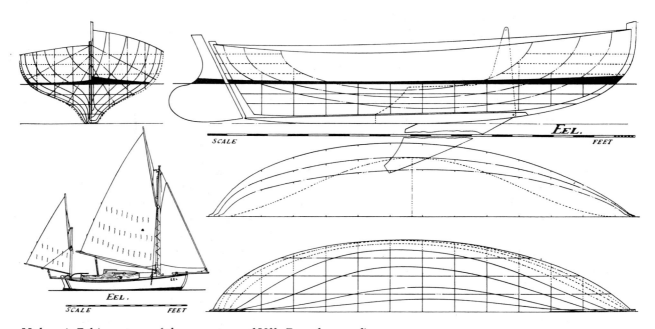

Holmes's *Eel* (courtesy of the executors of Uffa Fox, deceased).

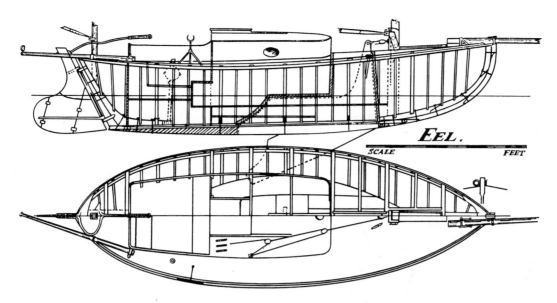

Holmes's *Eel* (courtesy of the executors of Uffa Fox, deceased).

casional canoe yawl yacht. The Humber Yawl Club in England published a wonderful year-book including plans of these cruisers many years ago. The most recent well known model is L. Francis Herreshoff's little *Rozinante*, a keel version of the type that is related to the original canoe yawls mainly in the long, slim form and title.

Eel I have named after Holmes's boat—a good name for a little ship designed for wriggling up the most tortuous backwater or breasting the open sea. Basically, our new *Eel* is, by today's standards, a big, powerful dinghy with a divided rig and 400 pounds of inside ballast in bags, which may be heaved ashore when beaching or when loading the boat on a trailer for transport to another water. The rig is closely traditional for the type but without the fully battened sails of the original canoes.

The time-honored gunter rig, which is shown, combines short spars—all fitting in the boat—with an efficient hoist-foot ratio. The jib-headed mizzen will make a neat little tent, balance the rig, and give her the appeal of a two-sticker. My first proper yacht was rigged in a similar manner to this one. The boat was a 12-foot lapstrake skiff that my dad helped me con-vert. The mainsail, which cost seven dollars, was financed by Grandmother's money, home

money being non-existent in 1931. The sail was beautifully made of boatsail drill with fragrant tarred hemp boltropes by the elder George Broom's Sail Loft. The transaction was made across Broom's broad, blue serge vest and gold, stud-link watch chain, which to my eyes looked about right for my yawl's anchor.

PHAROS MINOR.

John MacGregor lighting his cigar from a lighthouse flame.

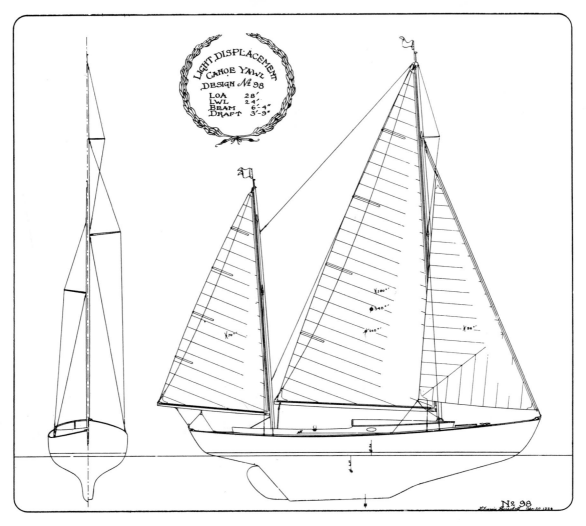

The canoe yawl *Rozinante*, designed by L. Francis Herreshoff (from *Sensible Cruising Designs*, International Marine Publishing Company, Camden, Maine).

Basic carvel construction is shown for the *Eel*, with 5/8-inch planking over bent oak frames. She will also adapt to strip or cold-molded techniques to suit your particular aptitude. Build her upside down on low horses set to the sheer sweep. The sheer harpin should be laid out on the floor, allowing for the greater length to be measured along the sweep of the sheer. Fabricate this harpin and deck structure, then lay it upside down on the horses, fit the deck beams, and set up the molds on 24-inch centers as shown.

Take reasonable care in sawing out the molds, but a few plane strokes and a fairing batten will true up any minor bumps prior to bend-

ing the ribbands. I usually fair any apparent bumps when I lay out the body plan and give it a final go-over when the boat is ribbanded off. Molds here can be made from shiplap or any rough lumber of about 3/4-inch thickness. In the case of strip building, I would retain the number of molds to ensure the boat's form, but strips can be 3/4-inch by 1-inch edge nailed, frames can be deleted, and a layer of fiberglass mat and cloth can be used as an overlay. If she is cold molded, a skin of three layers of 3/16-inch planks will do the job, and half a dozen ribbands can stay in as longitudinals.

Construction is on the rugged side for such a small boat, but the rather substantial members

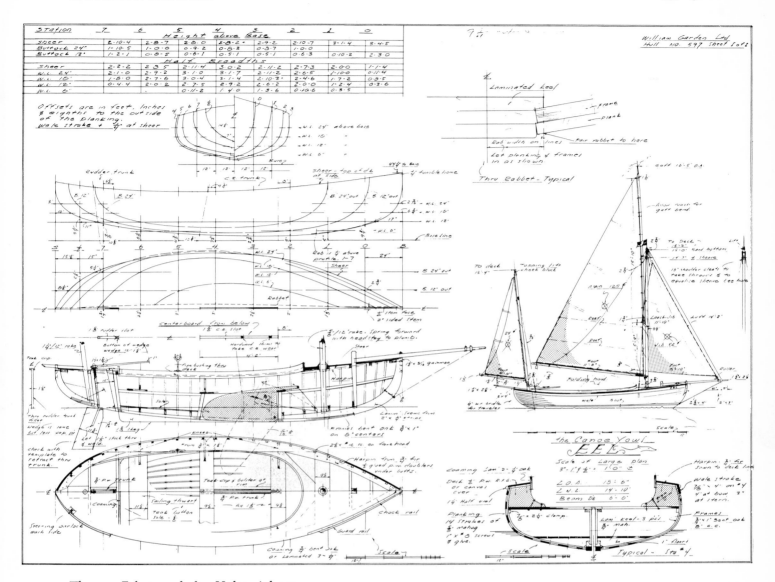

The new *Eel*, named after Holmes's boat.

simplify fastening and seem to go together with less trouble.

For sleeping on board, a few battens can be placed on the thwarts to form a base for sleeping bags. The canvas hood will provide adequate shelter, and, with primus stove, some water bottles, and spartan stores, she will be an interesting minimum cruiser.

The anchor could be about 15 pounds, on a 20-fathom, 7/16-inch diameter rode to double as a towline. Oars 8 feet long or thereabouts will be about right. Standing up facing forward will be the best rowing position, and one of the oars will do for steering when sailing in very shoal water. Fit chocks port and starboard along the side decks so the oars can be stowed out of the way, and she's ready to sail.

Color? I would paint her a soft gray, with a white boot, a red copper bottom, and varnished guards. She should have sand-beige decks and sails a good red or deep tanbark, if the cloth is available.

2 *Diane*, a Tabloid Cruiser

LOA — 18′ 7″
LOA (fiddlehead) — 20′ 0″
LWL — 15′ 0″
Beam — 6′ 10″
Draft — 3′ 3″
Ballast — 1,400 pounds
Displacement — 4,000 pounds
Sail Area — 290 square feet, 3 lowers

Diane, as she is to be called, is being built by my good friend Arthur Barnes, a boatbuilder who lost his sight and right arm in a dynamite cap explosion at the age of twelve. During the last twenty years, since moving back to the Coast, he has turned out an impressive amount of machine woodwork utilizing jigs and self-designed artificial limb attachments as required to maintain a point of reference. With time and patience he seems able to accomplish nearly any precision job. A daytime visit to his shop is impressive, but the true measure of the difficulty of his task got to me one night when I went into the blacked-out shop. As I turned to go out, thinking no one was there, he hailed me from where he was working—in the dark, under the boat.

Art is a natural craftsman with an intuitive feel for form and structure. He and I designed *Diane* with cardboard. We began with a cardboard section model to 3/4-inch scale. A deck plan was cut out in cardboard to the shape that he had in mind, next a midship mold was done, then a waterline shape. Each shape was first roughed out with scissors, then trimmed and faired. Art was a demanding client, with definite ideas of the boat in his imagination. With a minimum of suggestion on my part, we ended up with a little ballasted yacht of general Friendship sloop model. The length was dictated by the backyard shop available, and the other proportions suit a minimum cruiser. Construction is underway and gradually progressing. She will be a nice little sloop for day sailing, and what a boat she'll be for a couple of boys, even old boys who want a rugged day-sailer with the feeling, when underway, of a proper sailing vessel.

The waterline length of 15 feet encompasses a full-bodied hull form of 4,000 pounds displacement, with about 35 percent of the weight in ballast. Nine hundred pounds of lead will go in the keel and about 500 pounds will be fitted inside, amidships.

The length on deck from the transom to the rabbet is 18 feet 7 inches, the length to the fiddlehead is 20 feet 0 inches, and the maximum breadth outside the tumblehome is 6 feet 10 in-

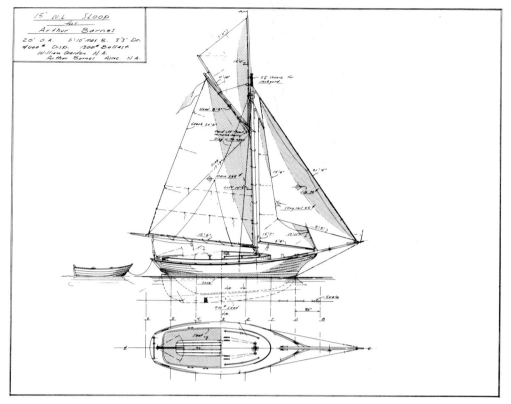

15' W.L. SLOOP
for
Arthur Barnes

20' O.A.   6'10" max B.   3'3" Dr.
4000# Disp.   1300# Ballast
William Garden N.A.
Arthur Barnes Assoc. N.A.

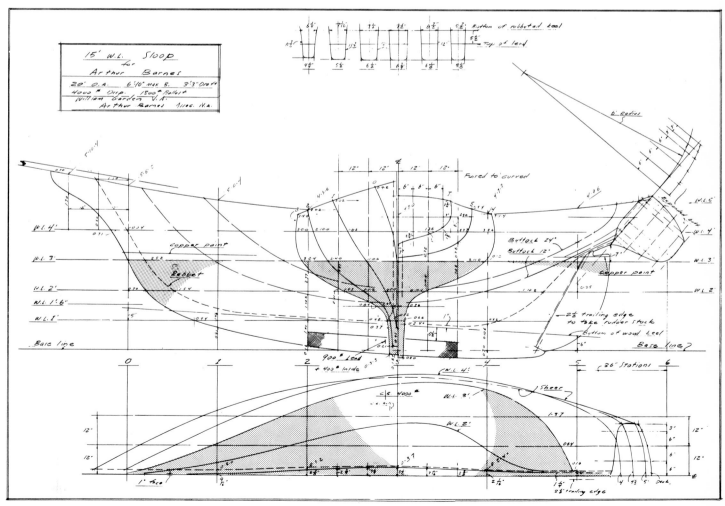

15' W.L. SLOOP
for
Arthur Barnes

20' O.A.   6'10" max B.   3'3" Draft
4000# Disp.   1300# Ballast
William Garden N.A.
Arthur Barnes Assoc. N.A.

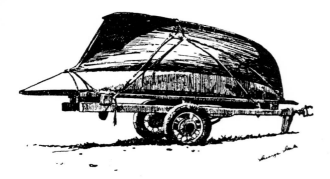

W. P. Stephens's little cutter *Snarleyow* (from the *First Book of Boats*, edited by William and John Atkin).

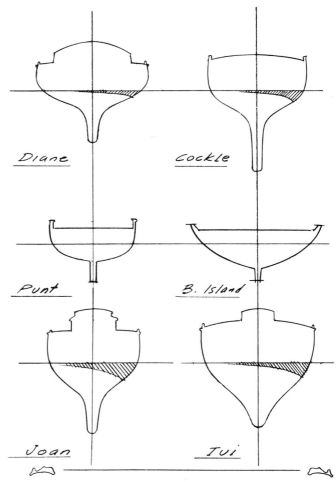

A comparison of the midsections of the boats discussed in this chapter.

ches. The draft with a couple of men aboard, and the anchor, water keg, sweeps, warps, and stores will be 3 feet 3 inches, making her a handy boat for areas requiring moderate draft.

These true tabloid cruisers have always had the charm of a good model boat, and, for a pleasant evening of browsing, I can't think of anything better than a dig through the old files and a study of the smallest possible ships.

At one time some of the major yachts carried miniature sailing boats on the davits for day sailing. We can find in the December, 1942, issue of *Yachting* an account by W. P. Stephens of his little cutter *Snarleyow*, built as a duplicate of one of these davit boats. Her length is 14 feet 10 inches and her draft is 3 feet with 900 pounds of bagged shot ballast, all inboard. The displacement of such a small ship would be close to 2,000 pounds. A one-ton dinghy!

Another one that has always interested me is *Cockle*, designed by J. R. Purdon around the turn of the century and rigged the same as a large cutter—3 headsails and a jackyard topsail—with all the gear and interest of her full-size counterpart. *Cockle* hailed from Marblehead, and she must have delighted the boys who had her in their care. She is about *Diane's* waterline length, but *Cockle* gains her sail-carrying power from ballast and draft, while *Diane* gains hers from both ballast and form stability or breadth.

Cockle's overall length is 18 feet 9 inches, waterline length 15 feet 11 inches, breadth 6 feet 3 inches, and draft is 5 feet 1 inch. Her ballast is 2,850 pounds of lead, all outside, and her displacement is 5,470 pounds. The structural weight of *Cockle* and *Diane* is only 20 pounds apart, with the ballast requirements varying due to breadth. *Diane* has 3,600 pounds of structure and 1,400 pounds of lead, and *Cockle* has 3,620 pounds of structure plus 2,850 pounds of lead for a ballast-displacement ratio of 52 percent. For a deep little boat, the *Cockle* is beautifully formed. Purdon had an eye for a boat.

Billy Atkin's delightful little *Joan* described as "18 shipshape feet" is another classic. She is described in Motor Boating Ideal Series Volume 15 as a "How-to-Build", and one of her model was once sailing on Puget Sound under a friend's house flag. *Joan* is just 18 feet 2 inches overall, 17 feet on the waterline, 5 feet 0 inches of breadth, 4 feet 4 inches of draft when light, and about 4 feet 7 inches when loaded and in sea trim. Her displacement is 6,200 pounds, with

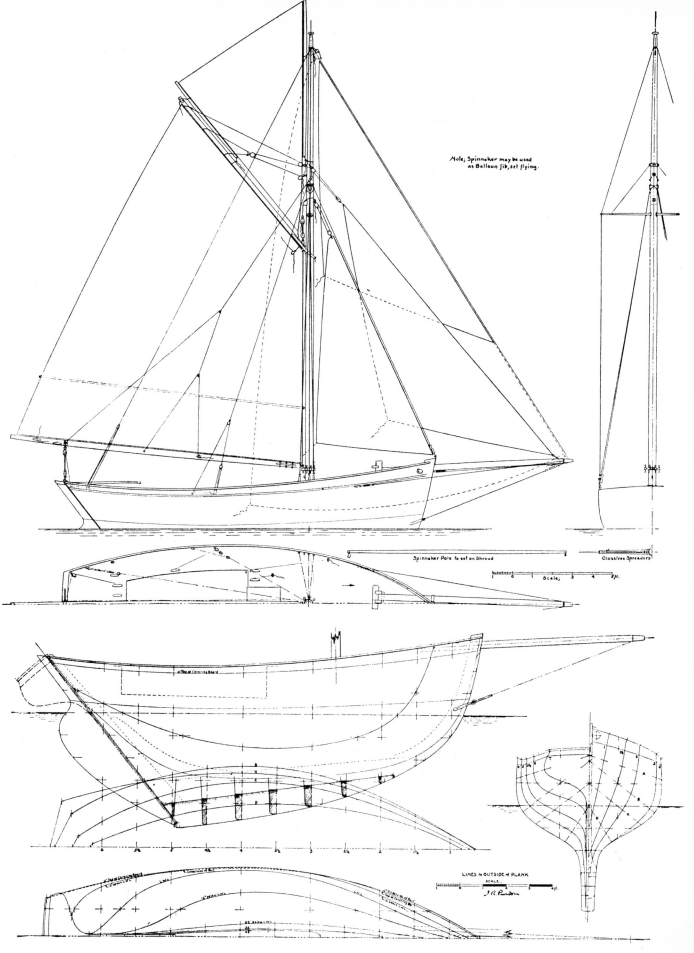

Note; Spinnaker may be used as Balloon Jib, set flying.

Spinnaker Pole to set on Shroud

Crosstree Spreaders

Scale;

LINES to OUTSIDE of PLANK
SCALE.

J. R. Purdon

The cutter *Cockle*, designed by J. R. Purdon.

2,600 pounds of ballast: 2,100 pounds in an iron casting and 500 pounds inside. With a three-foot bowsprit to supplement the knockabout rig, she is an excellent sailer. And what a nice little cabin to sit around in. One reach fore or aft in a cabin this size and you can have anything without moving. She has the smallest possible stove, the smallest possible engine, and a big measure of fun.

A little ship that I wanted desperately to build as a boy was the sloop *Tui*, a sturdy flush-decked three-and-a-half ton sloop designed by H. C. Smith of Burnham-on-Crouch. The old, faded, dog-eared article describing her, from an issue of *Fore and Aft*, outlines her dimensions as 17 feet 9 inches waterline, 20 foot length overall, 6 foot 9 inch breadth and 4 foot 0 inch draft. She has a nicely faired underbody and a displacement I would estimate at close to 8,000 pounds, with perhaps 3,500 pounds of this in ballast. Her breadth here is close to a practical proportion, for all little ships should have good beam to be useable.

One more I'll unfold is an Itchen punt, one of a class of 13 foot length overall sailing cutters of the 1880s sailed mainly, we are told in the 1884 edition of the *Manual of Yacht and Boat Sailing* by Dixon Kemp, by watermen such as

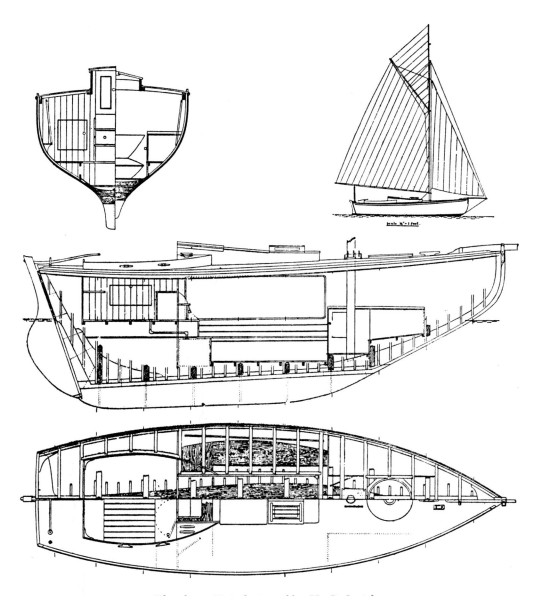

The sloop *Tui*, designed by H. C. Smith.

foremen at various shipbuilding yards, ship-wrights, and masters of yachts. The example noted is 13 feet overall, 13 feet on the waterline, 5 feet of breadth, and 2 feet 6 inches depth of hull. She draws two feet of water when in sailing trim with about 600 pounds of lead ballast outboard. She is a full-bodied little ship with a wineglass transom, plumb ends, outboard rudder, a bowsprit and boom 6 feet 3 inches and 5 feet outboard respectively, and lots of sail—the only way to make a fat little boat go.

But enough about tabloid cruisers of the past, and back to *Diane*.

Diane's rig is similar to that of a Friendship sloop, and, although two head sails on such a little packet is overdoing things, it is what Art had in mind and nothing else would do. The simple sloop rig—jib and mainsail—of one of the Friendship sloops in Phil Bolger's book, *Small Boats* (International Marine Publishing Co., Camden, Maine), would be my own choice for a sail plan.

The deck layout indicates a solution to accommodations, but, with Art's boat, we'll sit around on some boxes and, with battens and a few clamps, tailor a cabin to suit his ideas.

For the serious builder who has the room and funds, I would recommend a larger hull requiring a moderate increase in building hours and perhaps resulting in a more useful boat, but for the smallest-boat diehard, the sloop *Diane* is an interesting project.

For Art Barnes, without a dream, lots of drive, and a wonderful imagination, it would be a long night.

3 *Jelly Bean*, another Tabloid Cruiser

LOA — 21′ 6″
LWL — 19′ 6″
Beam — 8′ 8″
Draft — 4′ 6″
Displacement — 4,950 pounds
Ballast — 2,000 pounds
Sail Area — 291 square feet, 100 percent fore triangle

Jelly Bean is a prototype glass boat designed around the theme of the most boat for a given length, an approach that perhaps makes sense mainly if a boat were to be kept in a box or if there is an absolute length limit overall. For those who want the most in a short length, she is an interesting study.

The displacement here is 4,950 pounds, with 2,000 pounds of this in the cast iron fin. The length on deck is 21 feet 6 inches, the length on the waterline is 19 feet 6 inches, the breadth is 8 feet 2 inches on the deck and 8 feet 8 inches at the knuckle, and the draft is 4 feet 6 inches. The dimensions give a lot of room for the waterline length, with a pilothouse of 6 feet 6 inches headroom and a flush deck with 5 feet 2 inches headroom under. Twenty five years ago it would have been thought impossible to push this sort of freeboard to windward, however the flat-floored, beamy, stable hull combined with an efficient fin keel balances off the extra-tall, powerful rig for excellent performance and, due to the deck height above the water, banishes forever the "wet seat of the pants" associated with low freeboard.

Each year we seem to be getting one jump closer to boats designed by an electronic synthesizer, but the eye grows accustomed in time, and, assuming continued development, *Jelly Bean* will probably look shippy 20 years hence.

Power is by outboard in a starboard-side well; boarding flats will help the swimmer or provide general access, plus form a dinghy support. The cockpit affords good lounging space, with locker seats port and starboard for sails or gear.

The layout, with four berths, galley, and enclosed head, is a straightforward use of space. A folding table over each berth will keep the passage clear and still allow two on a side to eat in comfort. The toilet room is minimum but affords the privacy so important in a congested

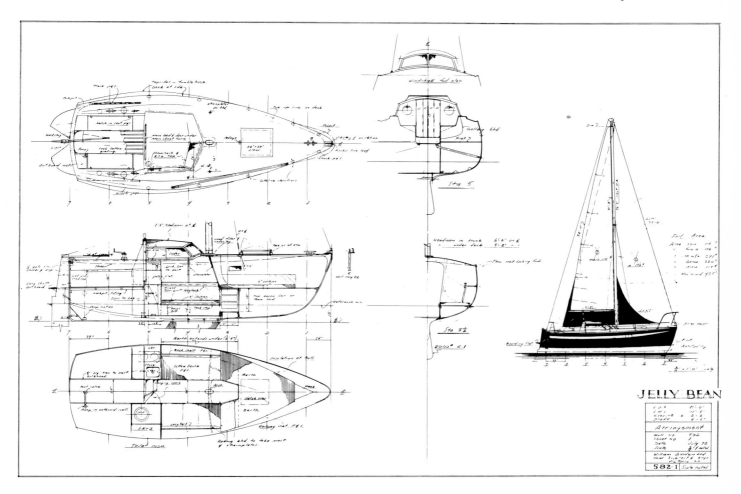

space. Forward are a pair of good berths with an access and ventilating hatch over.

The rig was designed to get the maximum sail-area-to-wetted-surface ratio and was intended to suit the light-air summer conditions of the Northwest. An intermediate headstay is fitted to support the mast at midpoint, rather than the usual forward lowers. The mainsail is a long, narrow slat requiring a vang, but it is a simple sail to set and handle.

"Tabloid cruiser" was once the designation for a little sloop of this sort—the most in the least for the man who has a 22 foot berth to tie up in and wants a small, practical cruiser.

4 *James W. Hart*, a Catboat

LOA — 23' 0"
LWL — 20' 9"
Beam — 10' 0"
Draft — 2' 3", board up
Displacement — 6,000 pounds
Ballast — 1,400 pounds
Sail Area — 420 square feet

"I've always liked the looks of a real cat on the water. They look so buoyant and able and hard to lick." Hiram Maxim wrote this about *Black Duck* in a story on catboats published in *Yachting* a long time ago. Jim Hart, a departed friend and a great cat fancier, once quoted it with a glassy stare, and we had a good laugh about how the early inoculation had taken. So this little cat is the *James W.* (for Whitney) *Hart*, 23 feet overall, 20 feet 9 inches on the waterline, 10 feet of breadth, and 2 feet 3 inches draft with board up. She differs from today's classic cats mainly in the old-time extended counter stern with tucked-under rudder.

Construction is straightforward, carvel or strip, as you choose. The backbone differs from that of a classic cat in that it is the same width from stem to stern, in this case 5 1/2 inches. The centerboard is on the port side of the keel and swings down through a slot in the garboard. The trunk rests on a heavy bed-log alongside the keel. This off-center board suits a cabin layout and minimizes the chance of a rock being jammed in the slot when the bottom hammers on a gravel beach. The big shoal-draft coasters used a similar board arrangement in past years. I

once built myself a small schooner this way with no noticeable difference in performance on the port or starboard tack, and I presently have a big, husky 14 foot sailing dinghy with the board alongside the keel. In fact, if the wind had come up this afternoon, I would be describing the *James W. Hart* on another afternoon.

So, shipmates, this is how I would set up a little cat. But before you start chopping, I would get *The Catboat Book* from International Marine Publishing Company for lots more lore and a bibliography of digging for the purist. Some dandy cats are illustrated, one of which might be closer to what you need. [All these plugs for our books are genuine, unsolicited testimonials. Honest. —Editor]

If you build the *J.W.H.*, keep the big rig to assure good performance, but fit foot ropes to tend the outhaul or the reef earings. With simple slab reefing on modern sail cloth, she can be easily shortened down as the wind makes up. The rig is the maximum size for the hull, so in the lightest airs she'll gurgle along at a delightful rate. As it breezes up, you will have to take in a tuck to match the conditions in order to keep her on her sailing lines and moving. Properly

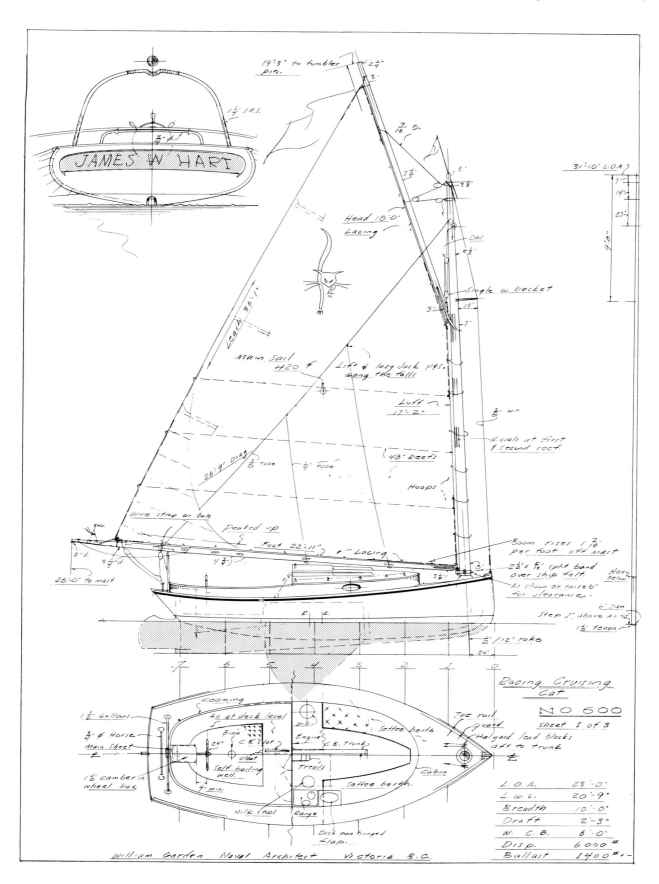

JAMES W HART

19'3" to tumbler pin.

Head 18'0
Lacing

Main sail 420 #   Lift & lazy Jack pts.
Gang the falls

Luff
17'-2"

48' Reefs

Hoops

Leach 36'-1

26:9' Diag   ⅜' rope   ½' rope

Wire strap or bale

Peaked up

Foot 22'11"   Lacing

Boom rises 1 ⁷⁄₁₆
per foot off mast

2½"x⅝" split band
over ship felt.
As shown or raise 6"
for clearance.

26-0" to mast

±/12" rake

Single w. becket

H. ovals at first
& second reef.

Racing Cruising
Cat

NO 600
sheet I of 3

Toe rail
guard
Halyard lead blocks
aft to trunk

Coaming
All at deck level
1½ Gallows
Binn
¾" ⌀ Horse
Main Sheet
1½ camber in
wheel box
milk stool   Range
Dish pan hinged
flap.
Settee berth
Engine   C.B. Trunk
Self bailing
well.
Settee berth.
Cabin
Treads

William Garden Naval Architect Victoria B.C.

L.O.A.	23'-0"
L.W.L.	20'-9"
Breadth	10'-0"
Draft	2'-3"
W. C.B.	6'-0"
Disp.	6000 #
Ballast	1400 #

handled and in average conditions, the *J.W.H.* will knock the spots off almost anything of her waterline length, but, for the jib-and-mainsail sailor, she'll take some getting used to.

Remember your topping lifts and that big main will be a joy forever.

Balance should be about right. The boom is long but the board is well aft to counteract it. The forefoot is slightly deeper than that of many cats, and it is compensated for by a strong keel drag with perhaps 20 percent more draft at the

heel than a really shoal draft cat. The drag will help the helm and give the rudder slightly more bite in ding-dong conditions while reaching and running.

On deck the trunk and general appearance are traditional, with a nicely rounded house and cockpit, a heavily cambered cabin top, and cat-eye ports. A little cat like this is a one-portlight-per-side size; two would be an affectation, and, at today's costs those shown will suffice. A sash is worked into the after bulkhead for additional

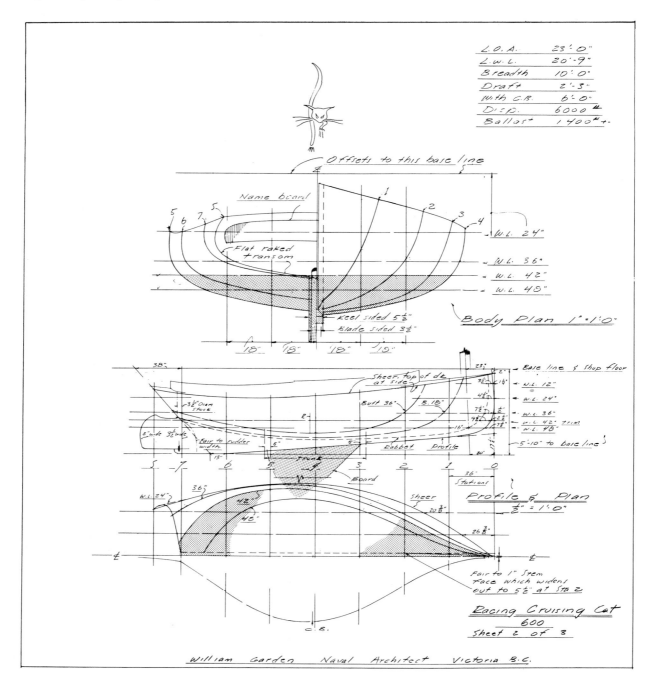

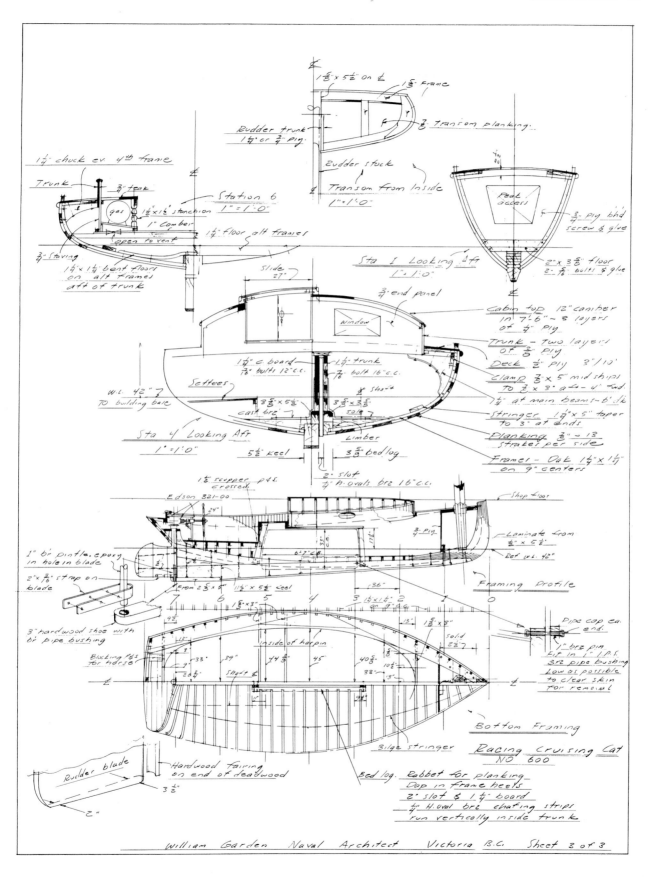

Rudder trunk 1¼" or ¾" Ply.

Rudder stock

Transom from Inside
1"=1'·0"

1⅝"×5½" on ℄   1⅝" frame

¾" Transom planking.

1¼" chuck ev. 4th frame

Trunk   ¾" teak

gas

Station 6
1"=1'·0"

1⅝"×1⅝" stanchion
1" Camber
open to vent

¾" Sterving

1¾" floor alt frames

1¾"×1¼" bent floors
on alt frames
aft of trunk

Peak
access

¾" Ply b'h'd
screw & glue

Sta 1 Looking Aft
1"=1'·0"

2"×3⅝" floor
2·⁷⁄₁₆ bolts & glue

Slide
27"

¾" end panel

window

Settees

1¼" c. board
⅞" bolts 12" c.c.

1¼" trunk
⁷⁄₁₆ bolt 16" c.c.

℄ shaft

3⅝"×5½"
cast brz

3⅝"×3⅝"
50/7

Cabin top 12" camber
in 7'-6" – 3 layers
of ¼" Ply

Trunk – Two layers
of ⅝" Ply

Deck ½" Ply 3"/10'

Clamp ⅞"×5" mid ships
to ⅞"×3" a⁴–4' 'ad
1¾" at main beams–b'lk

Stringer 1¾"×5" taper
to 3" at ends

Planking ¾" – 13
Strakes per side

Frames – Oak 1¼"×1¼"
on 9" centers

w.l. 42" 7
TO building base

Sta 4 Looking Aft
1"=1'·0"

5½" keel

Limber

3⅝" bedlog

2" slot
⅜" H. ovals brz 16" c.c.

1⅝" scupper p'ts.
crossed.

Edson 321·00
24"

6'-7"·C.B

33"

17½

¾" Ply

Shop floor

Laminate from
⅜"×5½"

Ref w.l. 42"

Framing Profile

1" brz pintle epoxy
in hole in blade

2"×⅜" strap on
blade

From 2⅜×5⅝   11¼"×5⅝" keel

From 2⅜×5⅝

3" hardwood shoe with
brz pipe bushing

Blocking p'ts
for horse

7   6   1⅝"×3" 5   4   3 1¼"×1¼" 2 on 9" c.c.   1   0

43¼

48¼

12¾

20½

33"   39"   44⅜   45   40⅝   10½   33"   13"

inside of harpin

13"

13"   1⅝"×3"

solid
2·⅜·7

9½

Pipe cap ea.
end.

1" brz pin
Fit in 1" I.P.S.
brz pipe bushing
Low as possible
to clear skin
for removal

Bottom Framing

Racing Cruising Cat
NO 600

Rudder blade

Hardwood fairing
on end of deadwood

3½"

2"

Bilge stringer

Bed log Rabbet for planking
Dap in frame heels
2" slot & 1¼" board
⁴⁄ H. oval brz chating strips
run vertically inside trunk

William Garden Naval Architect Victoria B.C. Sheet 3 of 3

ventilation and light, and this, with the slide hatch, will open her out in warm-weather cruising.

Traditional catboat details should be considered when selecting deck fittings. Handrails should be the old-time cast bronze or galvanized stanchions with a half-inch-pipe connecting rail. Halyard cleats may be hardwood, and the lines will run aft over the cabin top from lead blocks port and starboard of the mast.

The hull has a short counter stern and simple wooden rudder stock working through a rudder port. To my eye the stern seems to fit a cat better than the chopped-off termination and barn door rudder of the present. We pick up an after deck here as a bonus, so the short counter is well worthwhile.

The entry is sharp and easy for a short, beamy hull; the forefoot is deep to give the mast enough bury to carry the wringing effect of a mast without shrouds. Heavy loads are trans-mitted back into the hull, so all faying surfaces should be glued to keep her as structurally stiff and strong as possible. Heavy partners and the harpin construction will be the most practical way to put her together. A stem band and eye will take the headstay. The rig is heavily loaded on the wind, so the little jumper strut will do to take the thrust of the gaff and keep the mast straight.

This cat I notice is my data reference No. 600, about 17 miles of tracing paper from No. 1, and perhaps as enjoyable a little ship to design as any in between. Of the two thousand or so boats I have designed, built, or sailed, of all types and services, the smallest ones seem to give the most pleasure in development, being a spontaneous sort of creation. Each one is a simple piece of wooden engineering or design. I hope these little boats will give you a small measure of the enjoyment I've had at the drawing board.

5 *Spice Island Cutter*, a Seagoing Ship

LOA (fiddlehead) — 30'
LWL — 22' 6"
Beam — 9' 5"
Draft — 5, 4"
Displacement — 12,600 pounds
Ballast — 4,700 pounds outside, 1,000 pounds inside
Sail Area — 531 square feet, 3 lowers

At one time, we had a bunch of these cutters built, some on this side of the Pacific in softwood and some in the Orient of teak and yacal. Originally the boats were built with a straight stem, which seemed to match the rig; then the plan was pulled out forward to a clipper bow, which to my eye looks the best for the type and which we found to give an overall length more in keeping with the relatively high cost for such a short boat. This cost is due to the weight, mass, and resultant heavy rig required to drive her.

There's full headroom under the trunk, wonderful deck space for working the ship, and an overall seagoing feel that will appeal to the dyed-in-the-wool cruising man. Under sail she is fast for her waterline length—one of the little ships reportedly maintained four nautical miles per hour average during two trips from the West Coast to the Marquesas. Any boat that can do this under a mixed bag of sea conditions is sliding right along.

Two sets of lines are used, one with all inside ballast and the other with outside iron. Performance will be reasonably the same with either, but I would build the outside-ballasted

model as shown if a foundry is willing to pour the iron. Originally, she was built with all weight inside. The iron version was later designed for construction in the Orient, since a casting can be bolted up without much difficulty, but an inside-ballasted boat must only be done with loving care, as upon completion of the cementing, a poor job covering rubbish and faulty work will defy detection.

The choice of either inside or outside ballast may be set down about as follows:

Outside Iron—Iron ballast outside will bounce off coral or rock with little chance of sticking or damage. Using it will keep the bilges clear, provide better control of weight, and allow a slightly lower center of gravity. Outside iron also permits a slimmer form along the garboards and a higher center of buoyancy. Outside lead will have the same attributes as iron but will require less mass, hence a smaller casting, because of its greater density. Upkeep for lead is less than iron and best in every way, except when grounding. Should the boat strike at speed she is liable to receive a damaging jolt as the lead tends to hang up and form over rock or coral. A little cruiser feels her way into some

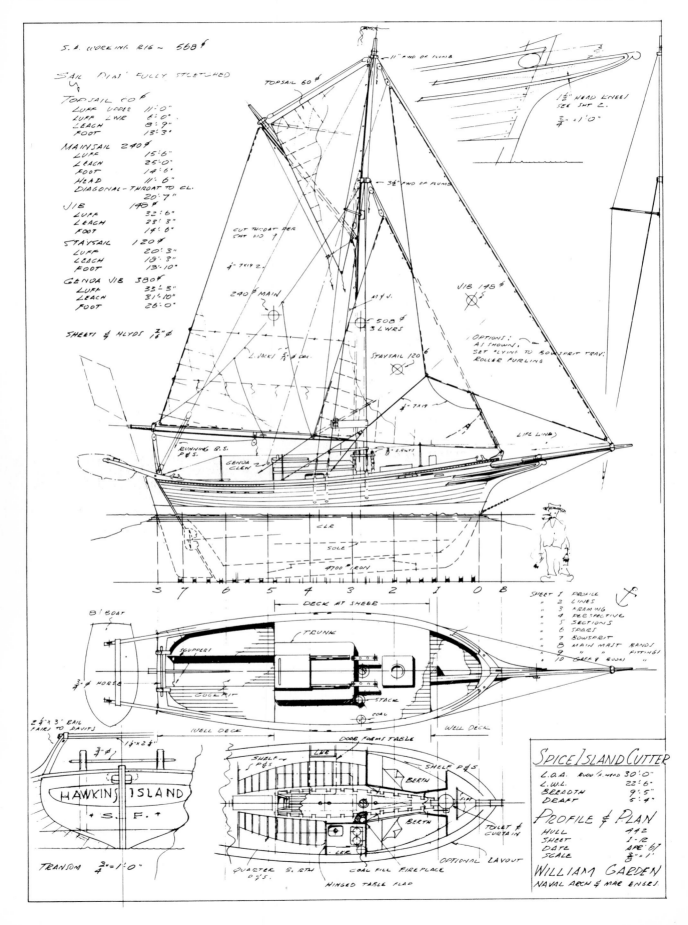

S.A. WORKING RIG ~ 568#

SAIL DIM' FULLY STRETCHED

TOPSAIL 60#
  LUFF UPPER   11'.0"
  LUFF LWR   6'.0"
  LEACH   9'.9"
  FOOT   13'.3"

MAINSAIL 240#
  LUFF   15'.6"
  LEACH   25'.0"
  FOOT   14'.6"
  HEAD   11'.6"
  DIAGONAL - THROAT TO CL.
                20'.7"

JIB 148#
  LUFF   32'.6"
  LEACH   23'.3"
  FOOT   14'.6"

STAYSAIL 120#
  LUFF   20'.3"
  LEACH   19'.3"
  FOOT   13'.10"

GENOA JIB 380#
  LUFF   33'.3"
  LEACH   31'.10"
  FOOT   26'.0"

SHEETS & HLYDS 7/16" Ø

Spice Island Cutter
L.O.A. BOOM & HEAD 30'.0"
L.W.L.   22'.6"
BREADTH   9'.5"
DRAFT   5'.4"

PROFILE & PLAN
HULL   442
SHEET   1 - 12
DATE   APR '67
SCALE   3/8" = 1'

WILLIAM GARDEN
NAVAL ARCH & MAR ENGRS.

TRANSOM 3/4" = 1'.0"

HAWKINS ISLAND
* S . F . *

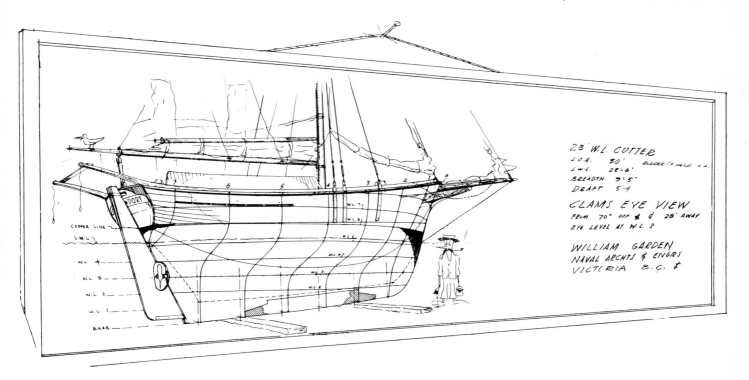

23' W.L. CUTTER
L.O.A.   30'   RUDDER/A HEAD O.A.
L.W.L.   28'6"
BREADTH   9'5"
DRAFT   5'4"

CLAMS EYE VIEW
FROM 70° OFF ⊄ & 28' AWAY
EYE LEVEL AT W.L. 3

WILLIAM GARDEN
NAVAL ARCHTS & ENGRS
VICTORIA B.C.

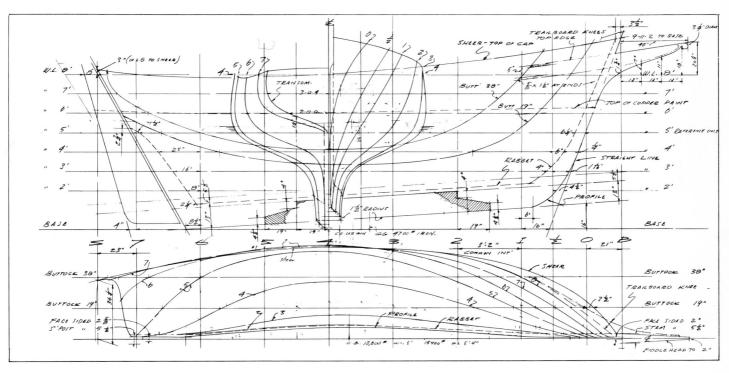

tight spots on occasion and iron would be my choice.

Inside Ballast—Inexpensive iron or lead scrap may be imbedded in concrete prior to launching for a relatively simple ballasting job. No mold or costly casting and bolts need be prepared. On the negative side, if she goes ashore and grinds awhile, the shoe and garboards can be badly chewed up. The shoe is wood and in a position that is most difficult to protect from worm. A metal plate under the hardwood shoe will help, but will add again to the construction cost.

For the home builder, installing inside

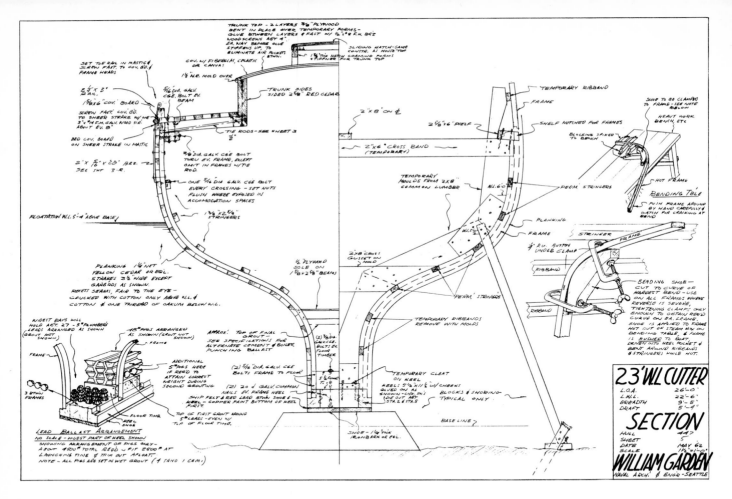

23' W.L CUTTER
L.O.A. 26'-0"
L.W.L. 22'-6"
BREADTH 9'-5"
DRAFT 5'-4"

SECTION

HULL 442
SHEET 5
DATE MAY 62
SCALE 1½"=1'-0"

WILLIAM GARDEN
NAVAL ARCH. & ENGR - SEATTLE

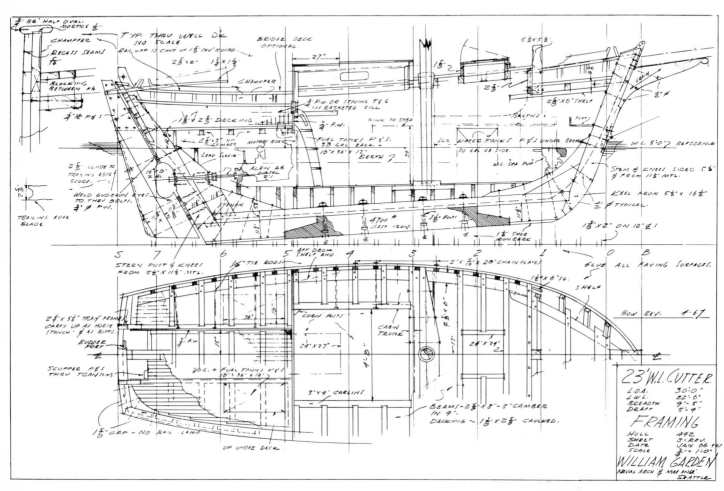

23' W.L. CUTTER.
L.O.A. 30'-0"
L.W.L. 22'-6"
BREADTH 9'-5"
DRAFT 5'-4"

FRAMING

HULL 442
SHEET 3 REV.
DATE JAN 06 '61
SCALE 3"=1'-0"

WILLIAM GARDEN
NAVAL ARCH & MAR ENGR
SEATTLE

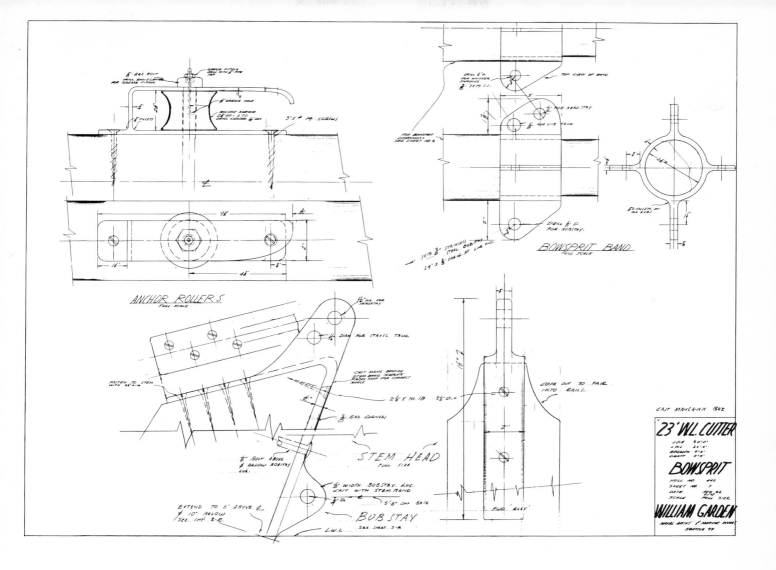

ANCHOR ROLLERS
FULL SCALE

BOWSPRIT BAND
FULL SCALE

STEM HEAD
FULL SIZE

BOBSTAY

23' WL CUTTER

BOWSPRIT

WILLIAM GARDEN

ballast is probably easier than installing outside ballast, but, if a boat is hauled for the winter freeze period, a space will open between the cement and wood because of alternate freeze drying and swelling, with the chance of rot eventually getting started in the voids. Cement should never be used above the waterline, since condensation can form between the wood and cement, with resultant rot. Below the waterline and in a boat constantly afloat, ballast in cement will result in economy and long life.

With concrete we can end up with a reasonably dense total. Concrete weighs 144 pounds per cubic foot. A ferro-phosphorus concrete mix weighs 300 pounds per cubic foot, and would be my first choice if available. Lead weighs 710 pounds per cubic foot; iron weighs 440 pounds per cubic foot.

The weight of inside ballast must be concentrated low, and the major portion must be in the middle third of the hull for best per-formance; the biggest chunks of metal that will pack reasonably well will do the best job. Boiler punchings in concrete are an old reliable, but nothing will match large-size pieces of scrap for maximum weight per cubic foot. To nest properly, a slurry of cement and sand mixed 3: 1 will best fill all bays and adhere to the hull without rot-producing voids. Galvanized common nails can be driven into frames and floors to key in the cement, and they will also help secure the heavy metal pieces. Install the ballast carefully. First get the inside of the hull bone clean, then wet it down, dump in a few pails of cement, and carefully work in the clean metal pieces, being sure that each piece is completely encased in cement and clear of the wood by about a half an inch. Work in about 3,500 pounds of cement and metal prior to launching, and, after she is rigged, the tanks are filled, and the gear is on board or its weight is simulated, complete the job. The cement should be topped

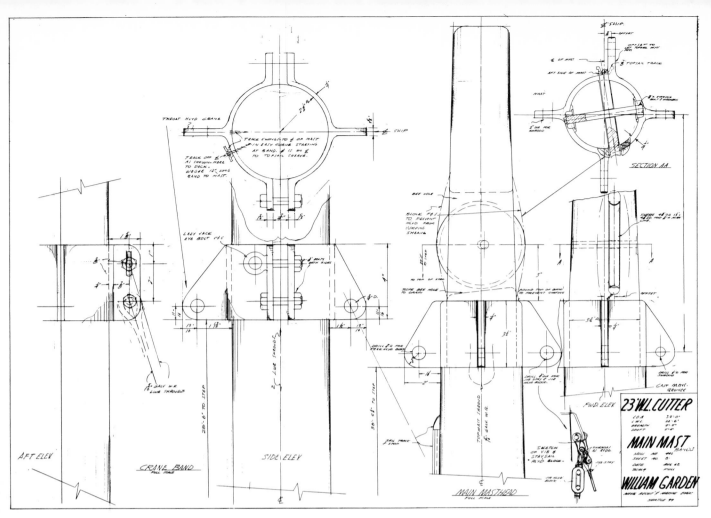

23' W.L. CUTTER

MAIN MAST BANDS

WILLIAM GARDEN

SECTION AA

CRANE BAND — FULL SCALE

SIDE ELEV.

MAIN MASTHEAD — FULL SCALE

AFT ELEV.

FWD ELEV.

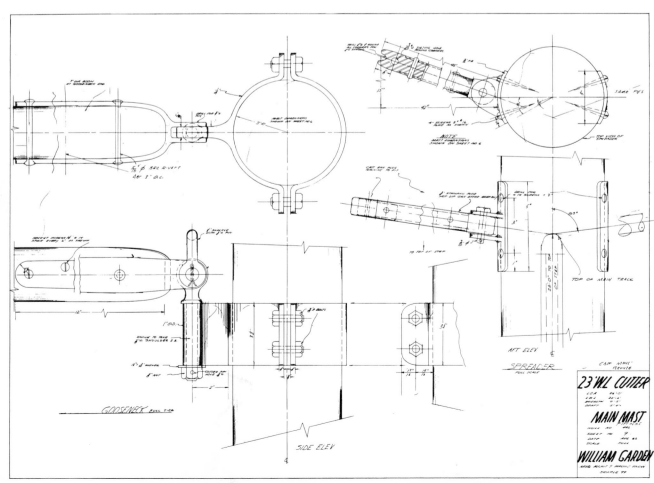

23' W.L. CUTTER

MAIN MAST

WILLIAM GARDEN

GOOSENECK — FULL SIZE

SIDE ELEV.

SPREADER — FULL SCALE

AFT ELEV.

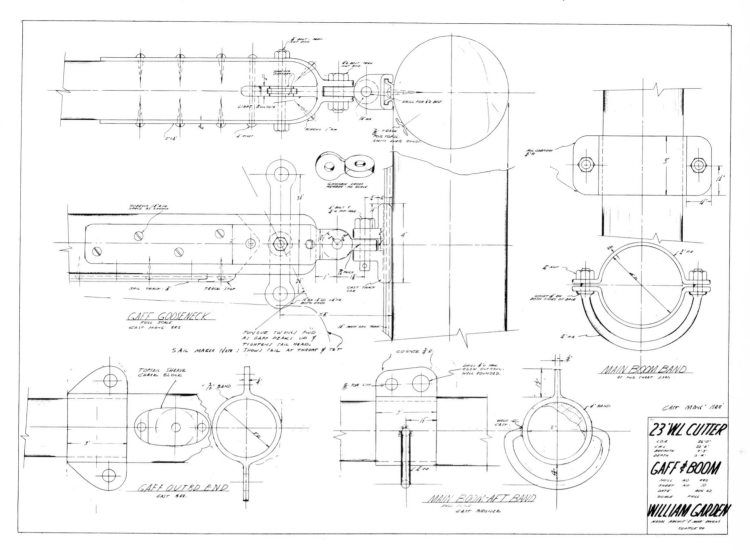

GAFF GOOSENECK
FULL SCALE
CAST MANG' BRZ

SAIL MAKER NOTE : SHOWS TAIL AT THROAT & SET

GAFF OUTBD END
CAST BRZ.

MAIN BOOM BAND
AT FWD SHEET LEAD

MAIN BOOM AFT BAND
FULL SIZE
CAST BRONZE

23' WL CUTTER

LOA	26'-0"
LWL	23'-0"
BEAM	7'-5"
DEPTH	3'-4"

GAFF & BOOM

HULL NO.	442
SHEET NO.	10
DATE	AUG 62
SCALE	FULL

WILLIAM GARDEN
NAVAL ARCHIT'T & MAR ENG'RS
SEATTLE 99

off with a slight vee to the centerline to strip any moisture back to the sump; give it the best finish possible in the interests of a clean bilge.

Let the cement dry completely, then give it two coats of cement floor paint and run about 12 inches up the inside of the hull port and starboard so the bilge will remain sweet and clean. It will be a joy forever, give or take a few years, and a dandy shock-absorbing base for a chopping block installed flush with the cabin sole.

The interior accommodation plan is practical, and the finish of the cabin will depend upon the owner. Simple bone-white areas with varnished hardwood beams, sole, and trim will suit many. Set off with the right cushions and books, such a scheme is hard to beat, particularly in a hot area requiring a light, airy effect. A very soft blue also wears well and picks up varying tones through the play of light and shadow. For a northern climate, the best choice might be the warmth of a varnished interior, brightened up with light, bright cushions. The mellow tones of wood seem to enhance a hideaway of this sort and might go best with the Spice Islander's theme.

Rigging is complex on a traditional cutter, no matter how small, and you will find that a 100-fathom coil of line is swallowed up easily with the parts of four halyards, downhauls, and sheets alone. For ease of handling, 7/16-inch diameter line is right, and it is big enough to grab and oversize for strength. Blocks to match will be 1 inch for each eighth of an inch of rope diameter, so 4-inch blocks will best match the 7/16-inch rope diameter.

Topsail gear may be lighter, and details of

the rig are shown on the sail plan. To clean up the jackstay, usually required to set a jib-headed topsail without going aloft, the mast here has both main and topsail set on sail track. The main gaff car replaces the usual jaws, and the main track is rugged enough to carry the gaff easily. The topsail then is set from a bag on deck and hoisted alongside the main with the sheet and downhaul bent on, the sheet being permanently rove off in the usual way through the block at the gaff's end.

With the main set and drawing, the topsail is run aloft and two-blocked, the downhaul hove down to tighten the luff, and the sheet set up to give the sail the required draft. If the topsail leech is too tight, the halyard must be eased and the downhaul reset to bring the sheets more in line with the block. The sheet fall runs forward and down to the lead block or lizard at the throat to avoid making a hard spot and spoiling the draft in the mainsail, then the sheet runs to its belaying pin at the gooseneck or boom jaw.

Notice that the foot of the topsail is cut back from the mast. This allows adjustment of both the foot and the sail's shape or draft as the tension and lead of the downhaul is varied. The downhaul runs down and *around* the mast, belaying on the opposite side at the pinrail. I stress this point somewhat, since topsails get blamed for their mismanagement, and not many sailors today have had the pleasure of getting one to set properly. There is something about topsails that give them a never-ending charm. They are admittedly impractical from the standpoint of on-the-wind efficiency, but still they are one of the most interesting and occasionally the most helpful sails that can be set. Club topsails, gaff topsails, or the spectacular jackyard topsails are all absorbing to watch, a pleasure when they are drawing, and sometimes a menace. Our simple topsail here, set on a track and up a pole mast, will be as docile and efficient as such a sail can be.

The rigging details and fittings of spars will take many evenings of pattern-making if of bronze, or fabricating if made from mild steel. Some can be simplified or altered to suit your inclination or skills, but I've shown the whole bag here to outline the pieces required.

"God save us from it," you will say, but persevere and the final fabric will be a source of endless pleasure and learning.

6 *Portage* 24, a Sailing Outboard Cruiser

LOA — 24′ 3″
LWL — 20′ 8″
Beam — 8′ 5″
Draft — 4′ 6″
Displacement — 4,000 pounds
Ballast — 1,750 pounds
Sail Area — 297 square feet, 100 percent triangle

A plywood hull with a glass skin overlay has great appeal to the backyard builder who wants a practical method to follow for a relatively simple boat. With the Portage 24, a simple hull is achieved with longitudinal framing over the bulkheads and some forming molds. The topsides are 3/8-inch plywood and the bottom is formed of two layers of 1/4-inch plywood; the skins are glued together and to the framing. Decks are double, glued ply, and general framing details may be followed on the plans. A bunch of these boats have been built with this layout and also with a more usual trunk cabin.

The layout shown is my choice for a pleasant day boat or for summer cruising. The cabins fore and aft give good separation for a family of four, and the roomy midships cockpit doubles as a galley and lounge by hinging up the seats at the forward end to expose a sink and

stove with lockers under. This area is under the folding hood where there is full headroom. Fitting side curtains and a longer fly permits the cockpit to be converted into a snug deckhouse.

The boat that I've sailed went along very well, balance was close to perfect, and the efficient rig was carried well by the 1,800-pound cast-iron fin.

She was designed about twenty years ago before outboard rudders were an accepted thing for other than dyed-in-the-wool cruisers. This and her freeboard at that time kept her from any degree of popularity. We called her then a sailing outboard cruiser. The idea still looks pretty good. The flush-decked hull is about as simple as can be built, and the cabin superstructure is made from a stock aluminum windshield with a canvas shelter, so that much of the time-consuming work of building a cabin house can be economically farmed out. Most of the

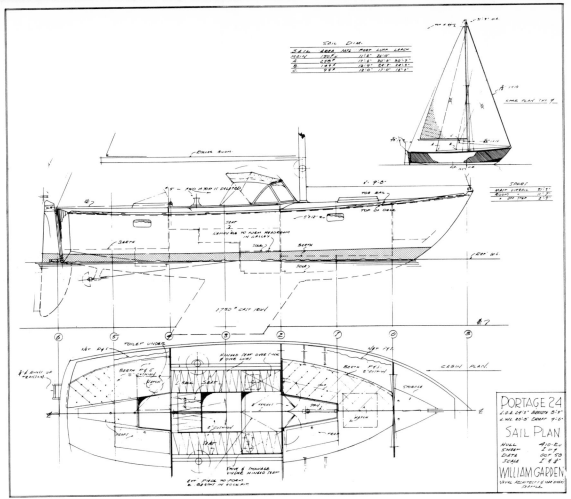

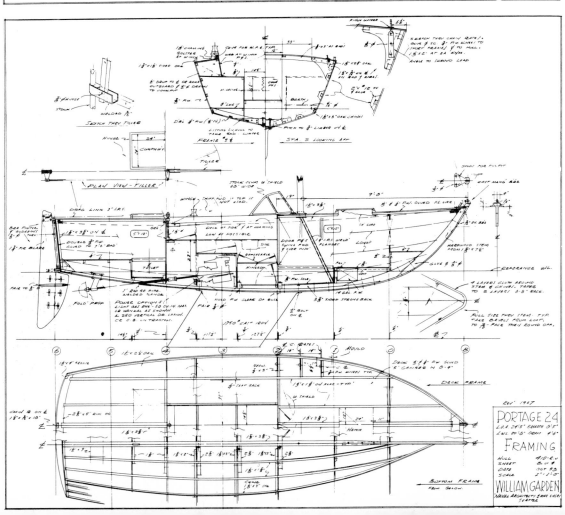

8 *Itatae*, a Cat Schooner

LOA — 27′ 0″
LWL — 25′ 4″
Beam — 9′ 8″
Draft — 4′ 0″
Displacement — 9,700 pounds
Ballast — 2,500 pounds outside, 700 pounds inside
Sail Area — 421 square feet

The cat schooner *Itatae* was designed for an Eastern sailor who wanted a handy day boat along with some reasonable accommodations. She was built in the early 1950s and seems to be a pleasant mixture of catboat, Block Islander, and old-time salmon boat — a change in pace from the usual jib-and-mainsail boat but admittedly not everyone's ideal ship. Edward Dane, her owner, had larger boats before *Itatae* and felt the pull of a small boat again. The charm of a boat without a paid hand or of a boat of single roast beef size is pleasant to contemplate after cruising and racing a double roast beef boat housing eight or nine mouths, however jolly they may be; so with *Itatae*'s size comes just two berths for overnighting, a nice day sailing cockpit, and a snug sail plan easily set and worked by one man if desired.

I've always liked the cat schooner rig. Basically, it is a two-masted sloop, the foremast being likened to a standing headstay and the overlapping foresail an efficient spread of sail despite the weight and windage of the foremast. Two masts make a ship and remind us here that these are all toy boats and variety is one of their main charms.

Years ago we built many little flat-bottomed cat schooners similar to double-ended skiffs with a foremast right up in the eyes, keel of a tapered 2 × 12, and a neat little cabin of vertical staving tumbled home from the sheer and just big enough for a couple of kids to cruise with. The rig always seemed handy, and we had lots of fun with the little boats. The rig was always a pleasure to use.

The *Itatae* is 27 feet by 9 feet 8 inches, drawing 4 feet, and carrying 421 square feet of sail on the 7-inch pole masts. The rig is short but reasonably efficient. A longer, spread-out sail-plan base would put her out of balance, and greater height would add more problems, so the rig is probably best on a fairly long, slim hull.

The short Block Islander gaff doesn't make much sense. In the other cat schooners I've designed, I've worked in a real foresail similar to the round-sterned schooner, which was developed on a power fishing-boat model that my old friend Black Dave used to build as a stock boat. The foresail-leach/main-luff relationship gives a good slot effect between the sails, and the foresail, which is broader across the head than those on Block Islanders, is a real horse for

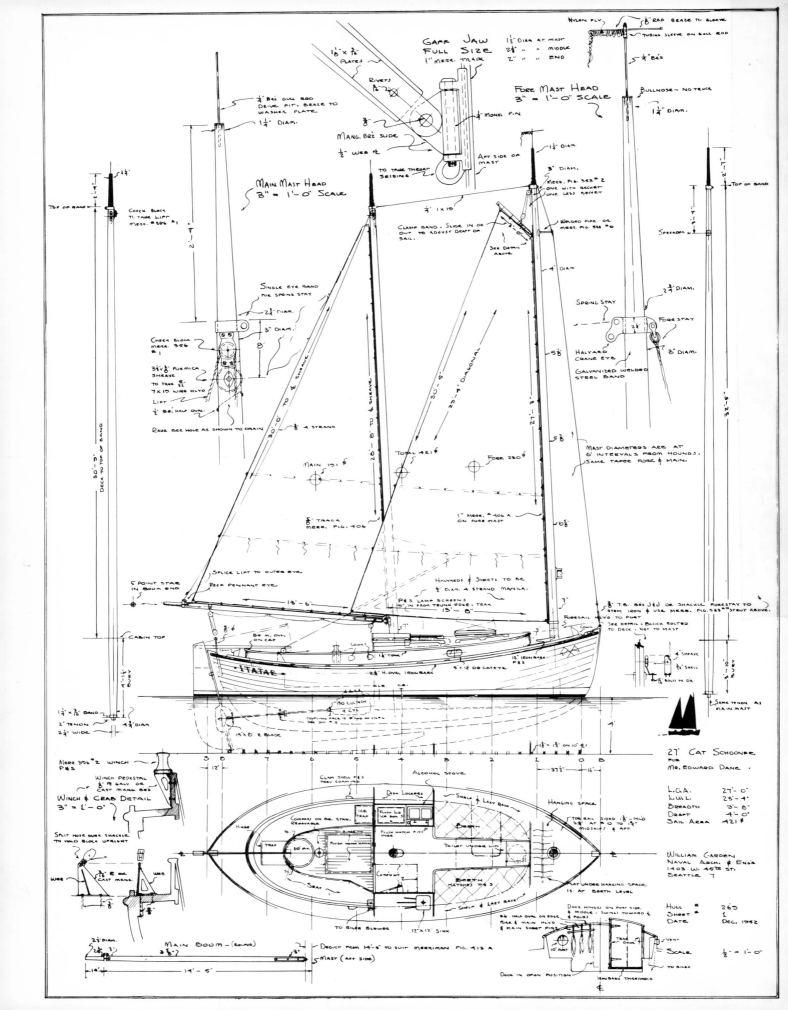

27' CAT SCHOONER
FOR
MR. EDWARD DANE.

L.O.A.   27'-0"
L.W.L.   25'-4"
BREADTH   9'-8"
DRAFT   4'-0"
SAIL AREA   421#

WILLIAM GARDEN
NAVAL ARCH. & ENG'R
1403 W. 45TH ST.
SEATTLE 7

HULL #   265
SHEET #   1
DATE   DEC. 1952
SCALE   ½" = 1'-0"

drive. Black Dave's heavier, round-stern schooner, incidentally, looks pretty square on deck, but she has a quick, high flare forward and a long hollow entrance, so all is not lost.

Itatae's model is very pretty in the shop and combines a pleasant wine glass section with a high bilge. The displacement to waterline four is 9,000 pounds, and ballast consists of 2,500 pounds outside and about 1,500 pounds inside.

The relatively long waterline allows easy ends, and the fore-and-aft lines are fairly flat. I've never sailed her, but she's supposed to go along very nicely.

The framing plan indicates a rugged structure without undue weight. Planking is 7/8-inch white cedar on 1 3/8-inch by 1 3/4-inch bent

STATION	8	7½	7	6	5	4	3	2	1	½	0
HEIGHTS											
SHEER	6 10 7	6 7 1	6 1 6	6 2 2	6 1 7	6 3 3	6 6 5	7 0 0	7 7 4	8 0 0	8 4 5
BUTTOCK 18"		4 8 4	3 9 5	2 11 3	2 7 5	2 7 7	2 9 4	3 2 4	4 1 5	5 5 6	
BUTTOCK 37½"			5 2 5	3 11 0	3 6 0	3 5 1	3 8 4	4 5 6			
RABBET		2 6 0	1 10 2	1 6 7	1 7 0	1 8 1	1 10 1	2 1 6	2 0 6	3 4 1	
HALF BREADTHS											
SHEER	1 4 0	2 9 3	3 7 0	4 6 0	4 10 0	4 10 4	4 8 0+	4 2 0	3 1 4	2 3 3	1 2 6
W.L. 7'-0"									3 0 1	2 0 4+	0 10 4
W.L. 6'-0"	0 9 2	2 6 3	3 5 6				7 7 5	3 11 6	2 8 4	1 8 2	0 7 0+
W.L. 5'-0"		1 9 2	2 10 7	4 2 6	4 8 4	4 8 2	4 4 1	3 6 3	2 2 0-	1 3 0-	
L.W.L. 4'-0"		0 10 0	1 5 2	3 3 4	3 11 3	3 11 6	3 6 0	2 7 0-	1 4 0	0 7 3	
W.L. 3'-0"			0 7 2+	1 7 2	2 1 6	2 2 4	1 10 4	1 2 4	0 4 6		
W.L. 2'-6"			0 4 0	0 10 1	1 3 3	1 3 0	1 0 4	0 6 7			
W.L. 2'-0"				0 5 4	0 9 0	0 9 2	0 7 3				
W.L. 1'-0"			0 1 3	0 2 5	0 4 1-	0 4 3+	0 3 4-				
DIAGONAL				4 2 0	4 7 6	4 8 0	4 3 7	3 7 0			
RABBET	0 2 2	0 2 2	0 2 2	0 4 0	0 5 6	0 6 6	0 6 04	0 4 2-	0 2 2	0 2 2	0 2 2
PROFILE	0 0 7	0 1 0	0 1 1	0 2 2	0 3 2	0 3 4+	0 3 0	0 1 6	0 0 6	0 0 4	0 0 4

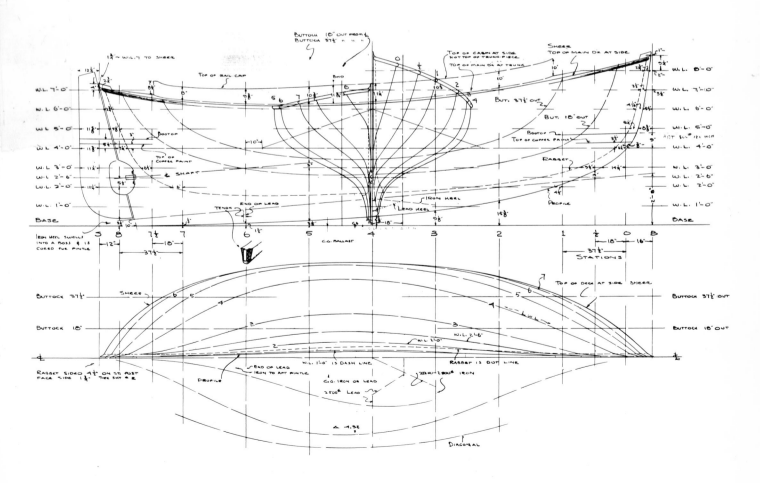

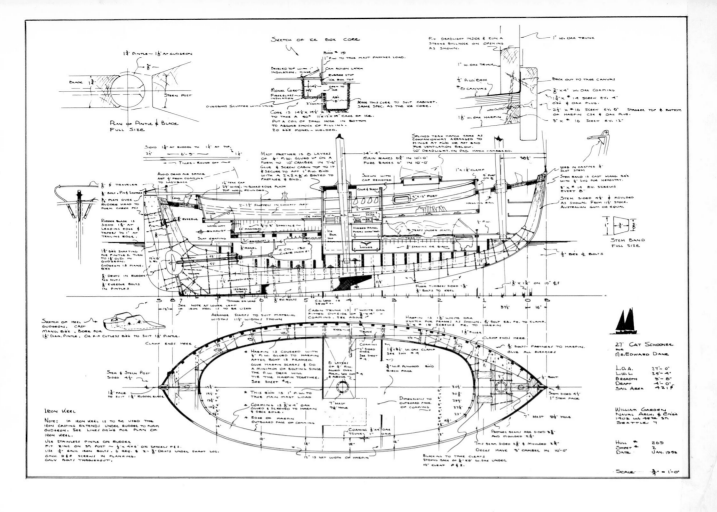

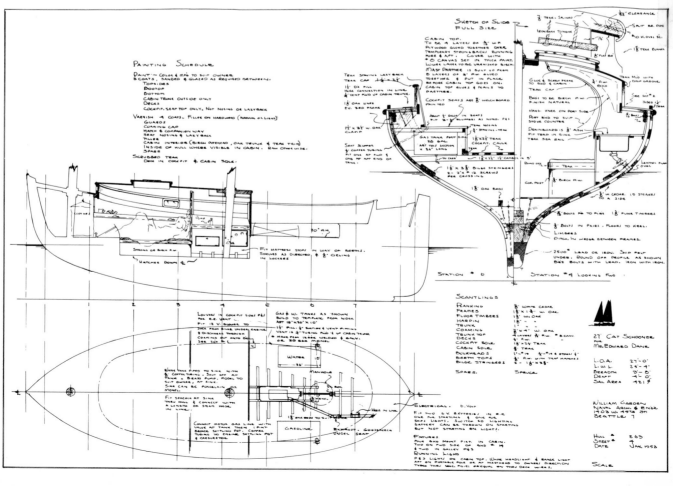

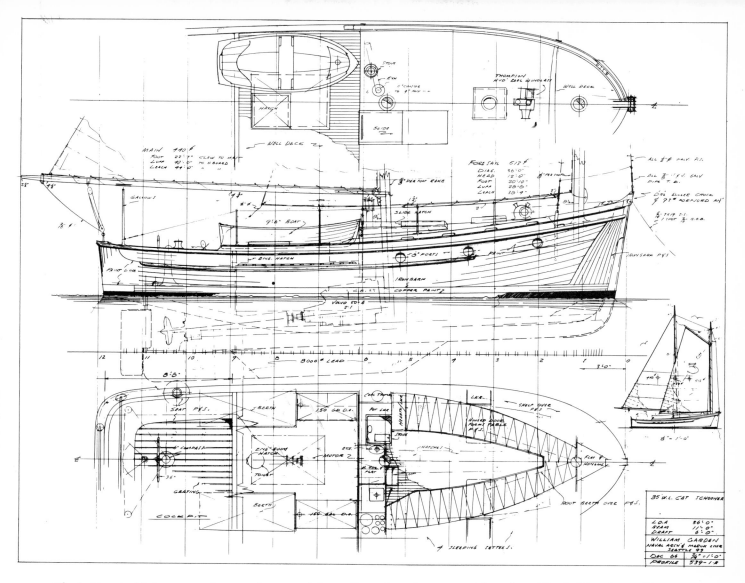

Black Dave's 36-foot cat schooner has a real foresail, rather than one with a short Block Islander gaff as in *Itatae*.

oak frames; the deck and house top are of plywood with eight ounce canvas over, and the cabin trunk is one inch white oak.

The midsection indicates clamps and floors and the inboard profile a backbone assembly with lots of meat to take the fastenings.

The size is good. At one time, the Alaskan Bristol Bay Canneries were serviced by a great fleet of double-ended salmon boats that were about this length and breadth, but with flat floors and a centerboard for taking the sand and working on the flats. We converted many of the boats into schooners, cutters, yawls, and sloops, and I always yearned for one with an "S" section to put the ballast low, so *Itatae*'s form is perhaps how things might have been.

Paul Luke built her in East Boothbay, Maine, to his usual high standards, so she should be good for a long time to come.

9   A Coasting Schooner

LOA (on deck) — 28′ 0″
LWL — 24′ 0″
Beam — 9′ 5″
Draft — 5′ 4″
Displacement — 16,700 pounds
Ballast — 5,200 pounds outside, 600 pounds inside
Sail Area — 627 square feet

This little coasting schooner is 28 feet on deck, 24 feet on the waterline, 9 feet 5 inches breadth, and 5 feet 4 inches draft, with a displacement of 16,700 pounds The sail area is generous for her length and wetted surface, the three lowers totalling 627 square feet in a gaff schooner rig set on pole masts. Her performance will be excellent with the lofty rig or when shortened down to deep reefs. A yard with course and topsail can be fitted for chasing off down the wind, but I would be inclined to rig her with the three lowers only.

The spars are from trees or solid timber, the boom and gaff jaws of wood, and the basic spar fabric can be worked up from a good wood lot. The deck plan is straightforward, with cockpit seats at the deck level surrounded by the cabin sides extending aft as coamings. A toe rail runs around the sheer and is topped off aft by the low taffrail and davits. Life lines of one-half-inch line will be rove off at the sheer pole height amidships, running aft to the davit bar and forward to the roller chocks.

Going below decks, the slide hatch leads down a three-step ladder to an excellent ship-shape cabin with good space for a 24-foot waterline vessel. To port is the coal range with a fuel bin filled through a deck coaling port, and alongside is a locker for pots and pans. Perhaps the most used of the latter could be a 10-inch iron frying pan, the maximum size to fit in the oven, with the pan handle shortened up to suit — a good pan for a roast or quick cooking on the stove top or over the primus.

The wet-gear hanging locker is on the port side of the engine, and to starboard in the galley are the sink and lockers, with an ice box under the cockpit seat and opening over the drain-board.

Accommodations are always a source of juggling, and here we could have quarter berths with galley and head between the cabins or variations as outlined in the little Bullfrog's description, which follows later in this book. I've shown her with four berths, with the toilet in the eyes of the boat. The toilet fits into her deep bow sections and uses up the area of liveliest motion, but, as an alternative, the forward berths could be pushed into the bow, the galley located on one side aft, and the head installed to starboard at the foot of the companionway. There is lots of room for variations

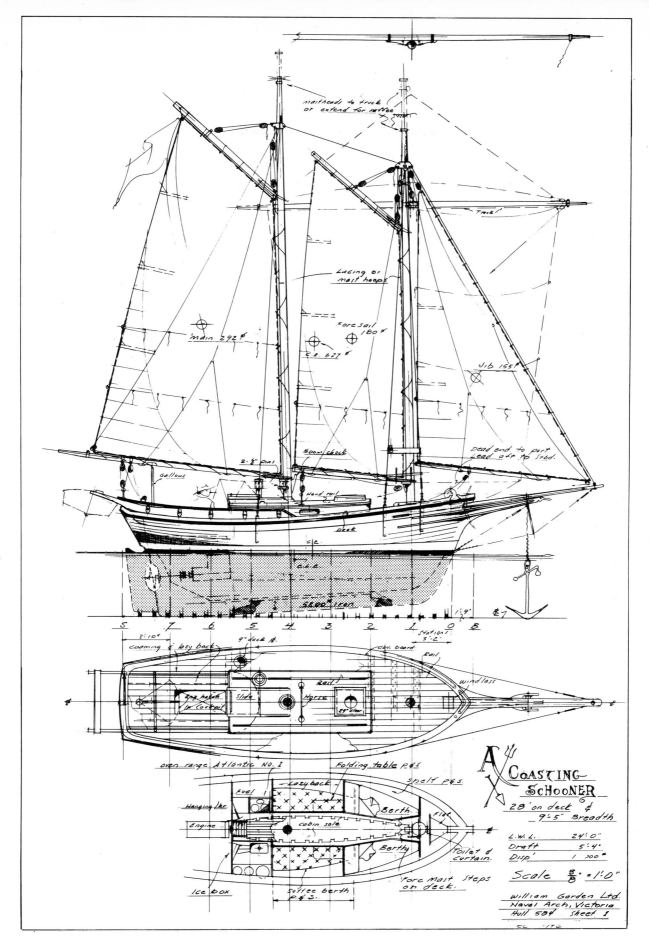

Figure 1.

in a cabin of this size, and it would be an interesting task to fit in the one that takes your fancy.

The schooner's construction is simple carvel planking on bent frames with the construction sections, profile, and deck plan as shown. The boat is currently being built in places as far apart as Maine and India. The Indian project is a hardwood ship and will settle down to the tip of the rudder blade with her greater timber weight. The softwood version will rest about as shown in the plans.

The rudder stock and trunk are built in the old-time manner, and the four-inch diameter stock fairs into the deadwoods aft, forming an easy release to the waterlines. The lines indicate a slippery form for this weight and length, and you will find her to be a chunky but handsome ship when in frame.

The numbered waterlines are in even feet to give the loftsman an even number for reference closer at hand than the baseline. The flotation line to the designed trim is at waterline 5 feet 4 inches, the painted copper line is at about 5 feet 8 inches, and the boot-top location is noted on the sail plan and lines. The shaded waterline in the plan view shows her form when at rest.

Of the schooner's 16,700 pounds total weight or displacement of water, 5,200 pounds of outside ballast and 600 pounds of inside ballast is in an iron keel and trimming ballast respectively — a ballast-displacement ratio of about 35 percent. With this weight, waterplane area, and displacement, she'll be a powerful boat for her size.

The lead of the center of effort to resistance is about right for the rig. As it breezes up I would tie a single reef in the main as the first reduction prior to shortening down seriously. Performance under any combination will surpass that of the short-rigged cruiser so often seen, and her appearance afloat will maintain her individuality in any anchorage or fleet under sail.

Traditional colors might combine light gray decks and house with white toe rails, oiled guards, black wale strakes, gray topsides, white boot, and copper-painted bottom. The cockpit could be picked out in fish blood red. An orange lapstrake pram would look nice on the davits. I would varnish the spars and paint the spar taper ends in black or white.

I include here a perspective drawing of the schooner, which was used to illustrate a *National Fisherman* article on the procedure of developing a drawing in perspective. This type of drawing is a great aid in showing how the boat will look from a bird's- or clam's-eye view. The projection of the lines of a boat in true perspective is a time-consuming exercise in marine drafting, and, although of questionable value in other than a decorative sense, it does give some insight into proportion and layout. For the student of design, the marine artist, or the practicing draftsman, the following outline of steps in making a perspective drawing might open a new field of interest.

We are concerned here with a relatively simple method of developing a true perspective whereby, from a set of lines, a perspective drawing may be made from any point in space, and, upon the boat being built, a camera positioned at that point will duplicate the drawing. After becoming familiar with the method, it will take a person about six to eight absorbing hours to produce a hull perspective. Several drawings done at a time will pull the process down to about four hours each. A computer-directed drawing instrument could do it in about two hours, I suspect, but here's a chance to help stamp out computers.

Perspective drawings have a long history. As long ago as 1768, Chapman's *Architectura Navalis Mercatoria* had some beautiful drawings of a full-bodied ship on her beam ends — one showed her hove down with her keel just clear and in very light trim for careening, and one indicated her in sea trim. These are probably isometrics showing not how the form would look to a camera, but how the sections would look superimposed on one another, with artistic license used to give them a reasonably accurate appearance.

In 1925 and 1926 issues of *Yachting*, the Urry brothers who were engineers, described the dreamboats *Cogge* and *Coggette* with perspective drawings that set generations of readers off dreaming about "Great Cabin" yachts. The drawings appear to be true perspectives arrived at by what the Urrys refer to only as a "fearsome project" without further elaboration.

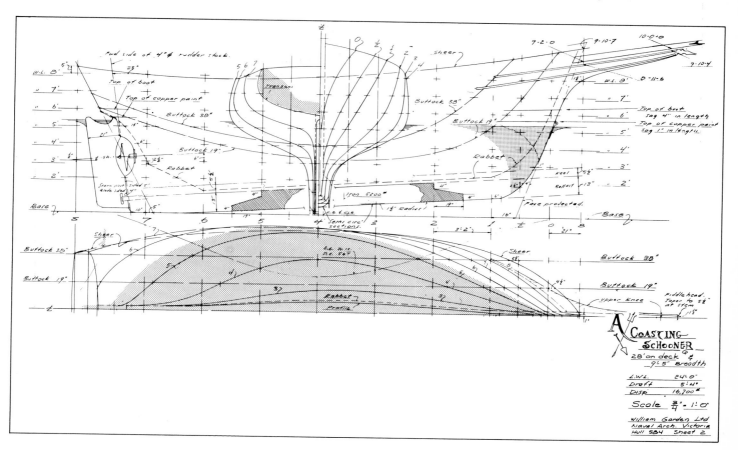

Figure 2.

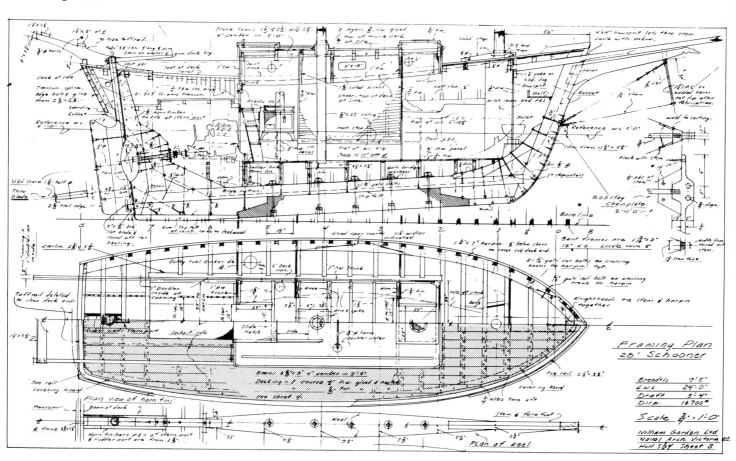

Harold Underhill's excellent *Deepwater Sail*, page 126, has a process description of deck perspective development, with many good drawings. British motor magazines, applying the technique to automobiles, have run many beautiful perspectives, particularly time-consuming cutaways of structure and machinery.

The architecture section of your library

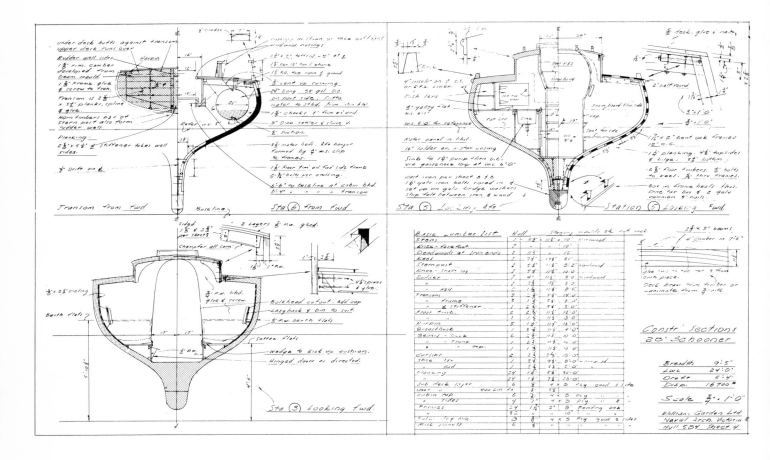

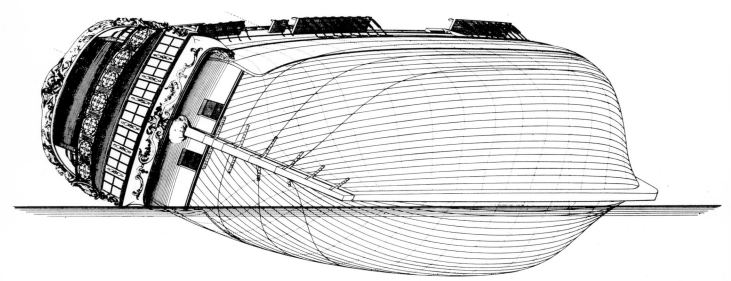

An English East Indiaman careened. Drawing by Fredrik Henrik af Chapman (from *Architectura Navalis Mercatoria*).

will have books that show methods of projecting buildings and regularly shaped units in perspective, and will also use the precise terminology. I'll hold herein to the "from-thumbtack-A-to-horizon-thence-to-B, etc." method. Things will go along well this way, and if you wish, you can polish up the correct terms to your satisfaction later. The method to be outlined was developed with my brother Lorne and based on a Royal Air Force method of making identification drawings of an unknown aircraft from an inflight photo. The method evolved seems ideal for boats, balloons, or even a mud-turtle portrait, if you have taken his lines off in plan profile and section.

Our 28-foot coasting schooner (Figure 1) has been chosen as an example to produce an interesting form for projection. In Figure 2, the lines are shown in normal format, with profile above, waterlines below, and body plan superimposed on the profile for simple projection and a condensed drawing; 3/4 inch to the foot is a good lines scale to keep the perspective drawing at a reasonable size if distant views are desired.

For a bow view, the lines drawing, Figure 2, is placed inverted in the upper right-hand corner of the drawing board as in the layout, Figure 3, but I've deleted the profile in this layout to clarify the projections. A view from aft would have the lines drawing placed in the upper left and the projection would be reversed. To show the stern view, as on the *Vega* headed to the right (Figure 6), a rough preliminary drawing is turned over and traced.

Refer now to Figure 3 and pick a viewpoint.

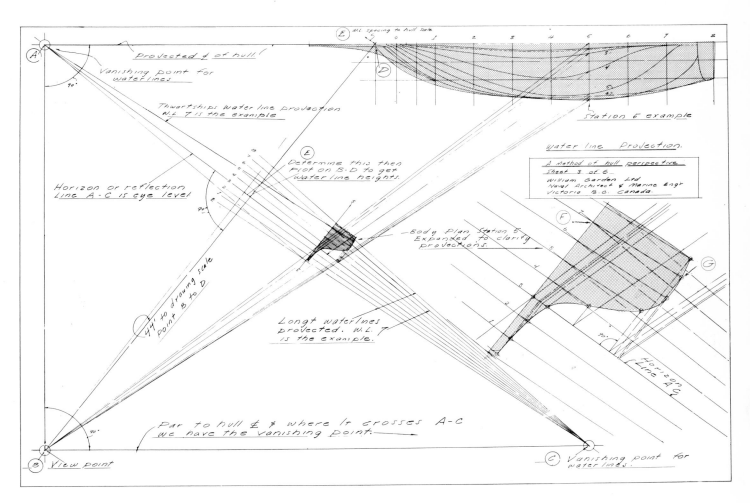

Figure 3.

For the first try, let's use the viewpoint that I've noted, which is 52 degrees off the centerline of the boat and 44 feet away.

Now draw a line *DB* from the forward perpendicular of the hull to the viewpoint.

Next extend the centerline of the boat to point *A*, which is determined when a right angle from it will hit viewpoint *B*.

From *B* run a line parallel to the centerline of the boat. This will form line *BC*.

On *DB* make a right angle that will cross point *A*; this line extended will cross line *BC* at *C*, forming the longitudinal vanishing point for waterline projections. *A* is the vanishing point for transverse waterlines. The line *AC* is the horizon and reflecting line. The point at which *AC* crosses *DB* is labeled *E*.

For true waterline heights, we must take the scaled waterline spacing (in this case, 3/4 inch equals 1 foot scale and 12 inches waterline spacing) and project the 3/4 inch from point *D* at right angles to *BD*. Where the *EB* line crosses *AC*, we measure the true distances the waterlines are apart and plot these above and below the horizon *AC*, then connect to *C* with light lines. The longitudinal waterlines at the hull centerline are now established.

Let's use station five as an example. Project station five at the centerline on the plan down to *B*. When it crosses *AC* (horizon), it then reflects back up at right angles to *AC*, and we have a station centerline for five. Next project waterline seven, station five, down to *B*, and, where it crosses *AC*, reflect it back at right angles to *AC* and draw a light line. Now from *A* draw a line through waterline seven where it crosses station five at the point noted as *F* on the drawing, and, where this line extended crosses the reflected line at right angles to *AC* established earlier from waterline seven, we locate waterline seven on station five point *G*. The other waterlines are projected in the same way, and the points established are then connected to form the outline of station five. Each station is done this way; then we're ready for the buttocks.

See Figure 4 for the buttock projection. Again, I've shown one section only, since the

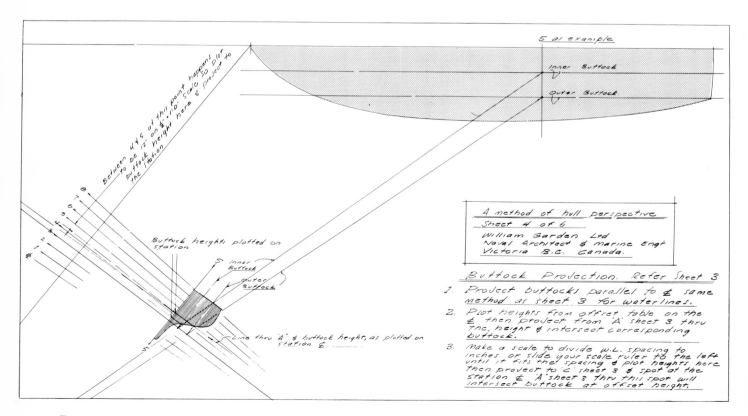

Figure 4.

completed drawing with all buttocks shown would be a blur of projecting lines. The buttock lines are projected onto the sections exactly the same way the waterlines were. After you bring points down to the horizon and project up to the crossing, the horizon should then be erased to clean up for the next section. Projection lines should be just sharp enough to follow.

With the sections drawn in, the waterlines, buttocks, sheer, rabbet, etc., can be drawn through their section marks, and the basic hull is in outline ready for miscellaneous details you might wish to add.

The sheet that the drawing is projected on can be tracing paper or bond. Tracing paper is good, since the completed perspective may be turned over and headed the other way as described earlier. I usually make the projection sheet a rough drawing only, then trace it and add details of rails, etc., as required. For cutaway drawings, the full sections port and starboard may be drawn, and whatever you wish to show inside the ship may be exposed by erasing the hull on the near side.

Upon mastering the underbody projection, the principle will be absorbed, and you will see

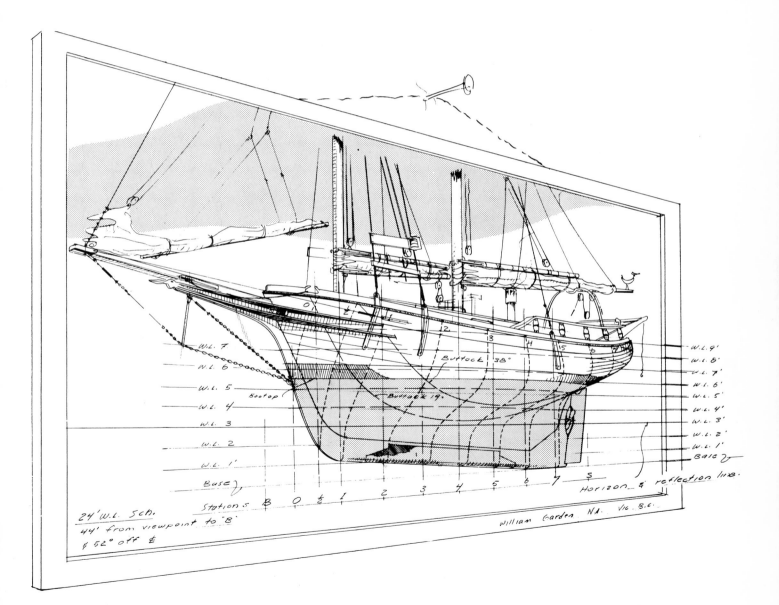

Figure 5.

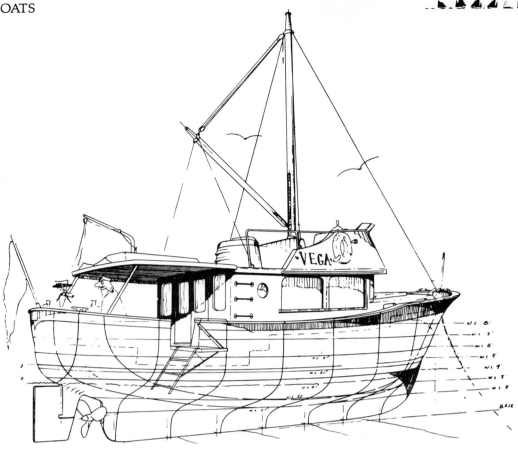

Figure 6.

that a view may be developed from any point in space with either a below (clam's-eye) or an above (bird's-eye) view. The latter shows the deck layout, breaks, deckhouse, and rig. The rig can be projected above the point that I have sketched in the example, but will appear short from the low angles of a below-waterline viewpoint.

The layout shown is used to keep the entire projection on the width of a 36-inch drawing board, hence the developing perspective is on an angle. The distance noted from the viewer to the schooner in Figures 3 and 5 makes a small perspective drawing, and, for the first try, I would suggest the 28-foot distance off as shown in Figure 6. On the grid explanation sheet (Figure 3), I have enlarged a body section to the right of the actual body section to clarify the projections.

Although your eye may be positioned above or below the boat, I would make the first try a basic underwater view. A close view will distort the hull to your eye, and a long distance view puts vanishing points at an impractical distance off the average drawing board, although should the need arise, another board may be put alongside the first to take the projections. With an angle that appeals, a set of permanent points may be established on your board, and any set of lines superimposed on them.

I usually place design waterlines for fairing at 12 inch intervals to simplify offset and lofting height measurements, which also helps in proportioning an odd scale height on the perspective.

For special tools, a 60 inch straight-edge is a help to reach the vanishing points without requiring an extension to the average tee-square via a triangle. Otherwise, the half-dozen curves and sweeps normally used in design will suffice. Heights of moldings and rails will be measured vertically and the drawing completed to suit.

10   *Toadstool*, a Schooner Yacht

LOA (on deck) — 29'
LWL — 23'
Beam — 9'
Draft — 5' 3"
Displacement — 6,800 pounds
Ballast — 1,500 pounds
Sail Area — 555 square feet

Toadstool, the little schooner shown here, is basically an old-time schooner yacht with a feel of the 1880s in rig and above-water form. Underwater she has had the wetted surface trimmed, stability and lateral resistance assured through a simple fin, and directional stability provided by an ample skeg and rudder well aft. One hundred years ago her forefoot would have been rounded down deeper and her keel run aft and down to about the same depth aft, but in one long sweep; the ballast would have been incorporated in her keel or perhaps inside. She would have been a better boat at sea — a steadier platform and more docile under some conditions — but would not have the lively feel that we'll get from the little *Toadstool* of today.

Her design is a compromise, which in this case was influenced by a friend giving me the fin from a *Thunderbird*. The hull size about matched a pile of old-growth planking that we had stacked away in the shop, and we needed a roomy, responsive day sailer and fast cruising boat. She's set up and about half planked at this writing. Another couple of weeks will see her closed in and ready to roll right-side up.

The ancestry of the little schooner is drawn

from all directions with the basic engineering elements warmed up by a period theme. She might be called a yacht miniature of the easy-lined fast packets and traders of a long time ago. A Currier & Ives print of 1856 shows one of her ancestors sliding along under a schooner rig with a short-gaff main rather than the leg-of-mutton main. She might stem from the Whitehall pulling boats of long, easy lines, but firmed up here to carry sail. The pictured schooner is long on the waterline and of the general *America* model, but with a plumb bow and much smaller than the *America* in size. The pulling boat model parentage is recognizable in the sketch, based on the old print (next page).

I can picture George Steers, the *America*'s designer, running up the harbor in a fresh breeze with a spritsail on a big Whitehall and thinking, "Something like this about 100 feet on deck would knock the spots off them." The model certainly came around the Horn to the Pacific, both afloat and in the molds and background of the watermen and boatbuilders who travelled there. It developed into some of the more powerful, but still fine-lined, schooners of the West Coast in the later nineteenth century.

(Above) A sketch of a fast packet originally pictured in a Currier and Ives print of 1856. *(Below)* The lines of a Whitehall pulling boat, which resembles in a way the hull of the schooner above.

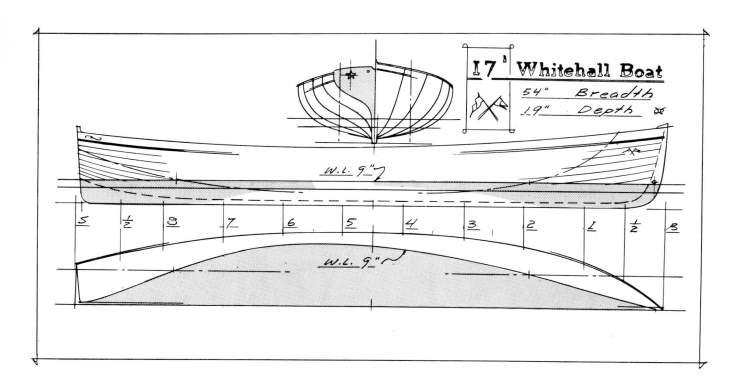

17' Whitehall Boat
54" Breadth
19" Depth

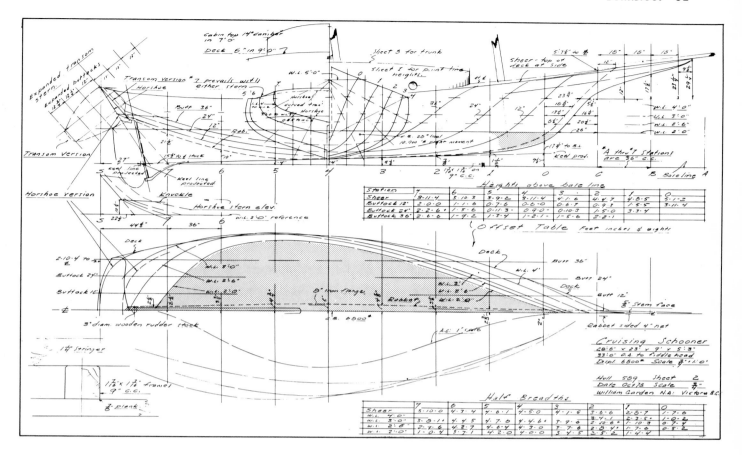

Toadstool's rig is simple and powerful, with the center of effort as low as possible for the generous sail area. The rig is long on the foot for maximum drive with a low center of effort. No light sails are carried, so for running down the wind we will have the main and a big foresail with the light foresail club to wing out the foot. In this area of British Columbia, the usual summer conditions are very light, so she is over rigged, with provisons for quick reefing to compensate as it breezes up. You will notice that the center of effort of the three lowers and the center of the foresail are in nearly the same position, so in a real breeze she will be snug and all inboard under foresail only.

The overlapping foresail must be handed through stays like any overlapping sail, but the jib is on a little poke-stick club, which makes it self-tending, so she's as handy as a sloop. In strong conditions, the foresail in the middle of the ship is in a good position for balance and ease of handling. This overlapping foresail is a wonderful driving sail. Rather than a gaff main, we've fitted here the simple jib-headed main of today, or historically, the "leg-of-mutton" main, such as was carried by the South Sea Island trading schooners and Bermuda boats.

In line with the *Toadstool*'s theme is the use of 1850 wooden engineering, requiring a minimum in costly hardware. Almost everything is within the capabilities of a handy woodworker. Spars are simple and solid, from young trees, and the standing rigging may be set up with thimbles and lanyards or galvanized pipe turnbuckles screwed up in white lead and tallow for long corrosion-free service. Deadeyes are a little overwhelming on a tiny ship like this and won't do anything that can't be matched by simple thimbles in the wire and a lanyard-eye chain plate. The headstay could be stainless steel to take the wear of jib snaps, but a galvanized headstay will last a long time, particularly if given some tallow or grease occasionally. Simple hanks can also replace the costly snaps. We can use a simple lacing of seine twine or light synthetic line to secure the sails.

In model, the *Toadstool* is a scaled-down larger boat in many ways, with the resulting

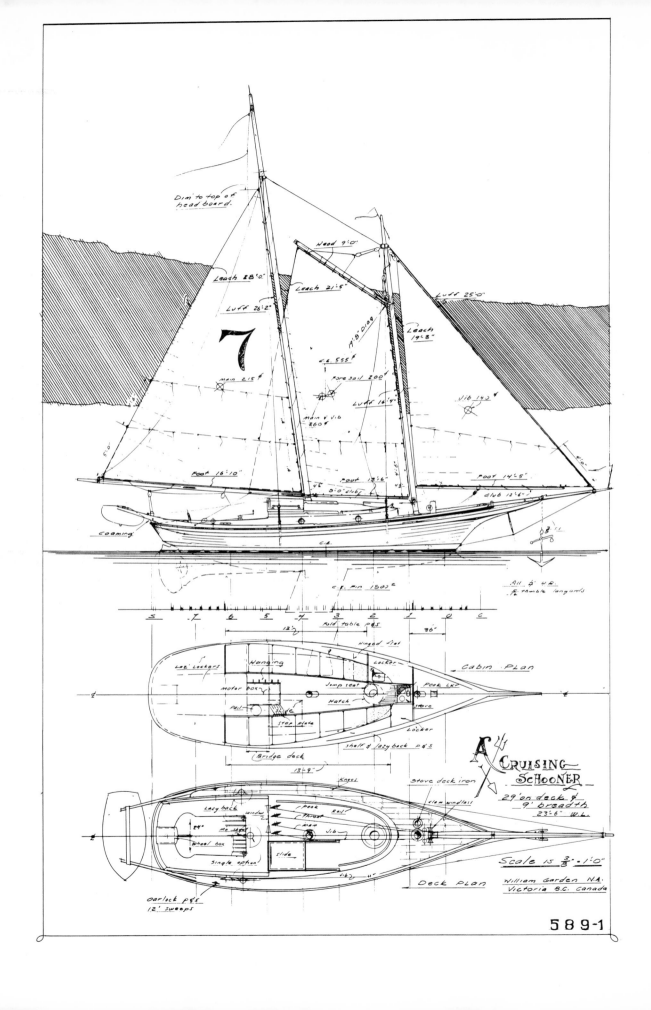

Dim to top of head board.

Leach 28'0"

Luff 26'2"

7

main 215#

Head 9'0"

Leach 21'5"

Luff 25'0"

4'0" Diag

C.E. 555#

Fore Sail 200#

Leach 19'8"

Luff 16'4"

Jib 140#

main & jib 360#

Foot 16'10"

Foot 13'6"

0'0" Club

Foot 14'5"

Club 12'6"

Coaming

C.E.

All ⅝" H.R.
& thimble lanyards

C.E. Fin 1800#

S   7   6   5   4   3   2   1   0   C

Fold table p&s

36"

Laz Lockers   Hanging   Locker   Cabin Plan
12'7
Hinged flat

motor box   Jump seat   Peak LKr
Pail   Hatch   stove

Step plate   Locker

Bridge deck   shelf & lazyback p&s

13'9"

A Cruising Schooner

Knee   Stove deck iron

Lazyback   window   Peak   Rail   Clam windlass
                      Throat
24"   Mo step   Main
Wheel box   jib
                          Single option   slide

oarlock p&s
12' sweeps   Jib   Deck Plan

29' on deck &
9' breadth
23'6" W.L.

Scale is ⅜" = 1'0"

William Garden N.A.
Victoria B.C. Canada

589-1

minimum accommodations. No attempt has been made to get stand-up space in the smallest possible boat, but rather the intent is to achieve a day sailer with a snug cabin for occasional cruising. The two settees will let two stretch out along with seabags, and four can sleep in a pinch since the settees are over 12 feet long. The woodwork is varnished throughout, and the frame and joinerwork is given a nice bead and chamfer as shown on the framing plan. Varnished out, with oil lamps lit, the right seat cushion covers, and a seabag to lean on, this cabin will be a nice hideout. Few structures give a feeling of shelter to match that of a tight, dry cabin with comfortable, sit-up headroom. Under sail she will be lively and hard to match in light airs, so we have a pleasant day sailer capable of very fast passages.

The fin will be the main jolt to the purist. A fin from any number of modern boats will do, and many coastal foundries will have a pattern of 1,500 pounds or 2,000 pounds that will fit with some improvising. This, along with the light, internal ballast, will make her stand up

and go with minimum wetted surface plus stability and draft for windward ability in rough water. The fin might be likened to a permanent ballasted centerboard, giving the boat self-righting qualities; major sail-carrying ability comes from the hull form.

The hull form is interesting to compare with the little schooner *Gleam*, one of her more recent ancestors. I built *Gleam* for myself in 1939, so she and *Toadstool* are about 35 years apart in time. Perhaps the best compromise would be *Toadstool*'s bow and *Gleam*'s stern.

Gleam had bulwarks and a short trunk with the engine hatch abaft the main mast and a bridge deck amidships forming mast partners; this arrangement shortened up the accommodations to a two-berth layout. She was a nice boat at sea and would run downwind like smoke. *Toadstool* has a lower center of gravity, less wetted surface, greater stability, and a bigger rig, along with no bulwarks but with a catboat type of coaming and house, so both boats will be about equally dry or wet under sail. Jerry Anderson and Bob Colwell are busy

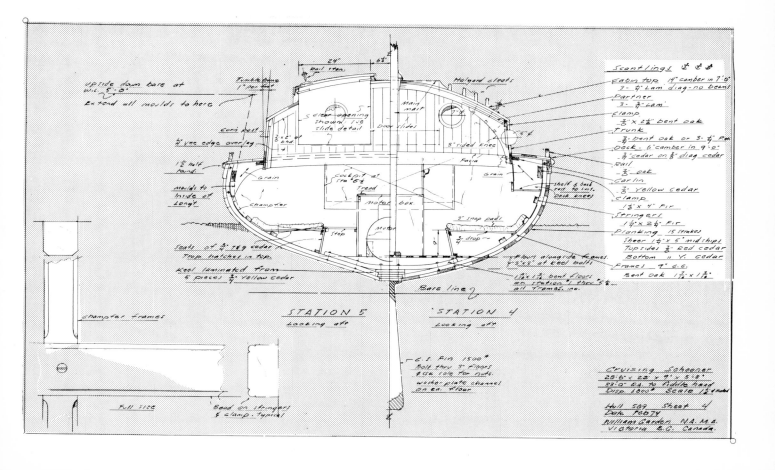

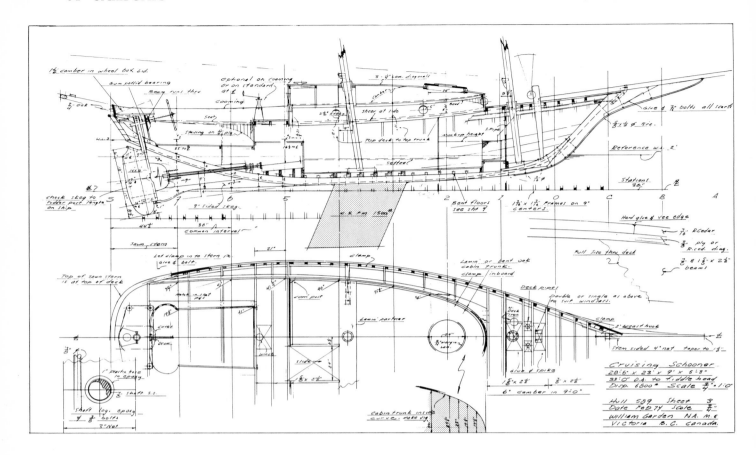

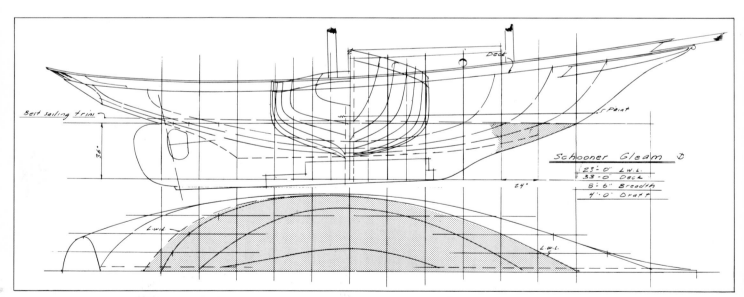

The lines of the schooner *Gleam*, which is a recent ancestor of *Toadstool*.

with the new ship out in the shop, and items of gear and material are piling up in the storeroom. We seem to spend as much now in a month as I spent back in 1939 on the whole schooner. The old account book shows a total expenditure in time of 1,621 hours, and the material cost was a grand total of $700.00, including a rebuilt Kermath 6-8 hp, two-cylinder engine. Not much money by today's shrinking-dollar standards, but then it was the residue after living expenses from the previous year's boatbuilding at 80 cents per hour.

Toadstool in the building shed, ready to launch (photo by Studio West).

For *Toadstool*, a round stern (on this coast a "horseshoe stern") and an optional transom are both shown, and, until we had the body plan half down, I hadn't decided on either, but a nice pile of yellow cedar 4 × 12s turned it in favor of the round version. The elliptical stern is an equally lovely form, and either will fit the clipper bow like tails do a top hat. The choice is yours.

Before leaving proportions, try to visualize her twice this size, about 18 feet in breadth and with a low trunk. There would be space then for stores, a rum room, and a boat on deck . . . but let's get on to construction.

She's probably best in wood about as designed. Over the years, we've had many hun-dreds of boats built in all sorts of materials and in all methods. Our attitude has been that whatever is on hand and suits existing skills is the best or most practical material and method to use, whether it is lapstrake, steel, ply, glass, aluminum, carvel, cold molded, double skin, canvas, or logs. *Toadstool* is a traditional sort, and our woodpile seems to favor simple bent-oak framing and carvel planking.

So that's it for *Toadstool*. There's a fresh westerly blowing across my island hideout today, good hard puffs coming off the weather shore, and a clear reach south leads off in flat water under the lee of the land. A wonderful day to blow the last shavings off the deck and try her out.

The newly launched *Toadstool* is a smart sailer.

11 *Privateer*, an Ancient Dream Ship

LOA (on deck) — 30' 1"
LWL — 25' 4"
Beam — 13' 0"
Draft — 6' 0"
Displacement — 26,000 pounds
Sail Area — 885 square feet
Ballast — 7,000 pounds

Fair laughs the morn, and soft the zephyr blows,
While proudly riding o'er the azure realm
In gallant trim the gilded vessel goes,
Youth on the prow, and pleasure at the helm . . .
— *Thomas Gray*

Privateer is sufficiently unusual to require some explanation in order to put her in focus. So before getting along with the boat itself, let's digress a moment and dwell on the past.

Among the earliest accounts of vessels for pleasure, or proportioned and rigged other than exclusively for commerce of war, are some misty references to Royal Yachts. References to these vessels outline scant details and dimensions, but perhaps especially fascinating is their brevity, which allows us unlimited speculation as to proportions, rig, and ornamentation. Phineas Pett, the naval constructor, notes in his autobiography that he received ". . . about January 15, 1604 a command to build with all possible speed, . . ." a little vessel for young Prince Henry to ". . . disport himself in about London bridge and thereby acquaint his grace with shipping and the manner of that element." The "proportions and manner of garnishment" were outlined to Pett, and the little ship was to

be 25 feet on the keel, 12 feet in breadth, "Garnished with painting and carvings both within and without, very curiously according to his Lordship's [Lord High Admiral Howard's] directions."

The request may have been made with a hint of the axe, since Pett "wrought night and day by torch and candle," and she went overboard on March the sixth. She sailed from Chatham, arriving on March the twenty-second in the Thames, where she anchored off Blackwall. Subsequently christened with a "great bowle of wine," she was named *Disdain* and noted in the Navy List of 1618 as of 30 tons burden. Apparently she was decorated and rigged after the *Ark Royal*, Howard's flagship against the Armada. Thirty tons indicates a deep and full-bodied model, with proportions beyond a quickly converted ship's boat, so the production time is impressive. With such an order today, backed by an open purse and assuming a similar

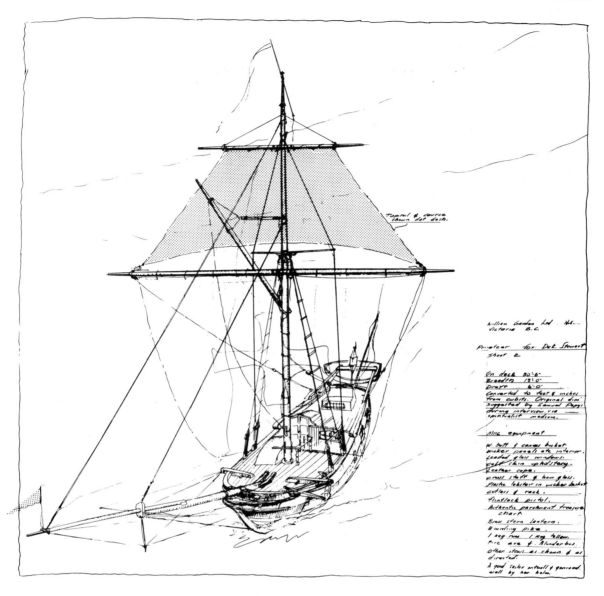

William Garden Ltd. Nk.
Victoria B.C.

Privateer for: Dk. Stewart
Sheet 2

On deck 30'6"
Breadth 13'0"
Draft 6'0"
Converted to feet & inches
from cubits. Original dim's
supported by Samuel Pepys
during interview via
spiritalist medium.

Misc equipment

W. butt & canvas bucket.
wicker panels etc interior.
leaded glass windows.
soft skin upholstery.
leather caps.
cross staff & hour glass.
Plastic lobster in wicker basket
cutlass & rack.
flintlock pistol.
Authentic parchment treasure
     chart
Brass stern lantern.
Boarding pike.
1 keg rum 1 keg tallow.
Fire axe & blunderbuss.
Other items as shown & as
directed.
A good sailor withall & guaranteed
well by her helm.

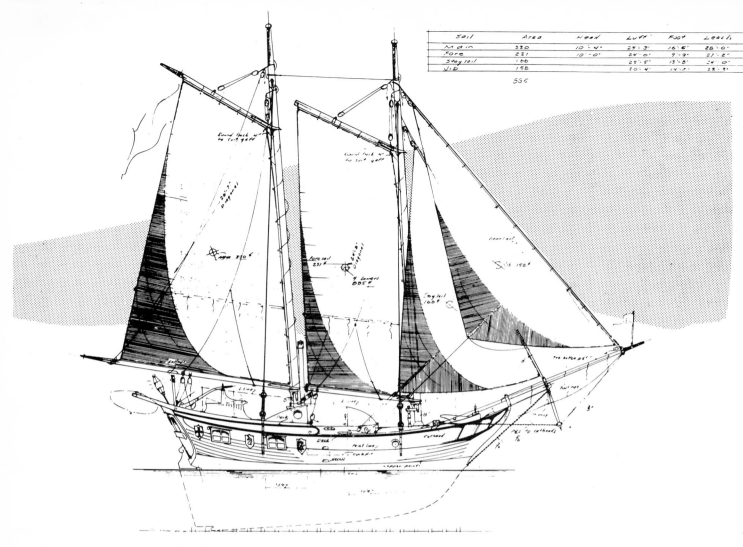

Sail	Area	Head	Luff	Foot	Leach
Main	330	10'·4"	25'·3'	16'·6"	28'·0"
Fore	231	10'·0"	24'·0'	9'·9"	27'·2"
Staysail	166		25'·5'	13'·8"	24'·0"
Jib	158		30'·4'	14'·7"	23'·8"

555

rather severe penalty clause, such as the gallows or the hulks, the building time of 51 days would be hard to match. Upon receiving the order, old Pett must have immediately leaned out the window and started shouting.

Rigging would have been started during the second week, and we can picture the complete masts with doublings, yards, and standing and running rigging being assembled outstretched on the shop floor, all being readied to step and set up to matching partners and chainplates. Sub-assemblies and components would be fashioned in every corner, and the major work of hull and decks would be swarming with every man the dockyard could position to lay hands on the vessel. A crew of six on each side would be hanging planks, two per side, lining off and getting them out and shaped. Beams would be fitted, carvers would be worrying about proportions, pit sawmen would be sweating away roughing out lumber, and old Pett would be co-ordinating, worrying, and thoroughly enjoying the rare chance of nearly spontaneous creation.

An estimate of 12,000 man hours for those times and equipment is probably safe for a crash program. A cost of £10 per ton in the 1600s might be realistic, and the Admiralty probably can still dig out a wrinkled statement to prove it, tear-sprinkled after perusal by a long-dead treasurer.

So we come to the noble *Privateer*, a little vessel in the ancient manner and based upon a nebulous concept of how things might have been, a time machine to transport us back to letters of marque and the days when a misty headland on the horizon would shelter some vast, unknown inlet with white beaches, lots to eat, and not a political thought in the minds of the kindly inhabitants.

She has an overall length including fiddlehead of 33 feet 5 inches, she is 30 feet 1 inch on deck, 25 feet 4 inches load waterline, 13 feet 0 inches in breadth, and will draw 6 feet 0 inches in her sea trim. This is a full-bodied little ship, requiring 885 square feet of sail to drive her. She is of massive sawn-frame construction, roomy

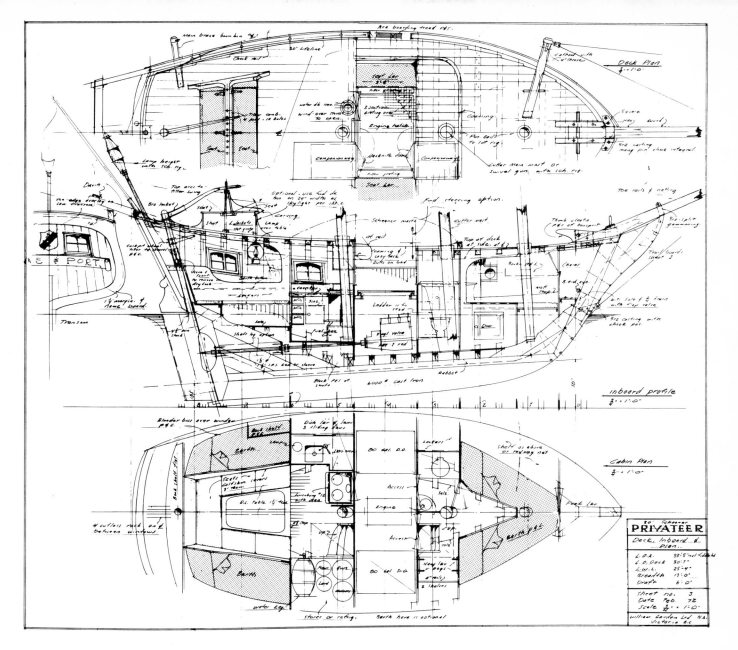

and able, capable of holding her own to windward in any company — with the assist of a good diesel engine. She will slide along beautifully for all normal cruising, and the ample rig with drive her in the lightest conditions.

Two sail plans were developed, the simpler and perhaps most practical schooner rig, or the old-time cutter, with a mile or so of gear for the man who owns a rope walk and likes to be busy roaming the deck with a handy-billy setting things up. With either rig nothing could be more pleasant than sitting on a cask contemplating the full curve of the mainsail as she bowls along toward the horizon.

Accommodations afford reasonable privacy and can be supplemented with a light deck awning for harbor use. The "great cabin" aft, of ancient lineage, comprises the heart of the ship in port, and the table laden with rich fare and surrounded by good company makes an enviable retreat. A wicker basket of lobsters, pewter service, and a few interesting bottles chocked off under the glowing lamp overhead are set off by cutlasses racked up and handy by the companionway. Oiled wood with heavy framing and joinerwork and rich book bindings contribute to the overall good smell of ship's rum and cordage. Captives we would keep forward and deal with as time allows.

So here she is. With a picked crew of tars, well laden with rich stores, a fully stocked rum room, and carrying a brass "long tom" amidships, the *Privateer* is a lovely way to go.

12 *Bull Frog*, a Cruising Double-ender

LOA — 30' 4"
LWL — 26' 0"
Breadth — 10' 0"
Draft — 6' 0"
Sail Area — 748 square feet cutter
Sail Area — 752 square feet ketch
Displacement — 18,500 pounds
Ballast, outside — 6,000 pounds
Ballast, inside — 600 pounds

The compulsion to build a boat is a long-rooted tangle down the genetic deeps, with perhaps only a whiff of salt beach to touch it off, and suddenly nothing else will do. In the complex mix that puts us on the water, it is the second element, of either competition or escape, that dictates the boat that catches us.

Bull Frog will be a choice for the traditionalist and reflects a couple of thousand years of double-enders that precede her, boats with proportions varying from the easy-lined Viking longships to William W. Nutting's chunky 42-foot 6-inch by 15-foot 6-inch cutter, *Leiv Eiriksson*, a fishing-cutter, yacht conversion lost somewhere to the westward of Reykjavik on her voyage home along the ancient route to "Vineland the Good" with a box of Viking bones from the Island of Yell chocked off on deck. She may have been hove down by a granddaddy wave, and the unsecured, rusty-red, pig-iron inside ballast may have gone thundering down through the lee berths and out the deckhouse. The working double-enders general-ly carried inside ballast, stowed in a hit-or-miss fashion. This is rough load to have loose when the boat is over past her beam ends.

The Scandinavian double-ender's ancestry and development goes back to the misty time of the first settlers of the northern coastlines. The planked boat might have gone north with them. The simple pulling boat developed into the long, lean Viking ship with its oar and square sail — perhaps the optimum seagoing, open boat. In their grim effect on European history, these beautiful, clinker longships of the Norsemen have few equals.

A most impressive collection of ancient boats is in Oslo, and, along with the awe-inspiring longships is a tiny pulling boat of exquisite model found in one of the burial mounds. It is very close in shape and construction to a 17-foot sailing and pulling boat that we once owned, bought from Norway in the early 1950s as a stock boat. The form has changed very little in a thousand years.

While the larger longship was the ultimate

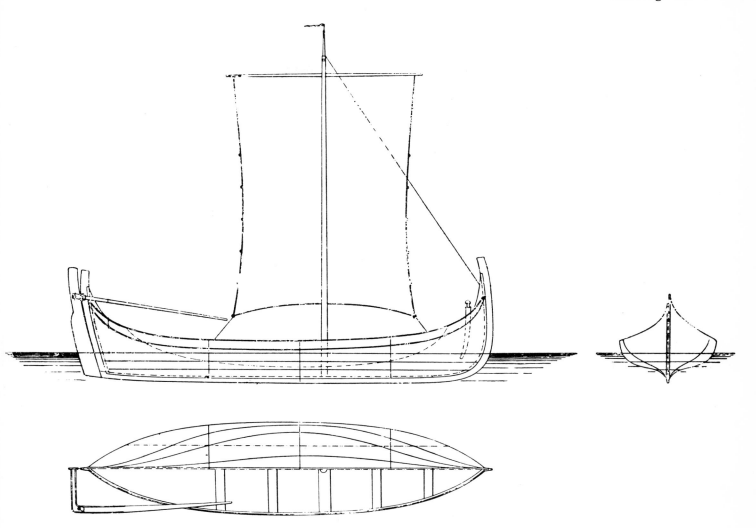

The Nordlands cod boat.

development for its service, the fisheries were carried on with longshore and beaching boats, still incredibly primitive until the introduction of the internal combustion engine. The Nordlands cod boat, shown here, is an example — open, high in the ends, but shoal bodied and relatively narrow with flaring sides. She had a square sail capable of reasonably close windward work, and, for winter fishing, a small cabin in the poop, with its stove, furnished minimum shelter. Essentially big rowing boats, these craft depended on oars for most windward work. Johan Bojer's wonderful *Last of the Vikings* (The Century Co., 1923) has a vivid description of the fishery. How hard things were then, is an indication of how hard they could be again.

On the coast to the south during the later years of sail, a more burdensome and weatherly model than the cod boat was developed similar to the cutters of Sweden and Denmark. Usually there was a sprit main with two headsails and a heavy pole mast; cordage was weak and the stout spars took the main load. This Hvalorbaad, similar to the herring boat illustrated, was the forerunner of the famed Redningskoite built for pilot and sailing lifeboat service by Colin Archer and his contemporaries during the latter part of the nineteenth century, prior to the development of power craft.

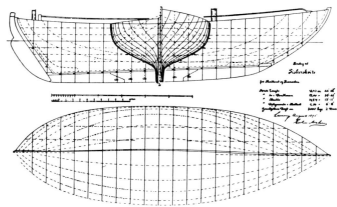

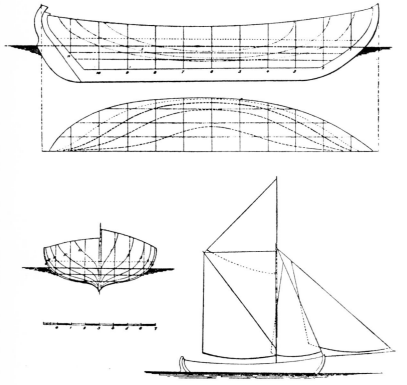

Lines of a 44-foot fishing ketch *(above)* designed by Colin Archer.

A herring boat *(left)*, forerunner of the Redningskoite, which in turn influenced many yacht designs.

The pilot boat was cutter rigged, on a similar hull to the fishing ketch illustrated, and a powerful, weatherly boat resulted. Later models used some outside ballast. This is the model so often seen converted to a yacht and written up in many cruise stories such as Erling Tambs's *Cruise of the Teddy*, Ralph Stock's *Cruise of the Dream Ship*, and countless cruising yarns in the old boating publications. These boats were of massive construction and even when half-rotten had enough solid structure remaining to be able to carry on for years. Timber was of oak and pine and was immensely strong by today's standards. For example, a 39 foot by 13 foot pilot boat would have 4 × 8 frames, 1¾ inch planking, 1½ inch decking, 4 × 4 and 4 × 5 beams, and a good, fat 12 inch diameter mast. Ballast would be about 30 to 35 percent of the displacement, with about half of it outside. The lifesaving ketch was also lined inside the frames with another skin of planking from the deck to the sole, giving her an inner watertight hull for additional safety. Outside ballast was concentrated well amidships to keep the ends light and lively. The weight of the outside iron increased with the boat's development, and

seemed to reach about half of the total ballast, the remainder being inside.

From these rugged old timers have descended the multitude of yacht developments of the "Colin Archer type." Billy Atkin designed some good ones, and his "Eric" design has probably made a record in the number built over the past fifty years. "Eric" and a host of others will reward a careful dig ohrough back issues of boating magazines and the library.

Our *Bull Frog's* most recent ancestor was another *Bull Frog* that I built and sailed down the coast many years ago. The original *Frog* was nearer the traditional Colin Archer, with about half of her ballast outside and half (cement and iron) inside. She had a gaff cutter rig, short trunk cabin, and deep bulwarks. In model she was much fuller forward than this new *Bull Frog*, the first one incorporating the symmetrical ends usually favored for the type. With eased sheets or in an easy sea to windward, the original was a good performer. On the wind in a fresh breeze and chop, the form gave room for thought, so the new *Bull Frog's* forward waterlines are sharper, her quarters are flatter, she has slightly more breadth on the waterline,

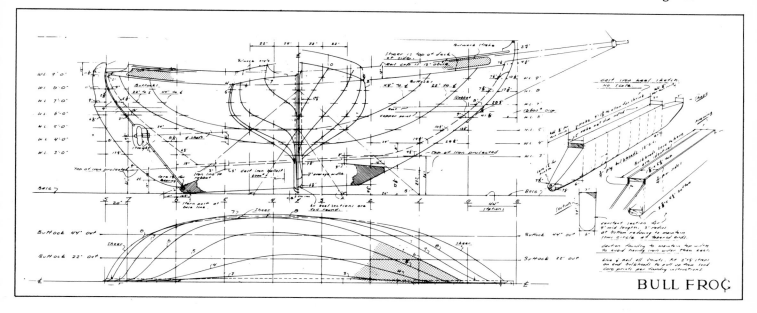

BULL FROG

and, for this burdensome a hull, she has an easy run. Nearly all ballast is outside, which will let her set and carry a more powerful rig, and the fore-and-aft length and weight distribution will be close to ideal. Not too much weight is in the ends, so she will rise easily and slip through a head sea with minimum fuss. This sail-carrying ability will enhance her worth for summer cruising and make her more exciting to sail, but will also result in a quicker, more tiring motion at sea, similar to the liveliness of the usual high-performance, racing-cruising boat. So we gain sailing ability for 90 percent of her sailing life and lose seakindliness in probably 30 percent of her time underway. Both *Frogs* will be equally able at sea, the lively one a faster, but more tiring, platform.

This performance under sail will be a revelation to those used to the stately plodding of the average little under-rigged, double-ended cruiser. Her rig's center of effort here is in the right fore-and-aft position and will be nearly the same whether she carries the flatter-leached boomed mainsail or the loose-footed sail with its lovely driving curve. With a ketch rig, the mast will be farther forward; the total centers of effort of each rig are noted on the sail plan. Balance will be close to ideal.

Under sail in the lightest airs, she will fan along with the topsail and the lower sails or with a big genoa jib; with the cutter's staysail and reefed main, she will be handy in a hard breeze — all inboard-rigged then — and simple in stays with the main and staysail self-tending. But be sure to fit the backstay runners noted on the rigging list to keep the jibstay reasonably straight when on the wind and also to lessen worry when running off before it.

A jib-headed cutter version and a boomed-mainsail gaff cutter rig are shown in dotted lines on the open-footed cutter plan. Note that the ketch rig has much less lead (the amount the center of effort is ahead of the center of resistance) than the cutter. With the ketch rig, the mizzen is taken in first as the breeze increases and a docile helm is maintained. A possible shortening down sequence is illustrated.

The masts and spars are solid and tapered to the dimensions shown by first making the timber four-sided, then eight-sided, then sixteen-sided. Finally the corners are rounded off to finish. Tree spars will do if the sapwood is skinned off. Shoulder cleats for shrouds, jaws, and other miscellaneous details are shown on sheet one. The rigging noted on the cutter plan is to be stainless steel with Norseman terminals, which are a neat way to terminate wires, but costly and probably not readily available. The ketch plan shows a detail of simple lanyards, which make an inexpensive option.

With the boomed mainsail, a boom vang may be fitted to keep the main quiet and drawing best. With the boomless main, the clew block can be a dangerous shipmate and more perilous than a main boom. Note that the leach is nearly plumb, so the block remains at about

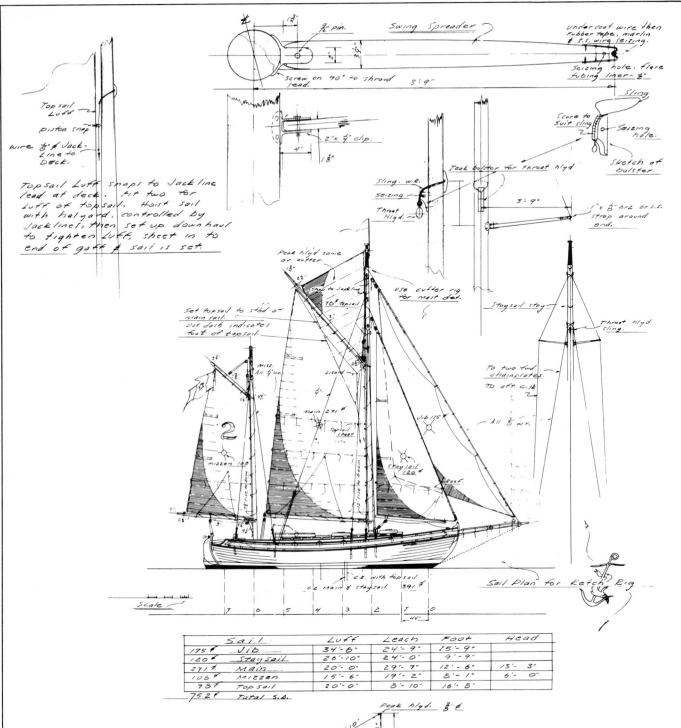

Swing Spreader

2/16" pin.

screw on 90° to shroud lead.   3'·9"

undercoat wire then rubber tape, marlin & s.s. wire seizing.

Seizing hole. flare tubing liner-3/4"

Topsail Luff

piston snap

wire 3/16"∅ Jack-line to Deck.

Topsail Luff snaps to Jackline lead at deck. Fit two for luff of topsail. Hoist sail with halyard, controlled by Jacklines, then set up downhaul to tighten luff, sheet in to end of gaft & sail is set.

2"x 7/8" clip.

Peak hlyd same as cutter.

Sling.

Score to suit sling   Seizing hole.

Sketch of bolster.

Teak bolster for throat hlyd

Sling. w.r. seizing

Throat Hlyd.

3'·9"

1"x 3/8" bre or s.s. strap around end.

Snap to Jackline 78# topsail

use cutter rig for mast det.

Staysail stay

Throat hlyd sling.

Set topsail to stbd of main sail. Dot dash indicates foot of topsail.

Mizz. All 5/16"w.r.

Lizard

Main 271#

Topsail sheet

mizzen 108

staysail 120#

Jib 175

Reef

To two fwd chainplates. To aft c.p.

All 5/16"w.r.

c.e. with topsail c.e. main & staysail 391#

Sail Plan for Ketch Rig

Scale

7 6 5 4 3 2 1 0

44"

	Sail	Luff	Leach	Foot	Head
175#	Jib	34'-6"	24'-9"	15'-9"	
120#	Staysail	26'-10"	24'-0"	9'-9"	
271#	Main	20'-0"	29'-7"	12'-6"	13'-3"
108#	Mizzen	15'-6"	19'-2"	8'-1"	6'-0"
78#	Topsail	20'-0"	8'-10"	16'-8"	
752#	Total S.A.				

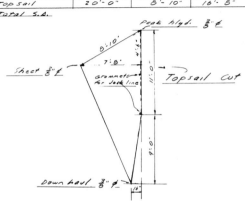

Peak hlyd. 3/8"∅

8'·10"

7'·8"

4'·6"

11'·0"

Sheet 3/8"∅

grommets for Jackline

Topsail Cut

9'·0"

Downhaul 3/8"∅

16"

BULL FROG

L.O.A	30'-11"
L.W.L.	26'-0"
Breadth dk	10'-0"
Draft	6'-0"

Ketch & layout C

Hull no.	580
Sheet no.	4
Date	1972
Scale	noted

William Garden Ltd
Naval Architects & Engr
Victoria B.C.

| 580-4. | Scale noted |

BULL FROG

L.O.A	30'-11"
L.W.L.	26'-0"
Breadth dk	10'-0"
Draft	6'-0"
Cutter Rig & Layout A & B.	
Hull no.	580
Sheet no.	1
Date	1972
Scale	noted
William Garden Ltd Naval Architect & Engr Victoria B.C.	
580-1	Scale noted

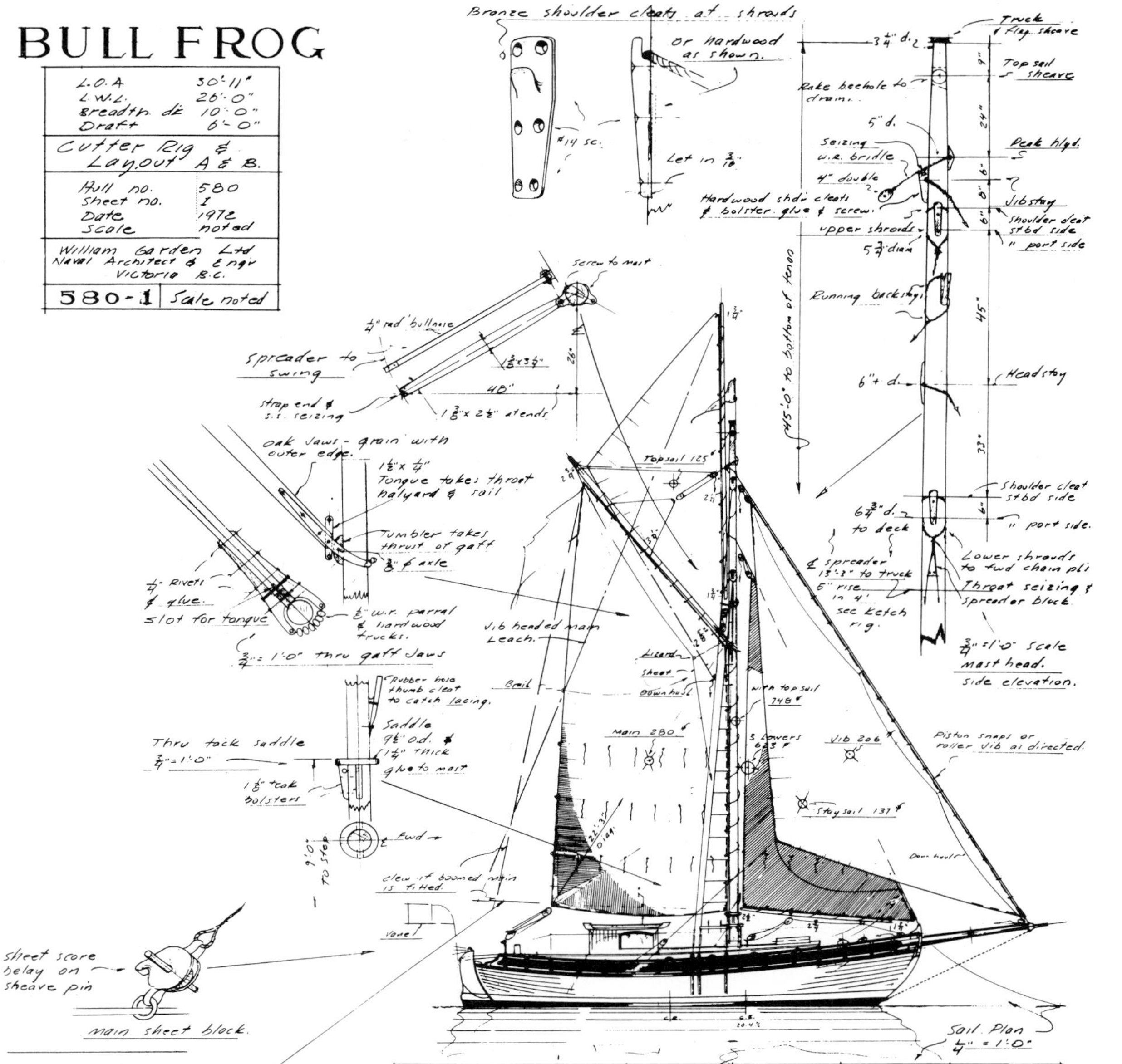

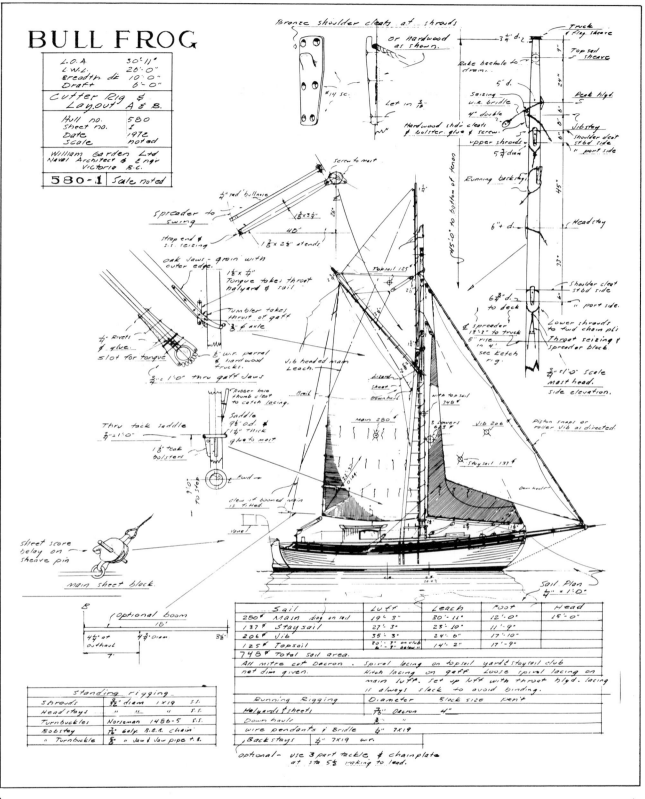

Bronze shoulder cleats at shrouds
or hardwood as shown.
#14 sc.
Let in 3/16
Hardwood shdr cleats & bolster. glue & screw.
Truck & flag sheave
Top sail sheave
Rake beehole to drain.
5" d.
Seizing w.r. bridle
4" double
Peak hlyd.
Jibstay
Shoulder cleat stbd side
" port side
upper shrouds
5 3/4" diam
Running backstays
Headstay
6" + d.
45'-0" to bottom of tenon
Shoulder cleat stbd side
" port side.
6 3/4" d. to deck
Lower shrouds to fwd chain pl.
Throat seizing & spreader block
3/4" = 1'-0" scale mast head. side elevation.
Screw to mast
Spreader to swing
Strap end & s.s. seizing
oak Jaws - grain with outer edge.
Tongue takes throat halyard & sail
Tumbler takes thrust of gaff
1/4" rivets & glue.
slot for tongue
w.r. parral & hard wood trucks.
3/4" = 1'-0" thru gaff Jaws
Rubber holo thumb cleat to catch lacing.
Saddle
Thru tack saddle 3/4" = 1'-0"
glue to mast
teak bolsters
Fwd
Topsail 125#
Jib headed main leach.
Brail
Lizard
Sheet
Down haul
With top sail 748#
Main 280#
3 Lowers 68.3#
Jib 206#
Piston snaps or roller Jib as directed.
Staysail 137#
Down haul
clew if boomed main is fitted.
Vane
sheet score belay on sheave pin
main sheet block.
Sail Plan 1/4" = 1'-0"

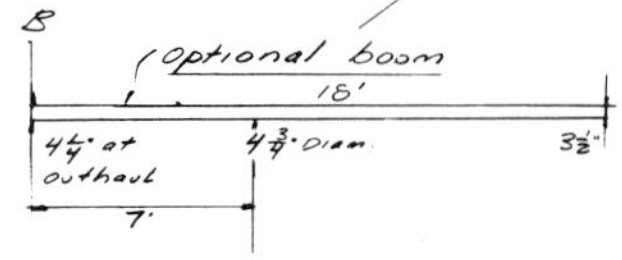

B
Optional boom
18'
4 1/4" at outhaul
4 3/4" Diam.
3 1/2"
7'

Sail	Luff	Leach	Foot	Head
280# Main diag on sail	19'-3"	30'-11"	12'-0"	15'-0"
137# Staysail	27'-3"	23'-10"	11'-9"	
206# Jib	35'-3"	24'-6"	17'-10"	
125# Topsail	20'-3" on club 6'-3" below	14'-2"	17'-9"	

748# Total sail area.

All mitre cut Dacron. net dim given. Spiral lacing on topsail yard & staysail club. Hitch lacing on gaff. Loose spiral lacing on main luff. Set up luff with throat hlyd. lacing is always slack to avoid binding.

Standing rigging		
Shrouds	9/32" diam 1x19	S.S.
Head stays	" " "	S.S.
Turnbuckles	Norseman 1486-5	S.S.
Bobstay	7/16" Galv. B.B.B. chain	
" Turnbuckle	5/8" " Jaw & Jaw pipe T.B.	

Running Rigging	Diameter	Block size	Rem'k
Halyards & sheets	7/16" Dacron	4"	
Down hauls	3/8" "		
wire pendants & Bridle	1/4" 7x19		
Backstays	1/4" 7x19 wir.		

optional - use 3 part tackle & chainplate at sta 5 1/2 raking to lead.

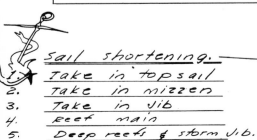

Sail shortening.

1. Take in topsail
2. Take in mizzen
3. Take in Jib
4. Reef main
5. Deep reefs & storm Jib.

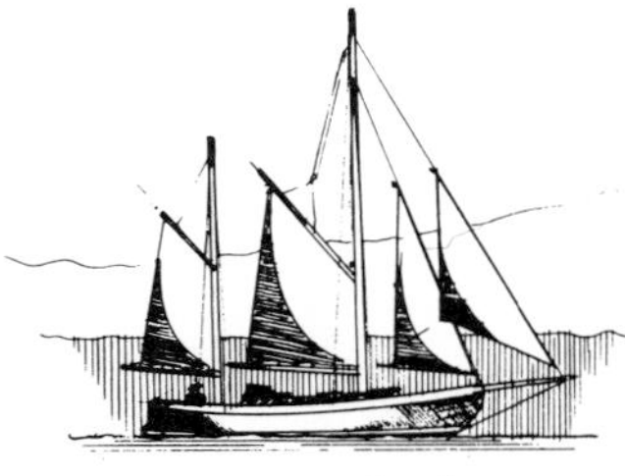

Deep reefed

Main & Staysail

With topsail

the same height whether the sail is sheeted home or slack. With a raking leach, the block would swing forward and wipe out the cockpit, a feature occasionally designed by an unthumped designer.

When reefing the loose-footed sail, the main is lowered about four feet, the tack is bowsed down, and the clew earing is secured to the main sheet block; then the throat and peak are set up again and the reef nettles are tied off to tidy up. The earing patches at the reefs must equal in strength the clew earing and have big grommets sewn in to take the reef pendant. Commercial quality blocks will do, but the lower main-sheet thumb block must be custom made, for there is nothing like this in an off-the-shelf item today other than the excellent cam-action jam cleat blocks, which are probably superior in action but might offend the purist.

The layout plans may vary, but in all cases I would leave the plan as is in the forward end. Plan A shows an arrangement to suit a trunk cabin boat, and Plan B fits only the pilothouse version, with quarter berths at the pilothouse

Layout Selection Chart

GOOD POINTS	BAD POINTS
LAYOUT A	
Quarter berths are at point of least motion and close to companionway.	Berths are under cockpit, with its noise.
Chart table is at companionway.	Spray or rain can wet bunks.
Easy motor access.	Folding chart table.
Sleeper is away from galley and off-watch noise.	Engine alongside berths - noisiest spot under power.
LAYOUT B	
Pilothouse has strength of permanent shelter; dry and warm inside, as is rest of ship.	Quarter berth tight access under decks at this height.
Inside auxiliary wheel and quarter berth at point of least motion.	No formal saloon.
Excellent motor access and space — stores, stowage, etc., under pilothouse.	
Galley stack forward clear of down draft due to the wind's pressure to windward of mainsail. Also clear of cockpit.	
Dinette's simple seating layout and table is out of passage. Cook can lean on it for brace.	
LAYOUT C	
Comfortable saloon clear of galley.	Crew must pass cook to go forward.
Galley aft under companionway for good ventilation and cockpit access.	Pilot berths are in main saloon.
Pilot berths port and starboard in quietest part of ship, clear of galley cockpit activity for those off watch.	
Icebox with deck fill can be fitted under seat in cockpit.	

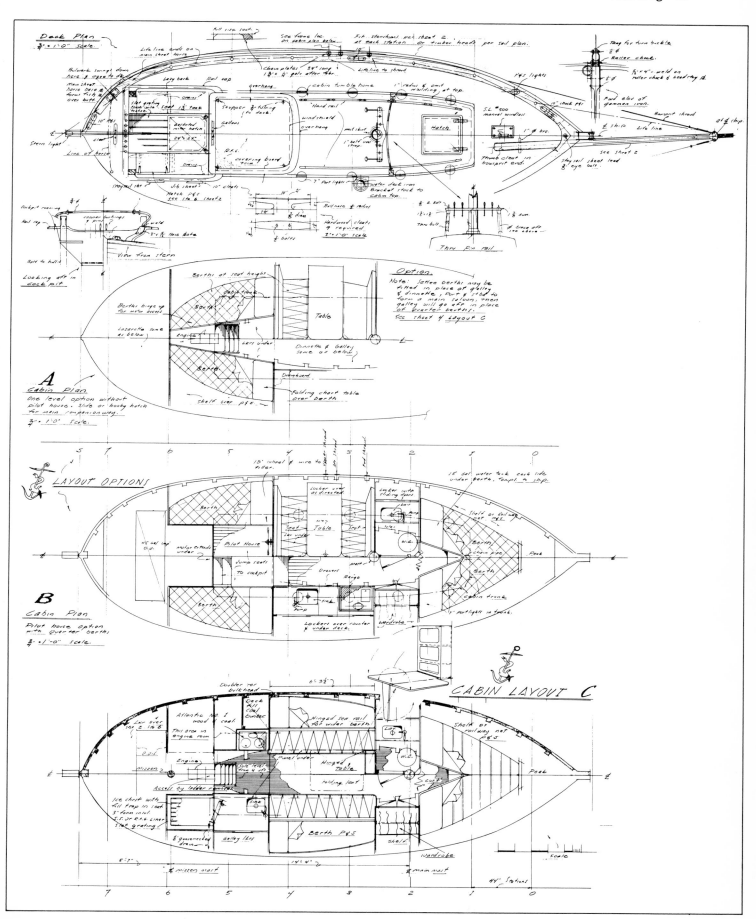

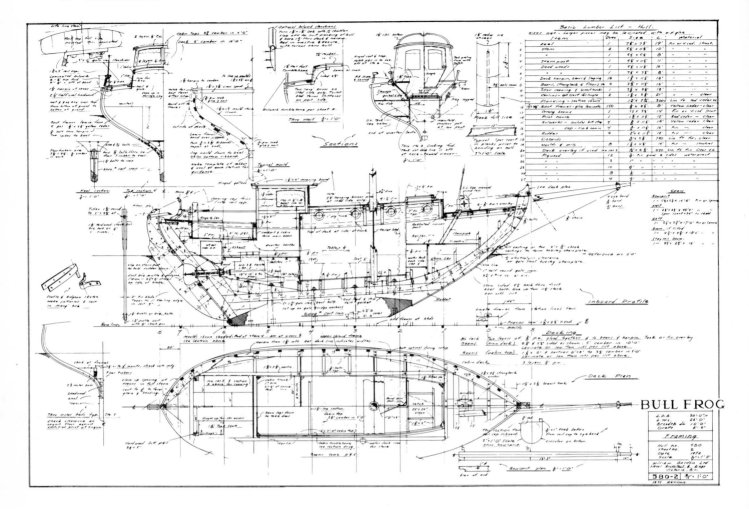

BULL FROG

sole level. These berths are kept dry by the enclosure of the pilothouse. With the trunk cabin and low quarter berths of Plan A, a waterproof curtain should be fitted to keep bedding dry under bad conditions. Layout C is perhaps my choice.

In any event, the layout selection chart which follows will help in selecting the best layout for your ship, and also will be a guide to developing layouts for other plans in the book. In all layouts, the forward berths are for coastal cruising, stowage, and the moored "live on board." The stateroom is roomy and affords room to sit up in bed to read; be sure, however, to fit two inch foam insulation under the berth panels to avoid hull condensation and damp bedding.

Bull Frog is of strip-built construction, with a minimum number of frames, which are laminated and glued up over the stringers. The normal building sequence is to make up the backbone timbers first and assemble them on

their side on blocks to keep them off the shop floor; this will provide bolt access and work room. Bolt the iron on next, patterned similarly to the drawing shown, then erect the backbone with the waterlines level and proceed with molds, stringers, etc. In strip construction, cleaning the glue off as you progress will be a timesaver later on and make a better job.

The bulwarks shown will secure to welded mild steel brackets, which are hot-dip galvanized after fabrication. An option could be simple 2-inch by 2-inch wooden top timbers. All special iron fittings requiring custom fabrication may be made locally at an ornamental iron works and shipped off via auto freight to the nearest source for hot-dip galvanizing. Electroplating will not last, so avoid it in fastenings and all coatings.

So, that's the *Bull Frog*'s outline and background. The boat is an ideal size to build and to sail. She's able, handy, and a home on the bright, blue sea.

13 *Buccaneer 300* and *Swoop,*
Two Contrasts

Buccaneer 300
LOA — 30'
LWL — 26'
Beam — 10'
Draft — 4'
Displacement — 9,800 pounds
Ballast — 3,500 pounds
Sail Area — 447 square feet 100 percent fore triangle

Swoop
LOA — 34'
LWL — 28' 3"
Beam — 10'
Draft — 4' 6"
Displacement — 16,500 pounds
Ballast — 5,700 pounds outside, 1,000 pounds inside
Sail Area (sloop) — 550 square feet 100 percent fore triangle

Swoop forms an interesting comparison with the Buccaneer 300; both have 10-foot breadths; overall lengths are 34 feet for *Swoop* and 30 feet for the Buccaneer. They are far apart in construction: The 300 is all fiberglass with minimal wood trim, while *Swoop* is of traditional wooden carvel construction. In form, layout, and theme the two boats are equally far apart: *Swoop*, despite the deckhouse, is a traditional seagoing model, while the 300 was developed as an ideal production, shoal-draft, cruising sloop. Yet, the 300 is not a warmed over, last year's competitive stock boat, but a boat designed specifically for the job.

Let's discuss *Swoop* first. Thirty years ago a deckhouse on a double-ender would have been unacceptable to the purist, but today it seems to fit our eye, and 30 years hence a deckhouse will probably signify a character boat, so the pattern changes. *Swoop*'s owner, Es Horne, is a sailor of long experience both on deepwater ships and yachts. From a boyhood familiarity with the big, power whaleboats of the Coast Survey, he has had a lifelong romance with the general model's strong sheer, sharp ends, shallow body, and light displacement. So when he wanted a new boat, he came up with the draft of a filled-

(Text continued on page 75)

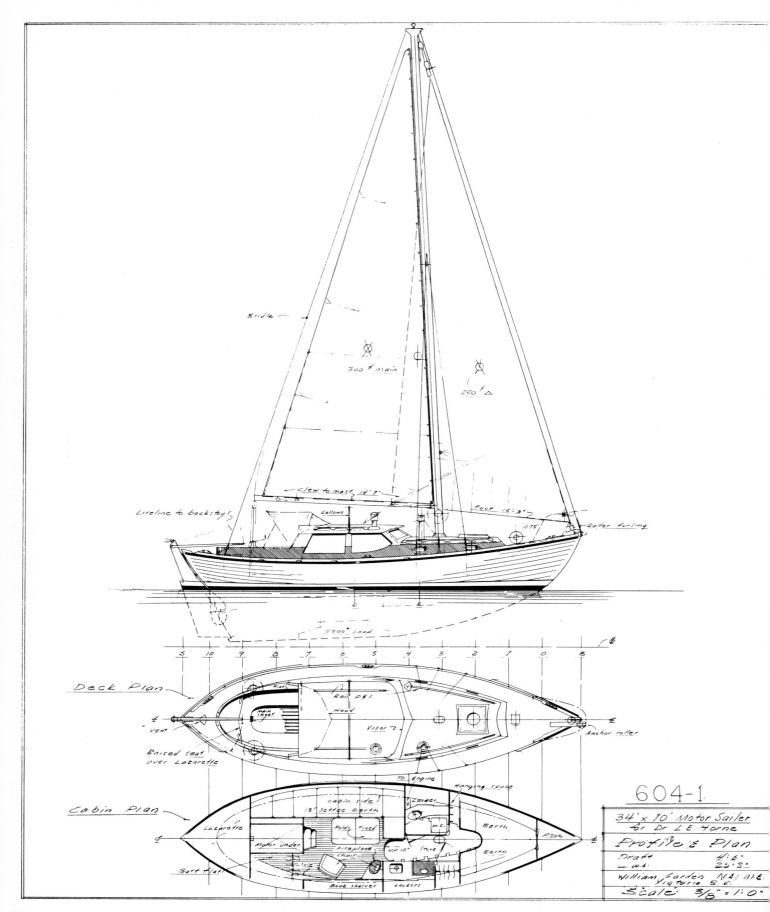

Bridle

300 # main

250 # ∆

Clew to mast 14'7"

Lireline to backstays

Gallows

Foot 15'3"

11.75'

Roller furling

5500# Lead

Deck Plan

Vent

Raised seat over Lazarette

main sheet

Rail p¢s

Hood

Visor 2

Anchor roller

To engine

Hanging space

Cabin Plan

Lazarette

cabin side 18' settee berth

Locker

w.c.

Berth

Peak

motor under

Fireplace Chair

Folds   Fixed

Up 10"   Stove

Berth

Butt Flat

Book shelves

Lockers

604-1

34' x 10' Motor Sailer
for Dr L E Horne
Profile & Plan
Draft   4:6
L.w.l.   25:3
William Garten N.A/M.E.
              Victoria B.C.
Scale: ³⁄₈" = 1:0"

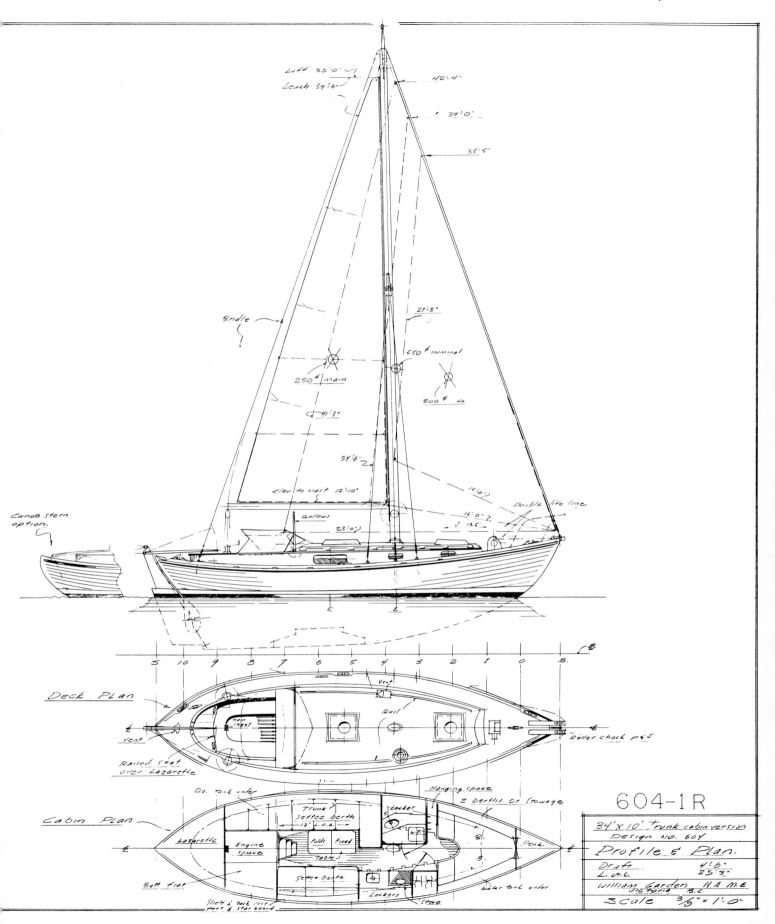

Luff 35'0"
Leach 39'6"

42'4"

39'0"

35'5"

Bridle

27'3"

550# nominal

250# main

300# ∞

41'3"

34'6"

clew to mast 12'10"

15'0"

Double life line

Gallows

16'0"

23'0"

J. 13.5

Canoe stern option.

5 10 9 8 7 6 5 4 3 2 1 0 B.

Deck Plan

Vent

Main sheet

Rail

Vent

Raised seat over lazarette

Roller chock p & s

Do. tank under

Hanging space

2 berths or stowage

604-1R

Trunk settee berth 18' L.O.A.

Locker

Cabin Plan

Lazarette

Engine space

Folds Fixed
Table

W.C.

Sl.

Sl.

Dk.

34' x 10' Trunk cabin version
Design No. 604

Profile & Plan.

Batt flat

Settee berth

Lockers

Stove

Water tank under

| Draft | 4'6" |
| L.W.L. | 25'3" |

William Garden N.A.M.E
Victoria B.C.

Scale 3/8" = 1'0"

Slide's back rest port & starboard

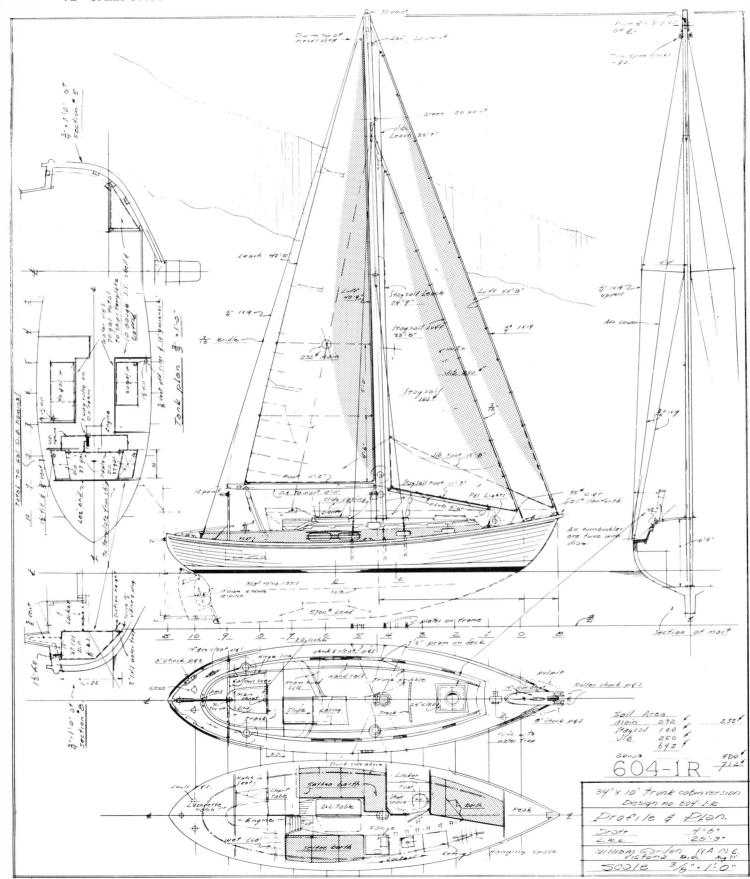

Sail Area
Main   232
Staysail   160
Jib   250
            642

Genoa   480

604-1R

34' x 10' Trunk cabin version
Design no. 604-1-R
Profile & Plan.
Draft   4'6"
L.W.L.   28'-3"
William Gorden N.A.N.E.
Victoria   Aug 75
Scale   3/8" = 1'0"

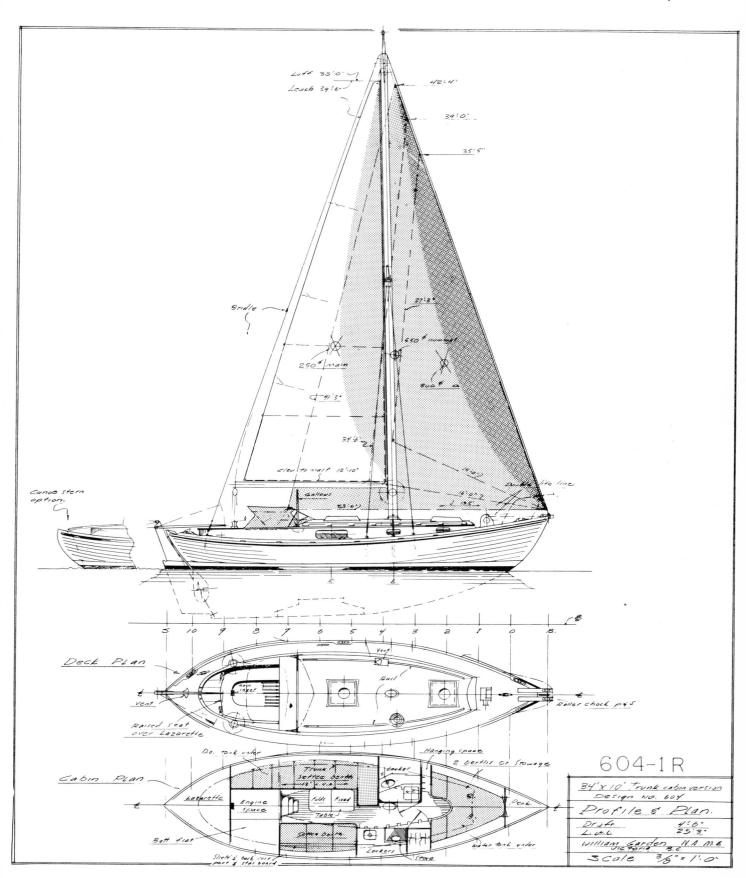

Canoe stern
option.

Deck Plan

Cabin Plan

604-1R

34' x 10' Trunk cabin version
Design No. 604
Profile & Plan.
Draft   4' 6"
L.W.L.   25' 8"
William Garden N.A.M.E
Victoria B.C
Scale   3/8" = 1' 0"

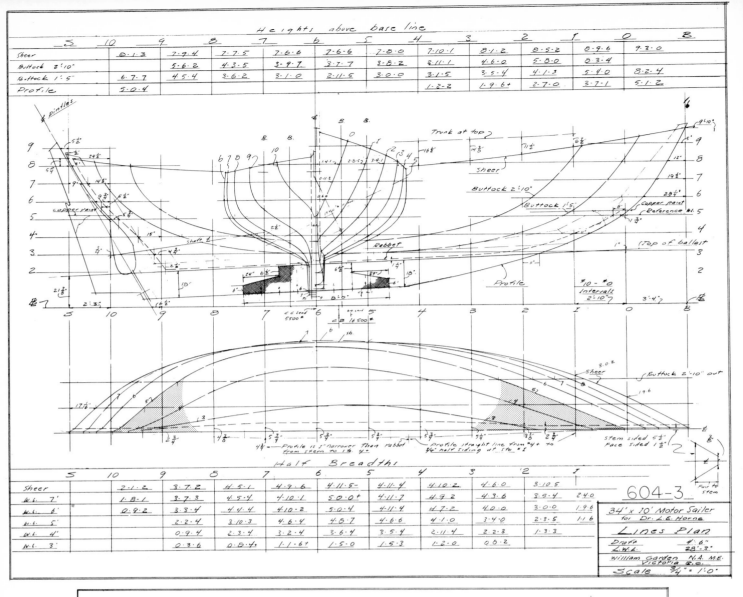

Heights above base line

	5	10	9	8	7	6	5	4	3	2	1	0	B
Sheer		6.1.3	7.9.4	7.7.5	7.6.6	7.6.6	7.8.0	7.10.1	8.1.2	8.5.2	8.9.6	9.3.0	
Buttock 2'10"			5.6.2	4.3.5	3.9.7	3.7.7	3.8.2	2.11.1	4.6.0	5.8.0	8.3.4		
Buttock 1'5"		6.7.7	4.5.4	3.6.2	3.1.0	2.11.5	3.0.0	3.1.5	3.5.4	4.1.3	5.4.0	8.2.4	
Profile		5.0.4						1.2.2	1.9.6+	2.7.0	3.7.1	5.1.2	

604-3

34' x 10' Motor Sailer for Dr. L.E. Horne

Lines Plan

Draft	4'6"
L.W.L.	28'-3"

William Garden N.A. M.E. Victoria B.C.

Scale 3/4" = 1'0"

Half Breadths

	5	10	9	8	7	6	5	4	3	2	1
Sheer		2.1.2	3.7.2	4.5.1	4.9.6	4.11.5	4.11.4	4.10.2	4.6.0	3.10.5	
W.L. 7'		1.8.1	3.7.3	4.5.4	4.10.1	5.0.0+	4.11.7	4.9.2	4.3.6	3.5.4	2.4.0
W.L. 6'		0.9.2	3.3.4	4.4.4	4.10.2	5.0.4	4.11.4	4.7.2	4.0.0	3.0.0	1.9.6
W.L. 5'			2.2.4	3.10.3	4.6.4	4.5.7	4.6.6	4.1.0	3.4.0	2.3.5	1.1.6
W.L. 4'			0.9.4	2.3.4	3.2.4	3.6.4	3.5.4	2.11.4	2.2.3	1.3.3	
W.L. 3'			0.3.6	0.5.4	1.1.6+	1.5.0	1.5.3	1.2.0	0.8.2		

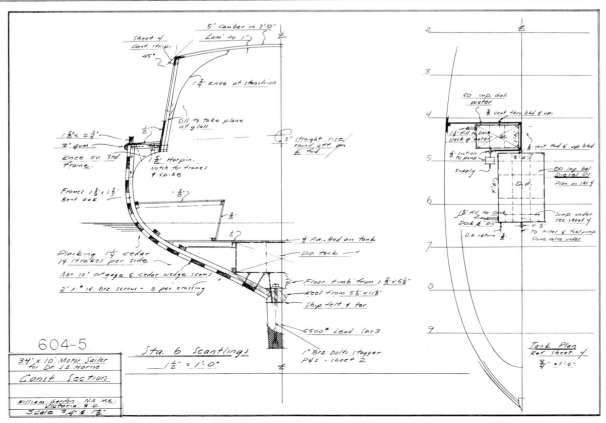

604-5

Sta. 6 Scantlings
1 1/2" = 1'0"

34' x 10' Motor Sailer for Dr. L.E. Horne

Const. Section

William Garden N.A. M.E. Victoria B.C.

Scale 3/4" & 1 1/2"

Tank Plan
Ref sheet 4
3/4" = 1'0"

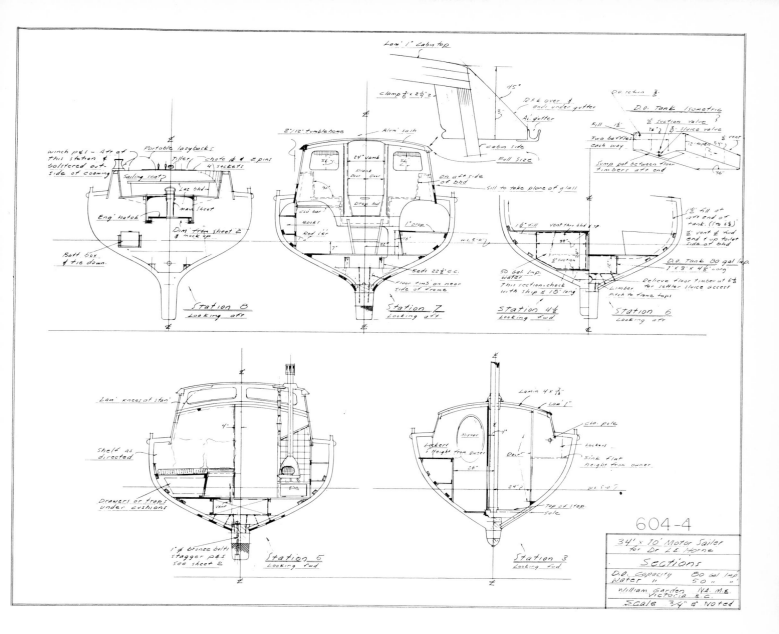

Station 8
Looking aft

Station 7
Looking aft

Station 4½
Looking fwd

Station 6
Looking aft

Station 5
Looking fwd

Station 3
Looking fwd

604-4

34' x 10' Motor Sailer for Dr L E Horne		
Sections		
D.O. Capacity	80 gal Imp	
Water "	50 "	"
William Garden N.A. M.E.		
Victoria B.C.		
Scale 3/4" & Noted		

out whaleboat's lines plan roughed out to give greater internal capacity than the original whaleboats. From this departure, we developed a model with half a plank again more freeboard, still fuller bilges with a greater waterplane area to increase sail-carrying power, and a generally more burdensome hull all around to accommodate the weights and required living quarters. In a hull this shallow, the height of the trunk cabin was dictated by a combination of the headroom requirements and the need to keep a general lookout while seated inside the sunken deckhouse. We've given her a 12-inch harpin shelf to form the decks along the cabin sides and have given the cabin sides a good tumblehome both to lower their apparent height and give leg room while going fore and aft on deck. Es's last boat was *Snoop*, so this one he has named *Swoop* the Sloop.

The Buccaneer 300, a production sloop, has been designed to a minimum weight for her length and cubic content. We needed a model incorporating moderate displacement and light ballast, using great form stability. The hull has fairly flat floors amidships, with wide, firm bilges and an easy entry fairing into powerful quarters. Draft was limited to four feet for shoal-water cruising without seriously affecting her good sailing qualities. A 3,500-pound casting of lead is fitted in the forward end of the fin for stability and self righting. The lead gives about 10,000 foot-pounds righting moment to match the cruising rig shown. A deeper 5,000-pound casting is designed to carry the largest rig option, though a deeper draft of five feet would be necessary to hang on for real performance to windward in broken water with the larger rig and this sort of freeboard. Over the years we've

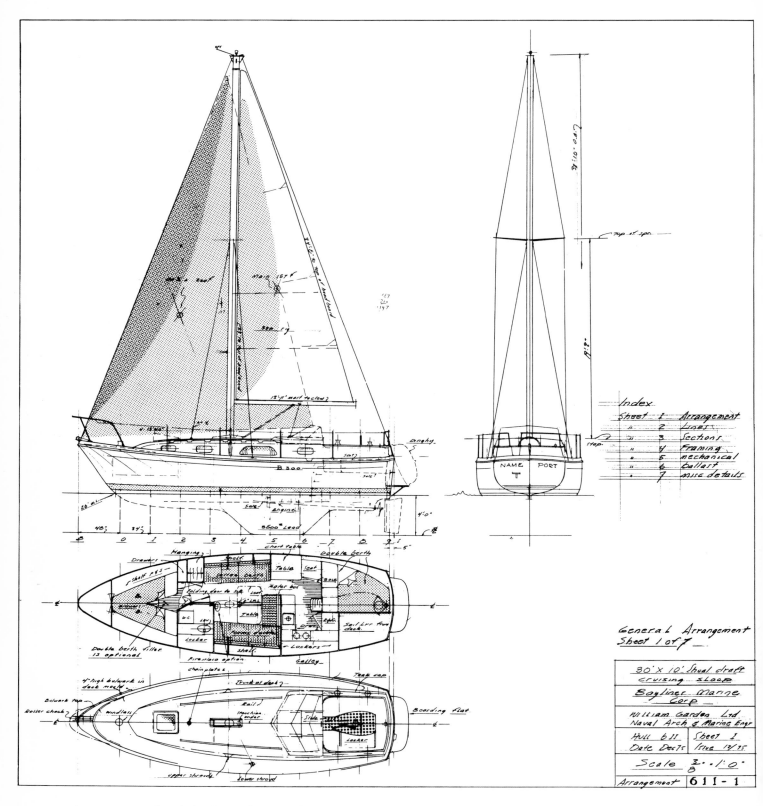

done many shoal-draft keel-boats for cruising and found them handy and wonderful cruisers, but for a ding-dong go to windward in open water with a real sea running, the addition of another foot of draft to this sloop will be required for really competitive sailing. But for nearly all family cruising conditions, the shoal-draft version is close to ideal.

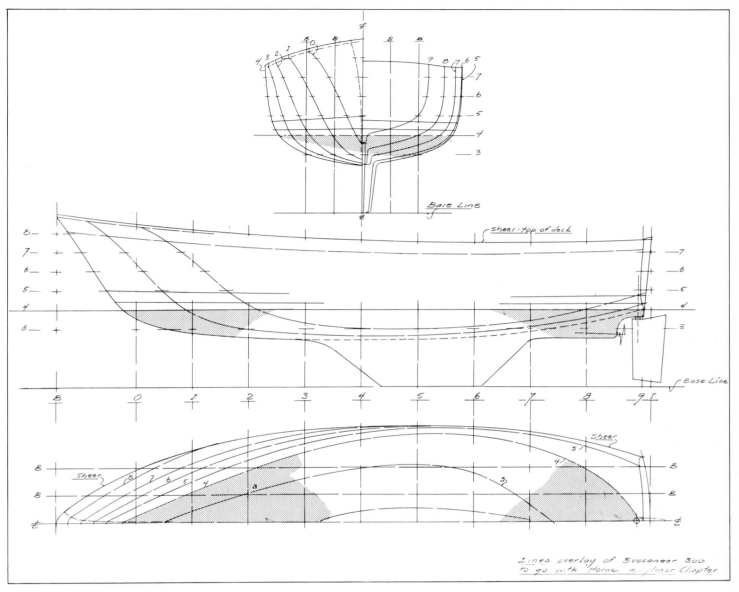

Lines overlay of Buccaneer 300
To go with 'Horne' Lines Chapter

So the Buccaneer 300 gets her sail-carrying power from a hull form of high initial stability plus ballast for ultimate stability and drive. *Swoop*, on the other hand, has greater deadrise, and her lower center of buoyancy requires greater ballast weight (total displacement is 16,500 pounds). She has worked out to be a slimmer form than a Colin Archer model, and her easy fore-and-aft lines make her less burdensome than most double-enders. She's an interesting compromise when compared to *Bull Frog* or *Seal* (next chapter), but is full-bodied when compared to the Buccaneer 300.

The draft of *Swoop* has been held to 4 foot 6 inches, which is about right for her lateral plane distribution and freeboard. Her rig is short, since she will be used for cruising mainly in local waters, but there is still enough base and

hoist to the fore triangle to carry some effective head-sails. For a larger rig, I would run the keel back in a long sweep from the existing forefoot, eliminating the spur shown and ending up with another 9 inches to 12 inches of draft. However, with the moderate draft shown, she will sail beautifully and be perhaps a handier cruising boat than a version with a larger rig.

The Buccaneer 300's bilge is of interest. The little ship actually has a bilge sump, a place for water to go and be pumped out. Some small, and a few large, production sailboats today have a lovely color-coded interior designed for maximum Boat Show impact, with nice warm colors and cozy carpetry underfoot. All this I'm told is mainly to get the sailor's wife to go along with the purchase, then off the ship goes under a press of sail, spray is flying, a port isn't dogged down, the stuffing box drips, the water tank clamp is loose, and the cozy floor carpetry is brine-soaked with no place for the good salt sea to go. Add a little vomit and a broken bottle of catsup to the sloshing bilge above the sole and a lot would be given for a sump. Carpet on the overhead I believe we invented, and for good interior decoration we once helped spend $40,000 on a large yacht's saloon and drapes, so I'm not anti-decor, but carpet in a small boat below knee height and below the waterline should be able to be rolled up and stowed when the breeze makes up. Above all, we need a place to gather bilge water under any rightside-up condition, and this the 300 has.

The 300 below decks is a real home afloat, with nearly the entire length utilized for accommodations. In a generally good, standard layout, we've stressed reasonable privacy for two couples. The feel of a much larger boat is achieved. The layout seems to afford a lot of comfort and convenience for 30 feet of deck, with full headroom fore and aft. There is a nice forward stateroom, a double-berth saloon, and away aft a snug quarter berth for a couple or for stowage. The saloon has ample lounging space, the head is roomy, and the galley has stove, sink, refrigerator, and ample lockers. The diesel engine is seated over the keel with the weight in a good spot, and the after end of the cabin, usually reserved for an engine, has been retained for a roomy double berth and stowage.

Swoop's layout, in comparison, is worked up around an open arrangement with accommodations in one general area. One excellent feature is that the cook is able to see out while below fixing something on the stove, a desirable thing, particularly for the singlehander. The galley is a step below the saloon in order to fit under the trunk forward, and this break makes a pleasant relationship in height when people are seated and the cook is working in the galley — both are at about the same eye level.

Both boats have cockpit shelters, which are so necessary for off-season cruising at any latitude. The 300 has an optional hardtop on aluminum sash, and the *Swoop* has a folding pram hood for cockpit protection. The 300's low bulwarks will be a helpful feature for general handling of ground tackle or deck work, and her low trunk cabin gives fair footing when working forward. The rig of the two boats requires about the same amount of work; the simple sloop, particularly with roller headsails, is close to the ideal for a cruiser of this general size.

Power is an Osco Ford diesel with $1\frac{1}{2}:1$ reduction gear in the double-ender; a four-cylinder Universal gasoline engine is standard in the 300.

Dinghy stowage is a problem. The 300 has an easy solution by affording stowage on the transom step. This will bother the traditionalist, but be a real pleasure to the practical cruiser. The double-ender will do with a towed dinghy while cruising, and both will carry inflatables.

The Buccaneer 300 is a stock boat with the Bayliner fleet and takes advantage of the economy of quantity production. The double-ender is a custom, one-off boat built by Bendt Jesperson in Sidney, British Columbia, and she hails from the Royal Victoria Yacht Club.

The trunk cabin, cutter-rigged version of *Swoop* is Joe Monrufet's boat, which is being completed as this is written. Of the two models, this is my choice aesthetically, but a deckhouse is a real temptation.

14   *Seal*, a Larger Double-ender

LOA — 37' 4"
LWL — 32' 4"
Beam — 11' 8"
Draft — 6' 0"
Sail Area (cutter) — 921 square feet
Displacement — 32,000 pounds
Ballast — 8,500 pounds outside
2,000 pounds inside

Seal is one of our old favorites. Designed originally as a gaff ketch, she has been built with a gaff main, a short jib-headed rig as illustrated, and with a flush-decked cutter configuration, which is also shown in profile along with the flush-decked optional cabin layout. The cutter or gaff ketch would be my choice.

Seal is a double-ended jump up from *Bull Frog* with a slimmer form for her length but, due to greater length and breadth, a much roomier hull. The two layout plans form an interesting study and can be set up in a plus-minus chart similar to that shown with the *Bull Frog*. The choice is difficult; greater sleeping privacy is achieved with the toilet room between the cabins, but the aft position of the toilet room might give it greater privacy. The quarter berth aft is an appealing feature, particularly for the single hander. Each layout has a chart area about equal, but the flush-decker's galley looks better. I'll leave it to you.

On deck, the ketch and the cutter are both basically flush-deckers, the ketch having a wider companionway forming a small deckhouse. The deck boxes on the ketch, so treasured on a cruising yacht, fit between the

cabin and the skylight, giving the effect of a longer trunk cabin. Either layout has ample deck space; the cockpits are identical and well decks are fitted forward on both. The bulwarks give the feeling of a reassuring bit of security, especially when muzzling a sail, handling ground tackle, or otherwise working forward.

The lines show an easy model, not so lively at sea as a beamier Colin Archer hull, but adhering to the traditional features. Ballast outside is 8,500 pounds of cast iron in a simple shape to form and to mold. Inside ballast of about a ton will be required, the amount varying somewhat whether she is a hardwood or softwood ship, and depending on what her stores, equipment, etc., will be.

Construction, you will note, is traditional carvel; a mold is illustrated on the lines plan to show the deductions that must be made from the hull lines plan to arrive at the net mold size prior to set-up. This set-up is by far the simplest since the sheer harpin contols the deck line and rests directly on the molds to align them athwartships and to take the deck beams. This harpin provides a backing for guards and frame-head bolts. The main clamp bends around under the

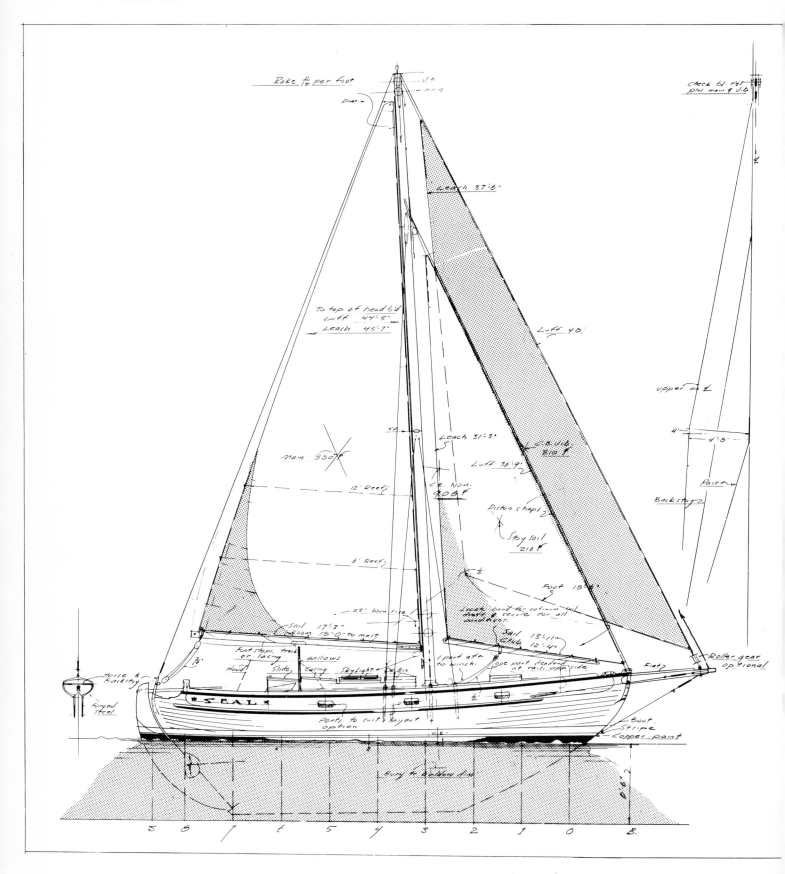

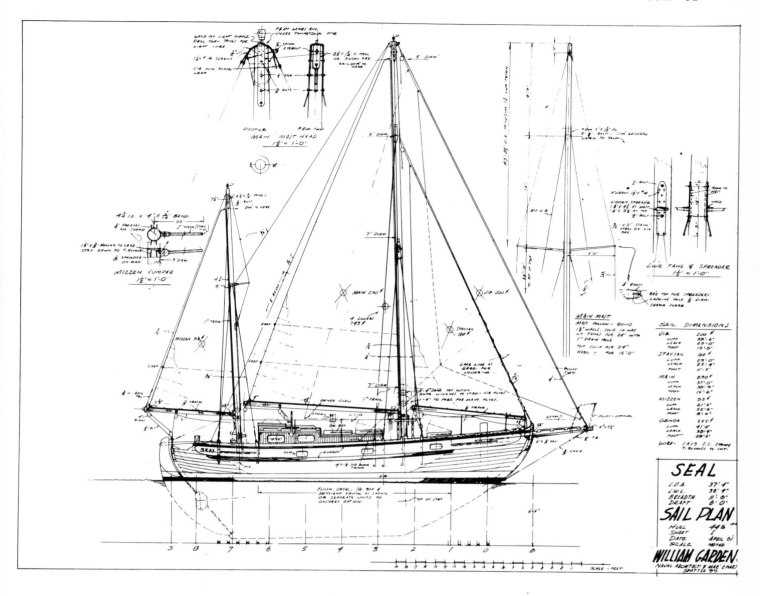

well-deck beams, and a short shelf is fitted in the ends to form the time-honored clamp-shelf configuration. Bilge stringers and ribbands also bend around the outside of the molds, and, when she is framed, these members take the place of ribbands and almost all may stay in, helping to retain the boat's shape. Remember to expand the sheer into the half breadth when laying out the harpin to ensure getting the true length.

In skimming the plans for further commentary, I notice a lack of deck obstructions to hang my big toe on while going fore and aft.

The 11-inch well deck forward and the shallower deck aft look about right. I like the big lodging knees from the rail to the tiller rack and the husky quarter bitts. I can picture her stepping out to windward in a fresh breeze with the tiller half a pin to weather, my back resting on a kapok cushion against the weather quarter knee and bitt, my feet up, and some nice little rainbows of spray blowing off the weather bow. There is something fitting and traditional about the Colin Archer theme; they are sturdy, seaworthy, and pleasant little ships under sail.

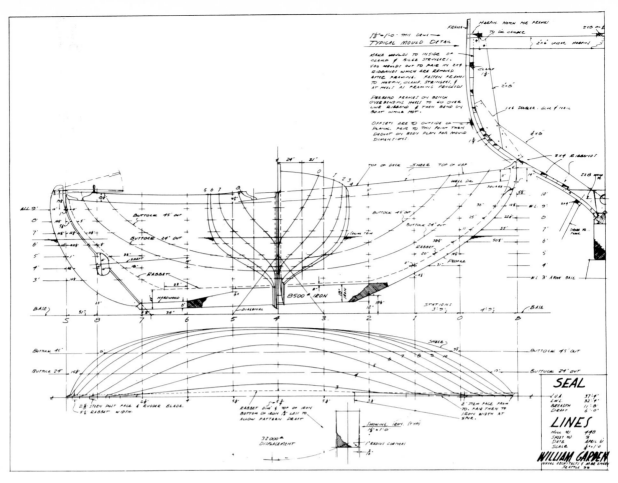

SEAL

LINES

WILLIAM GARDEN

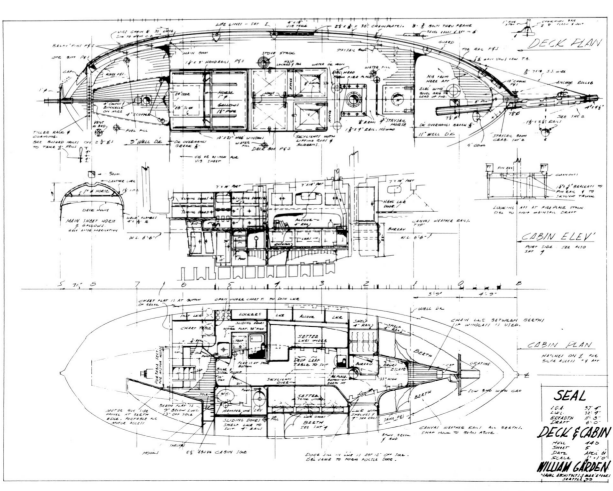

SEAL

DECK & CABIN

WILLIAM GARDEN

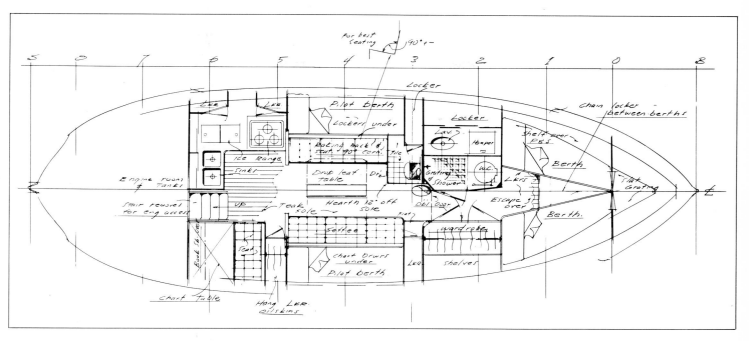

Accommodation plan for the cutter version of *Seal*.

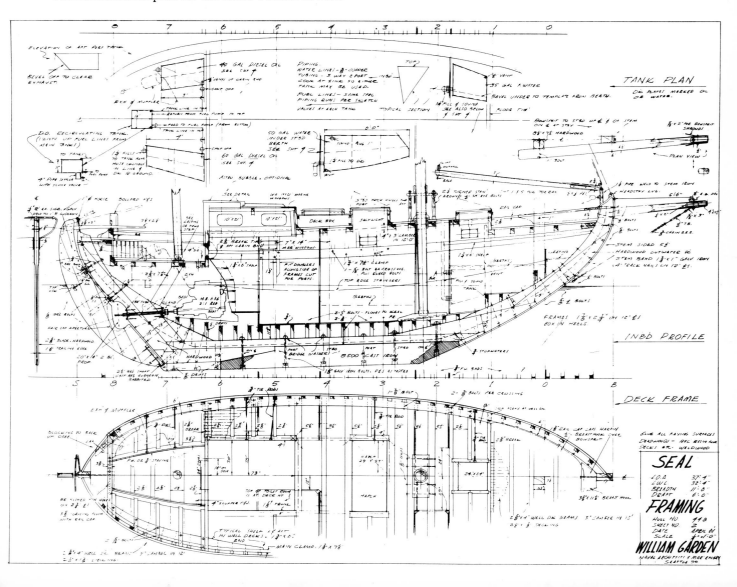

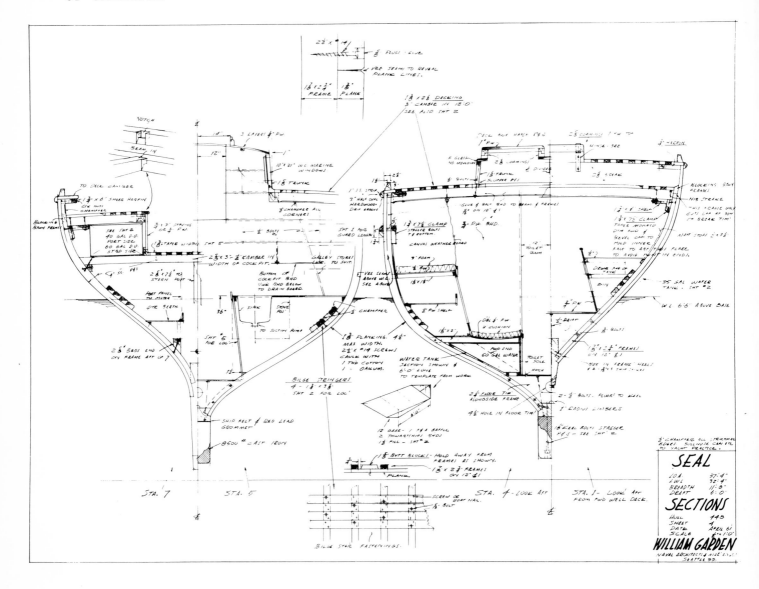

STA. 7   STA. 5   STA. 4 - LOOK AFT   STA. 1 - LOOK AFT
                                                           FROM FWD WELL DECK.

SEAL
LOA   37'4"
LWL   32'4"
BREADTH   11'8"
DRAFT   6'0"

SECTIONS
HULL   443
SHEET   4
DATE   APRIL 61
SCALE   ¾"=1'0"

WILLIAM GARDEN
NAVAL ARCHITECT & M.S.E. LTD.
SEATTLE 99

15 *Walloon*, a Cruising Ketch

LOA (on deck) — 37' 0"
LWL — 27' 6"
Beam — 10' 10"
Draft — 6' 3"
Displacement — 23,400 pounds
Ballast — 7,000 pounds outside, 1,000 pounds inside
Sail Area — 762 square feet, including 100 percent of the fore triangle

With a given pile of lumber, fastenings, machinery for propulsion, and gear for outfitting, the choice of the type of boat to build can vary widely depending on service, prejudice, or the builder's inclination. With the type of model decided on, we are still up against the best size and proportion to utilize the materials on hand.

The decision that perhaps a boat 34 feet overall by 28 feet on the waterline will suffice for our needs is disturbed when the idea of having an after cabin or adding a couple of feet on the waterline eventually creeps in. The sketching begins again to see if the changes can be made without reaching the next step up in equipment sizes and cost. With the waterline length and breadth fixed, it is usually possible to ease out the ends of a hull for a little more deck room, easier lines, or aesthetic appeal. Such increases can usually be done at very little added cost, but these adjustments, when developed, indicate the need for another 18 inches of waterline length to loosen up the layout again, and we are off to the next jump in equipment, plus another $500 in ballast, and the budget is shot.

Dr. John Tytus's *Walloon* has a practical layout for her size, but she is a boat requiring much time in finish work. Here we have every piece usually worked into a much larger boat, in this case condensed, which always adds to the cost. *Walloon* is a lot of boat for her length, both in accommodations and in form. Construction hours will be close to those for a *Porpoise* (chapter after next), and for the stock builder, a loosened-up, larger version will bring in a much higher return with slightly more cost, so she is at the bottom of one of the size jumps. Although relatively costly to build, she has proven to be a most pleasant little ship, handy under sail and extremely comfortable for extended cruising.

A live-aboard boat of this size should be supplemented by a shoreside dockhouse or nearby basement. *Porpoise*, I feel, is about the minimum size for a home afloat over extended lay-up periods and even for her, a big cargo hold or shoreside dockhouse would be ideal for storage.

For *Walloon*, an all-around cruising boat, a length on deck of 37 feet and a waterline of 27 feet 6 inches is about right, since a boat this size

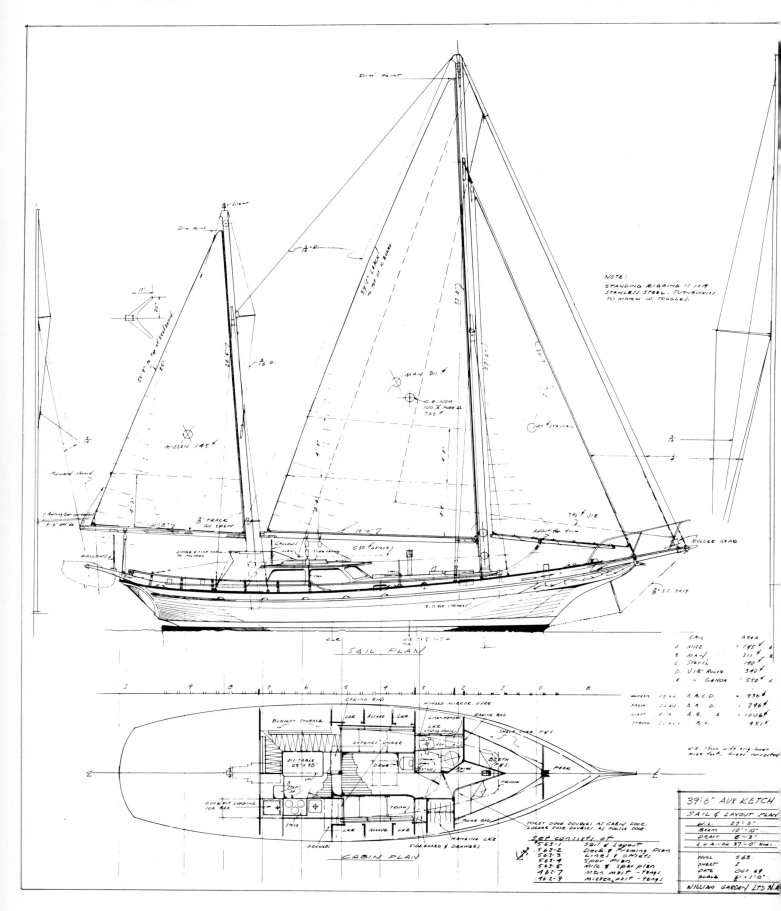

SAIL PLAN

CABIN PLAN

SAIL		AREA
A. MIZZEN		145
B. MAIN		311
C. STAYS'L		140
D. JIB - ROLLED		340
E. " GENOA		550

39'-6" AUX KETCH

SAIL & LAYOUT PLAN

W.L.	27'-0"
BEAM	10'-10"
DRAFT	6'-3"
L.O.A.- DK	37'-0"

HULL	563
SHEET	1
DATE	OCT 69
SCALE	⅜"-1'-0"

WILLIAM GARDEN LTD N.A.

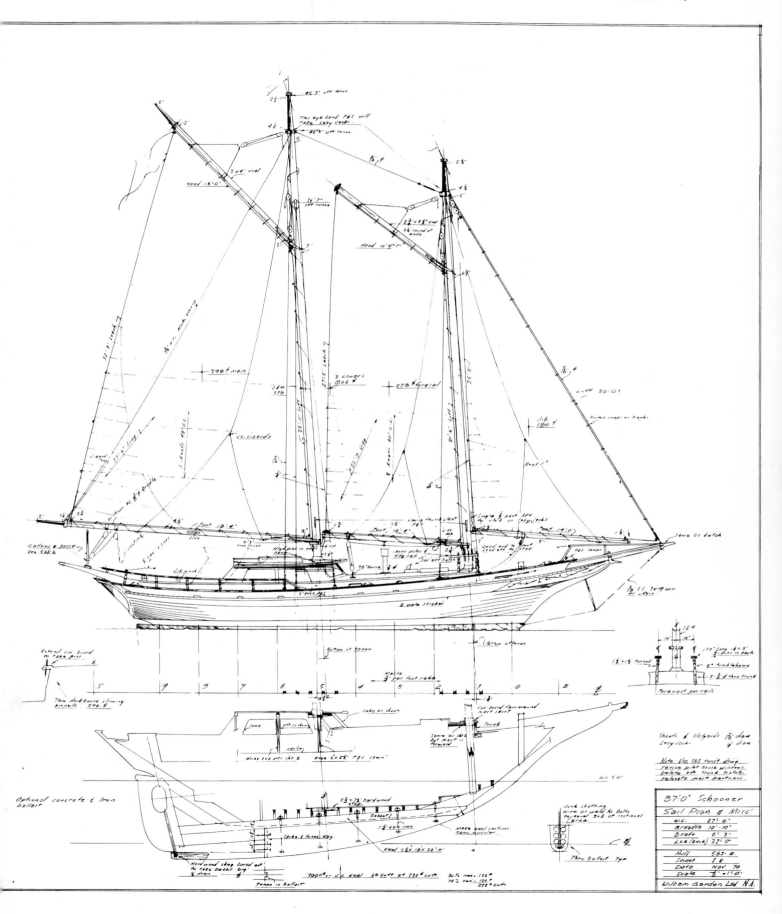

37'0" Schooner
Sail Plan & Misc'

W.L.	27' 6"
Breadth	10' 10"
Draft	6' 3"
L.o.a (deck)	37' 0"
Hull	563-R.
Sheet	I B
Date	Nov 70
Scale	⅜" = 1'0"

William Garden Ltd N.A.

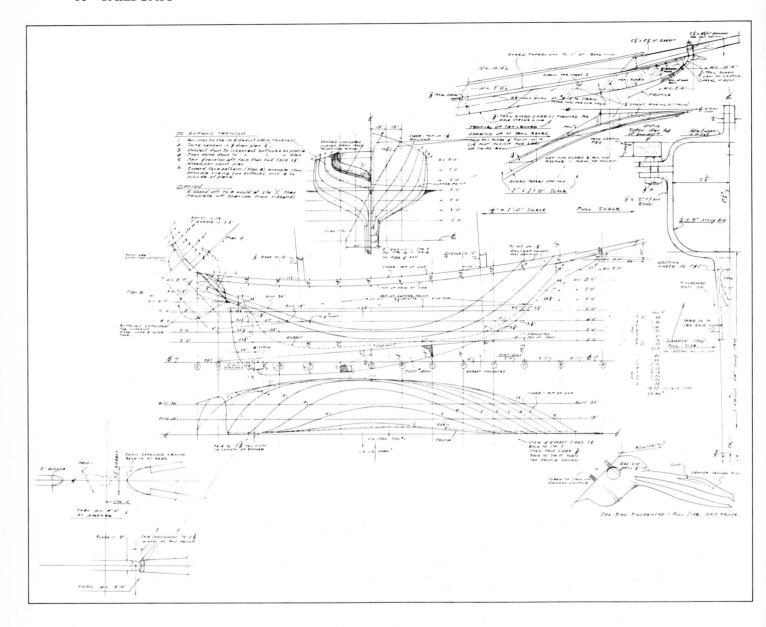

is easily singlehanded and can still accommodate four people in fair comfort. She has a breadth of 10 feet 10 inches and a draft of 6 feet 3 inches with an iron keel weighing 7,000 pounds plus 1,000 pounds of ballast inside. In a softwood version, this ballast is about 34 percent of her displacement, giving her enough power to carry sail and enough lateral plane to hang on in a seaway to windward. The lead of the center of effort ahead of the center of lateral resistance is 21 percent, so she will balance well under lowers as the wind makes up.

There are two ways to rig a ketch: one as *Walloon*, which is in balance until a reef must be taken in, and the other as a boat that balances best as a cutter, with the mizzen intended only as a light-air sail that is taken in as soon as the wind makes up, in order to avoid excessive weather helm. I am happier with the first method, which is the "balance-in-any-whole-sail-breeze" approach. In the second method, the "out-of-balance-in-any-sort-of-breeze" approach, the mizzen at best seems like a poor substitute for a bigger headsail for light weather, and at worst is a nuisance cluttering up the cockpit. Eventually, the out-of-balance rig seems to end up as a cutter full time, with the costly mizzen gear used mainly to support an

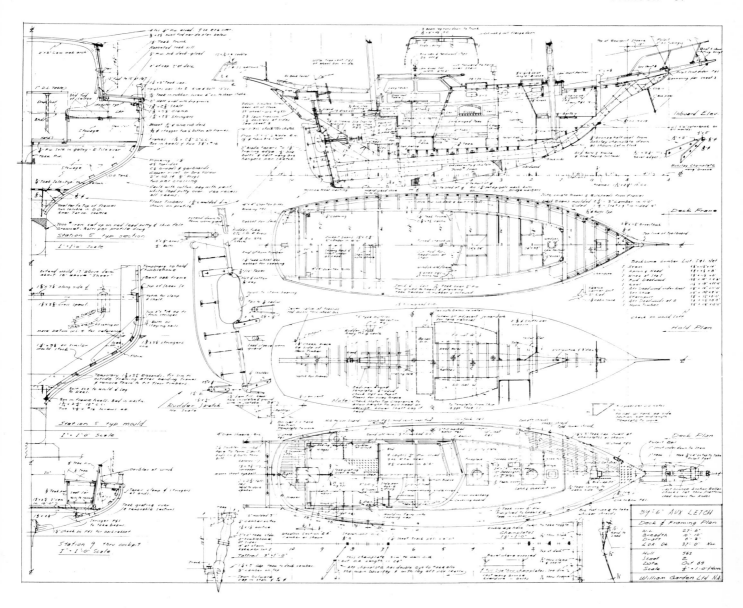

awning.

Walloon's general construction plan can be followed on the drawings, and details are noted for scantlings and method. She was built for John Tytus in Taiwan. George Fryatt has built a softwood duplicate in the corner of his Bel Air shipyard in Vancouver. The alternate schooner was developed for two boats utilizing reinforced concrete ballast keels, with proportionaly greater draft to accommodate the required bulk of the cement and scrap iron, the latter so important to get the required weight.

The layout is a practical solution to the need for a galley and dining-lounge area in a deckhouse. The length is divided up into three practical living spaces with a stateroom or sea stowage forward, a roomy saloon where the waiters can wait with a drink while the cook is putting a meal in shape, and the sunken deckhouse built over the engine space, which results in seated visibility with the galley shelter handy to the helmsman. A table may be set up below if the usual dining table is made into a chart table. With the separate saloon or sleeping cabin option, the crew is clear of the cook and they can have reasonable privacy when off watch amidships while ship's business is going on in the deckhouse.

16   *Tillicum*, a Scow Schooner

LOA — 41' 0"
Beam — 17' 0"
Draft — 2' 3" board up, 8' 0" board down
Sail Area — 1,029 square feet 3 lowers
1,519 square feet with topsail and fisherman staysail

I've always had a yearning for a scow schooner, a real old-time hay scow massively constructed with deep bulwarks, a big, thick wooden centerboard with hoisting tackle to the mast doublings, a chopping block on deck, a chicken coop, and a real hold with bins of nails, tool racks, firewood, and stores. The scow crews must have had some pleasant sails close reaching along with a cargo of fragrant hay bales stacked up in the waist under a lumber-reefed foresail. A whiff of salt flats would come drifting down from the weather shore mixed with the smell of new-mown hay and tarred lanyards and spiced by the occasional scent from a chicken bubbling in the pot below. Once upon a time, I had a whole carload of prime fir lined up for such a ship, but I ended up building a keel schooner instead and I've always regretted it.

A nicely proportioned scow is a handsome vessel and in alongshore conditions will gurgle along at a great clip, something like a huge pram dinghy. The sailing cargo-scows seem to have originated in the Great Lakes, but perhaps simultaneously with their development in the San Francisco Bay area. New Zealand was a scow-schooner stronghold, and the earliest ones there were named after the Great Lakes. Clifford Hawkins's excellent *Out of Auckland* (Pelorus Press, Aukland, New Zealand, 1960) has some good data on them. The Smithsonian Institution has a wealth of data and photographs on the American scows; some of the plans were taken off existing scows during the 1930s by the Works Progress Administration as a make-work project. These are reasonably accurate and well authenticated with dimensions and photos.

It is well to look at re-drawn plans or reconstructions of old timers with suspicion unless the delineator's source data is shown. Bjorn Landstrom's excellent book *The Ship*, although containing some minor errors, such as rowing ports being backwards, usually includes the data on which the drawing or reconstruction is based, which gives us an approximation of the amount of artistic license used. In other sources, an occasional beautifully rendered recon-

90

(Above) The big scow schooner *Undine* just launched in San Francisco in 1902 (courtesy of the Smithsonian Institution). (Right) New Zealand scow *Zingara* (courtesy of Clifford Hawkins). (Below) *Mary* outward bound and heavily laden. She was built in San Francisco Bay in 1891 (courtesy of the Smithsonian Institution).

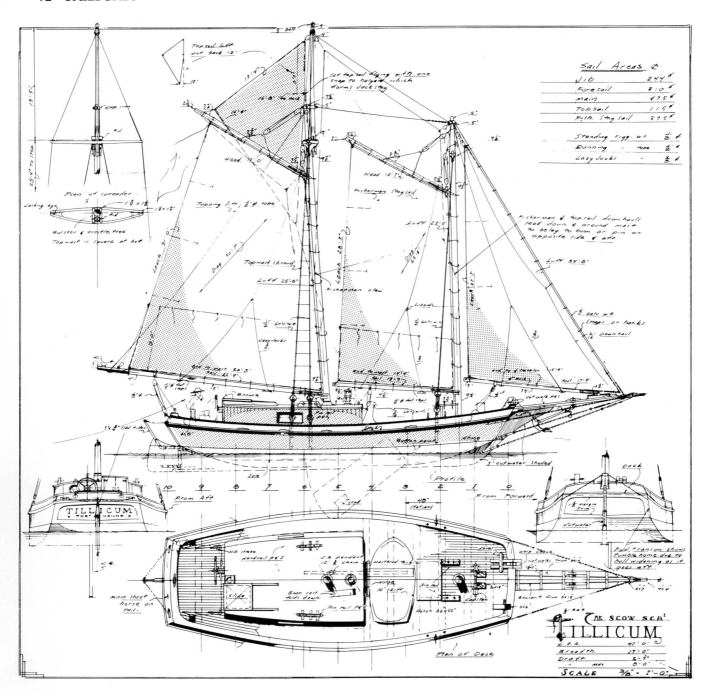

struction of a type has turned out to be based solely on an old photograph of a hulk on the beach.

We must bear in mind that, aside from boats for state occasions, the average working craft was probably a crude and well-hammered piece of pit-sawn carpentry. Yet the major ship-building centers built some outstanding boats in every era — and many of them even belonged to the mud flat fleet. The simple form and proportions of the best examples of the sailing scows have a shipshape quality that catches the imagination.

Construction of the scow *Tillicum* utilizes simple framing and structure, but, in spite of the relatively easy box shape, she will still tax the ability of an amateur builder. The time and material cost should not be underestimated, but

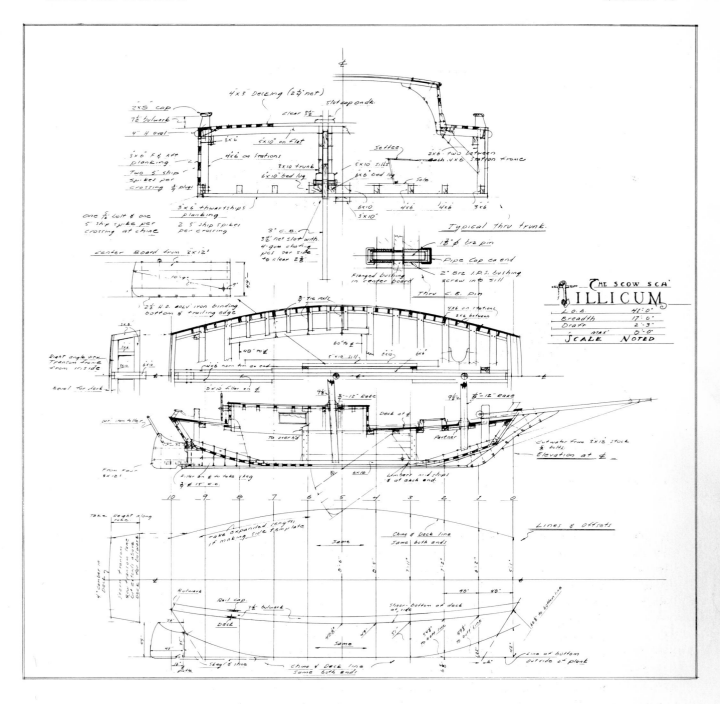

a man used to working with tools can tackle the job with a minimum amount of shipbuilding skills.

The hull is the same on both ends, so opposite members may be duplicated. Building is begun with the bottom upside down, since it is much easier to work downhand on the bottom. First you should lay down on timbers or on the shop floor all of the straight bottom longitudinals, including the centerboard bed logs. Next the bottom planking should be given a bevel for caulking, then counterbored and drilled for the spikes. Spread the planks out on the longitudinals, which have had limbers cut through on four-inch centers, then wedge the planks together and spike them down for the length of the longitudinals. You're ready now for the chine logs, which have to be sprung to the topsides' curve. To bend these members, block out with 2 × 4's from the outboard

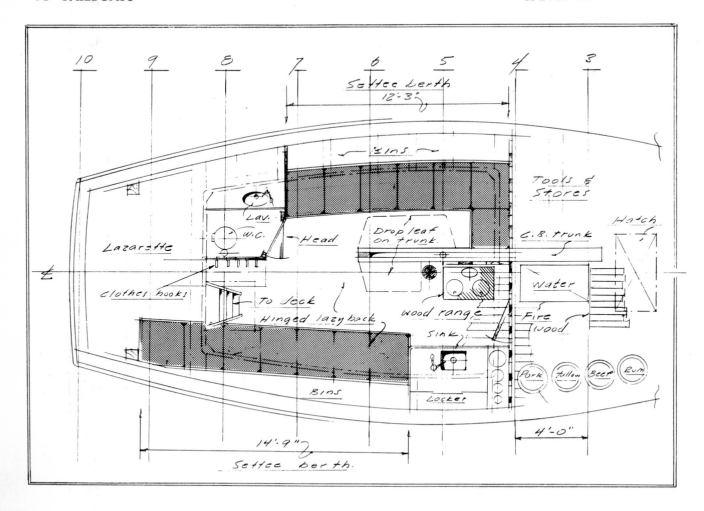

logitudinal to the chine position, spring the steamed 3″ × 6″ chine pieces around, then spike them in place. The bottom is now ready for a thread of caulking cotton and one of oakum before the bottom is rolled right side up. The bottom planks may be left long until the first side planks are fitted. When she's right side up, the raked ends can be completed.

With the bottom blocked up and trued about 30 inches off the shop floor, you can proceed with the 4″ × 6″ vertical station frames, which are erected on four-foot centers and notched for the bottom chine and sheer chine pieces. Cross braces will hold the frames vertical while the steamed sheer chine is sprung around. A pattern of the rake shape will establish the rake timbers, which continue the bottom logitudinal structure on up to the transoms. The centerline 6″ × 10″ timber is connected to the transoms by horn timbers along each side with a filler piece between, while the

4″ × 6″ longitudinals simply scab alongside their rake counterparts and are through-bolted.

The transoms may be fitted next; then the side intermediates, which are nailing pieces between frames, are fitted and the sides are planked up. The rake planking may be left off until the last to facilitate loading lumber and climbing in and out of the hull. If you wish, however, she can be closed in now, and access to the inside of the hull can be provided by staging that reaches to the deck level.

The deck framing is shown. Lots of board feet of lumber are needed here but very few pieces. The decking is 2¼ inches thick net, caulked with cotton and oakum, with a final paying of hot pitch.

The centerboard trunk and board are edge-bolted with 5/8-inch galvanized rod. Counterbore for the bolt heads, and bore the body size with a barefoot ship auger that has a welded-on extension made from cold-rolled round bar. A slow-turning half-inch drill will be required for this job. The ship auger without a worm requires a starting hole, but then will track cleanly and not follow grain and knots, as will a worm auger. After you have stuck the auger a few times, you will become adept at taking a small cut and then backing the auger part way out to clear it. By the time the scow is half built, you will have gained enough' experience to be able to push through a 30-inch hole with accuracy. The centerboard is built up from three-inch planks. On all these long bores, go through one plank and half an inch into the next, then check for direction and see if you are running off. If you are, correct in the second plank and check again. An aid when boring is to tack a sight stick alongside the hole and have a friend help sight the auger.

Fit a lead billet in the centerboard to give it just enough negative buoyancy for it to go down, but not make it too heavy to handle when the pin is pulled so the centerboard can be dropped clear and fished up alongside for inspection prior to dry docking and painting. A centerboard pin should always lie inside the ship where it can be pulled while afloat. This makes the board easy to check. With the simple board we lack a stop should the pendant break, but the gear is heavy and should last a long time. Any board can be a potential problem, but shoal draft opens up a world of marshland and weedy cruising that is closed to the long-legged yacht.

One of the handiest pieces of equipment in a scow yard is an electric plane, a tool worth much on a timber-working job of this sort. It and an electric chain saw are perhaps the biggest work savers when scow building.

An alternate deck may be made with ½-inch plywood, the 1 5/8-inch (net) decking overlayed in fiber gum, spiked into the beams with countersunk 5-inch common nails. These will take ½-inch deck plugs; a plug cutter will make piles of plugs from miscellaneous scrap lumber. The plug cutter should be driven its depth into the wood, then the wood should be run on its side through a table saw and the plugs will fly out into a cardboard box. Urea glue will do to set the plugs in. The deck seams can be caulked and payed with pitch or just payed with roof gum.

The bulwark logs are sawn and fitted, painted on all four sides, and then bolted in place. Next the cap is fitted, and on deck she looks like a real little ship. The bowsprit, chainplates, and ironwork can be the next job. The cabin trunk is from timber through-bolted to the carlin and sill.

The steering gear is bone simple, with the usual scow iron tiller swinging the wooden rudder. The traditional iron wheel and wooden drum handles a simple rope or twist-link-chain tiller line. The pintles and gudgeons are of iron.

The spars are to be from young trees — solid, simple, and easily recycled into rollers or firewood 50 years hence. They are the original way to carry sail and still not too far from the best. Heavy turnbuckles can be used or deadeyes as shown. Simple iron-wire rigging will suffice. *Tillicum* has great initial stability, so the weight of the rig low down as it is will not be noticed.

Remember to limber all bottom framing so the bilge water can run across to the pump suction. Fit a pump at each side so she can be stripped on either tack.

Tillicum will need about 6,000 pounds of scrap iron to settle her down and give inertia through stays as she goes scrunching around on the other tack. The ballast can be adjusted when you get the feel of her, and, remember, she is safe as a church with proper handling, but an inside-ballasted shoal hull is happy right-side up or upside down. Our *Tillicum* and Slocum's *Spray* have this trait in common. Without ballast she'll sail like a big dinghy, but your hiking weight will be about proportional to half a dozen tomcats on the rail of an International 14, so settle her down with ballast and sail her like a ship.

How far will she go? If there were a reason for it, I'd sail her most anywhere in the boating season; buoyant as a duck and well rigged, she will make some pleasant passages, but, as a shoal water houseboat cruiser, she will come into her element and be a wonderfully handy mudthumper and backwater cruiser.

17 *Porpoise*, a Home on the Ocean

LOA — 45' 9"
LO Deck — 42' 4"
LWL — 33' 4"
Beam — 13' 4"
Draft — 5' 8" nominal
Ballast — 8,700 pounds keel, 1,000 pounds inside
Sail Area — 950 square feet, 4 lowers
Engine — Mercedes-Benz OM636 (34 hp)
Fuel — 200 gallons U.S.
Water — 200 gallons U.S.
Displacement — 34,000 pounds

Porpoise is an ideal size for cruising or for living on board, and over the past years she has been one of our most cherished designs, with well over a hundred versions sailing the seas.

Originally, *Porpoise* was a very simple ship with outboard rudder and concrete keel, but gradually additions and refinements have been made to develop her into a most able and complete little vessel that is capable of any normal passage in comfort and safety. Some *Porpoise*s have been backyard projects built many miles from the sea and others have been built along most of the world's coastlines. Many have originated in unlikely spots. One well-remembered photo showed one of the ships nearly up to her waterline in snow. But all *Porpoise*s have been built with the same dream of distant voyaging. A stamp collection could be based on their travels. Today I received a note from "*Kapdura,* 420 miles S.S.W. of the Azores," mailed from Horta on the homeward

leg of a voyage from builder Robin Fung's yard in Hong Kong. This one is a real little ship, all teak, and the owner is an old Cape Horner, having made a grain-ship passage in the 1930s.

Some *Porpoise*s have been excellently built, and some have been barely recognizable when their proud owners have brought them by, but all owners seem to feel that the enormous effort of giving birth to a *Porpoise* is worthwhile. So, gentle shipmate, she is a project requiring great effort, patience, skill, and cost. She is about the maximum-sized structure advisable for a part-time effort. Many thousands of hours from the start you will begin to see the end of such a building program. Relating the hours to the 2,000-odd hours of workdays in a year, you can appreciate the amount of time and effort involved.

With a breadth of 13 feet, 4 inches, *Porpoise* has a length on deck of 42 feet 6 inches, and a moderate draft of 5 feet, which will in-

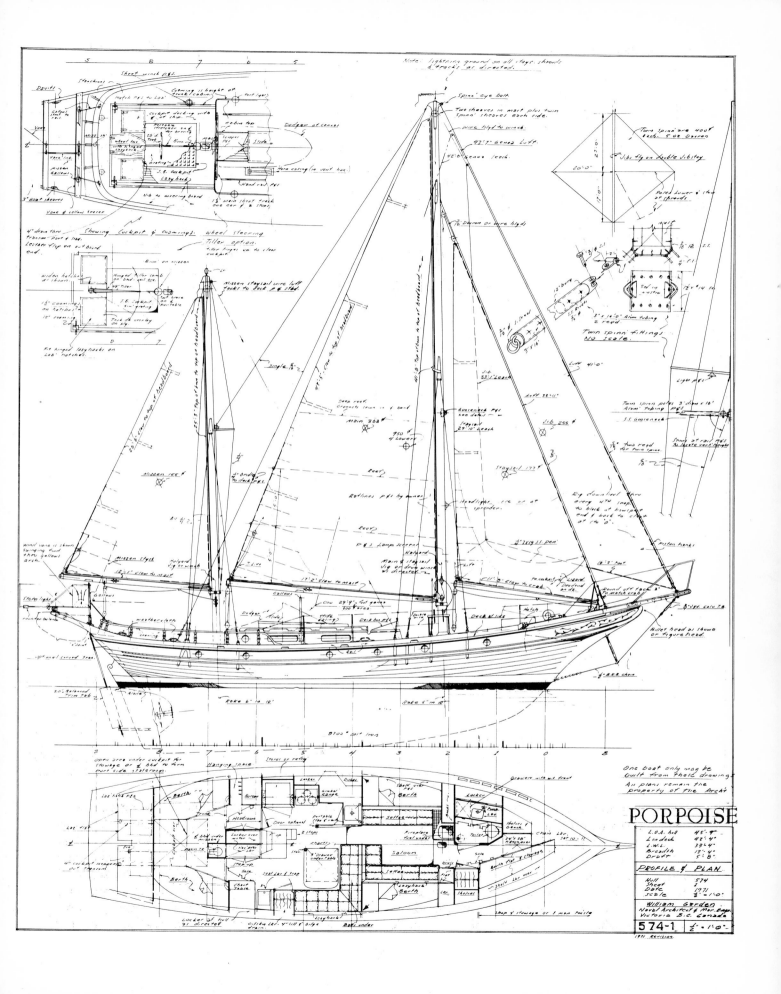

PORPOISE

L.O.A. hull	45'-9"
Len deck	42'-4"
L.W.L.	33'-4"
Breadth	13'-4"
Draft	5'-8"

PROFILE & PLAN

Hull	574
Sheet	1
Date	1971
Scale	½" = 1'-0"

William Garden
Naval Architect & Mar. Engr.
Victoria B.C. Canada

574-1   ½" = 1'-0"

1971 Revision

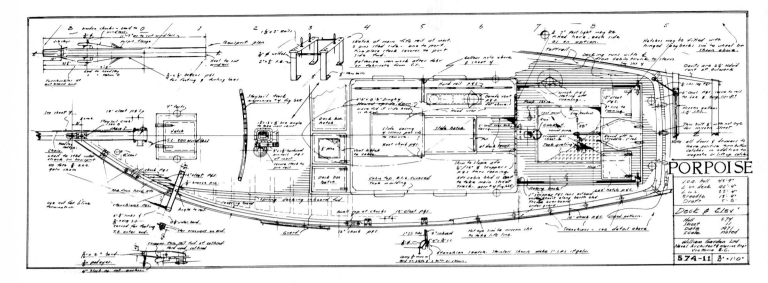

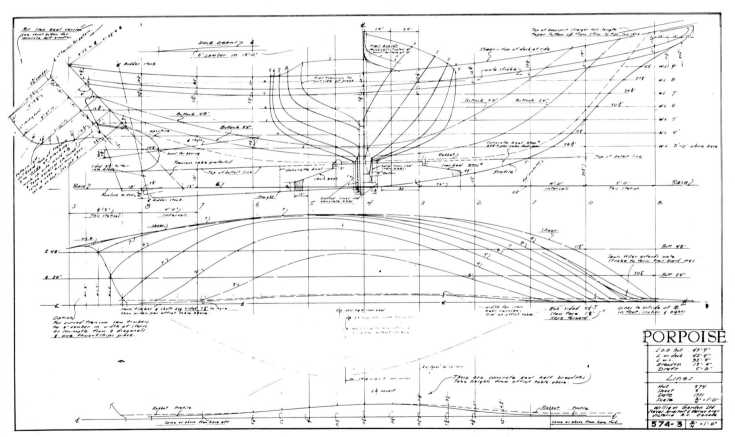

crease by about 3 inches when the boat is loaded down in sea trim for a long voyage. The model is one we've found ideal for offshore voyaging — long on the keel to make her docile on the helm, clipper bow and a broad plank bowsprit to give the sail plan sufficient base and still balance, and a snug ketch rig, which is ideally suited for chasing off before the wind under boisterous conditions. When running before it, a twin set to windward and a flattened-down jib to leeward will be a good combination with just the mainsail, the mizzen being stowed. The vane gear will hold her on course. The tall mast well forward allows her to carry twin spinnakers, and, with the four lower sails, several sail com- (Text continued on page 104)

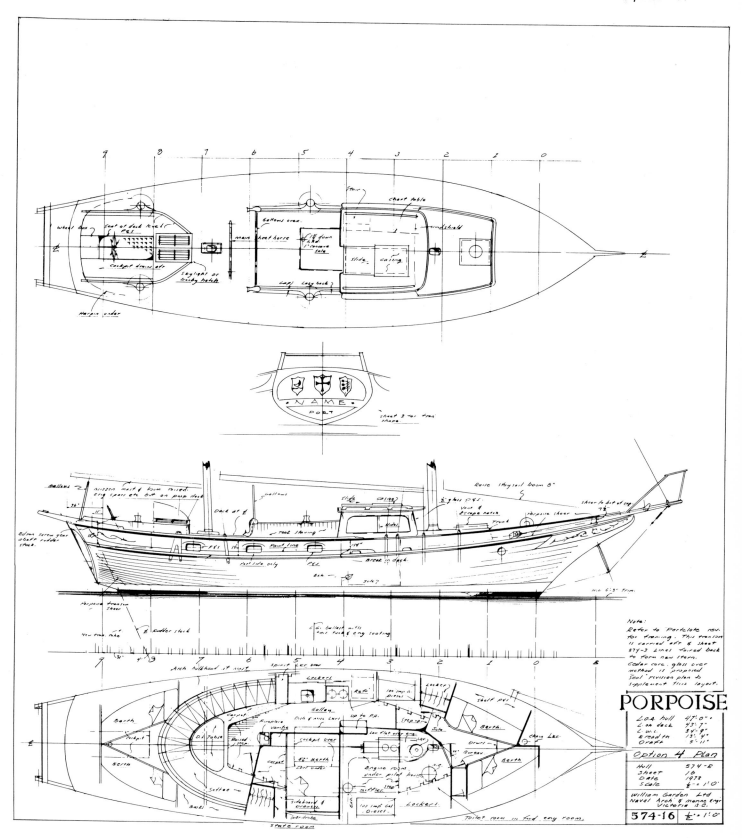

Gunther Lehman's motor-sailer version. Within these dimensions a number of layouts will fit.

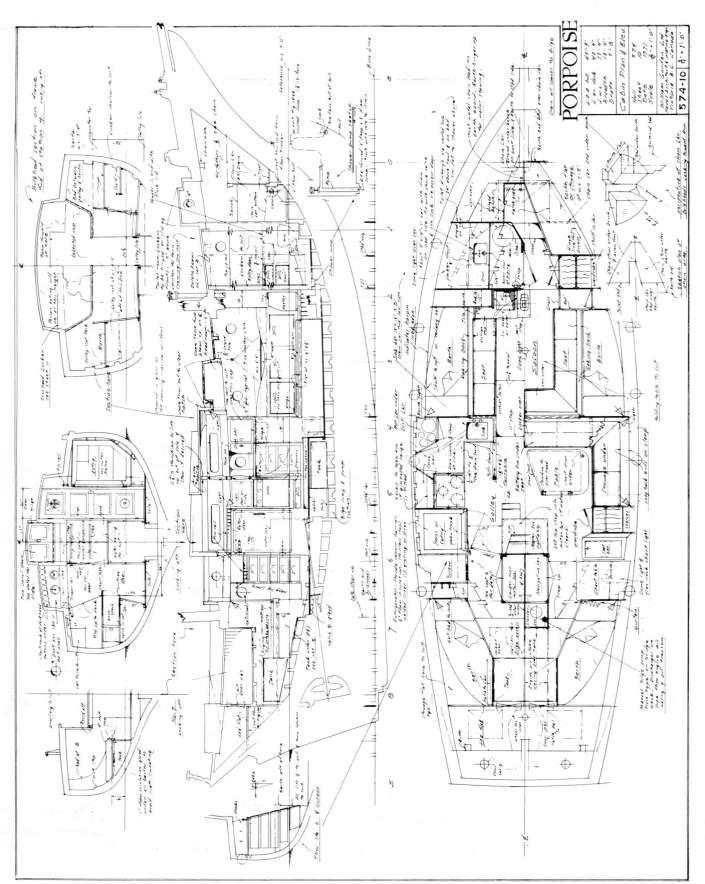

Steve Dickinson's *Kapduva*, built by Robin Fung in Hong Kong. Below decks she is snug and shipshape.

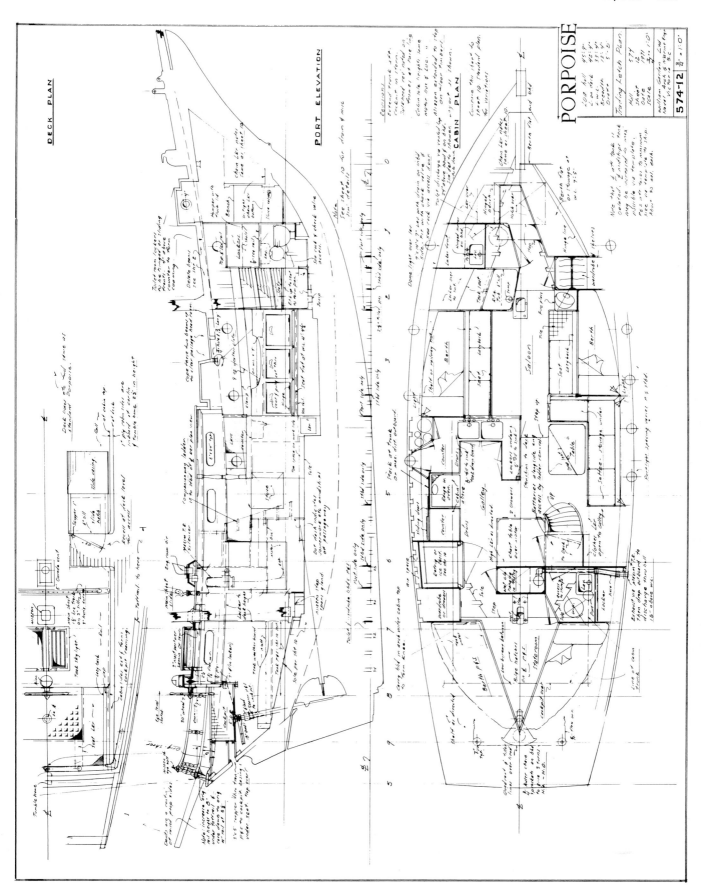

The trading ketch option with long trunk and the lazarette opened up for accommodations.

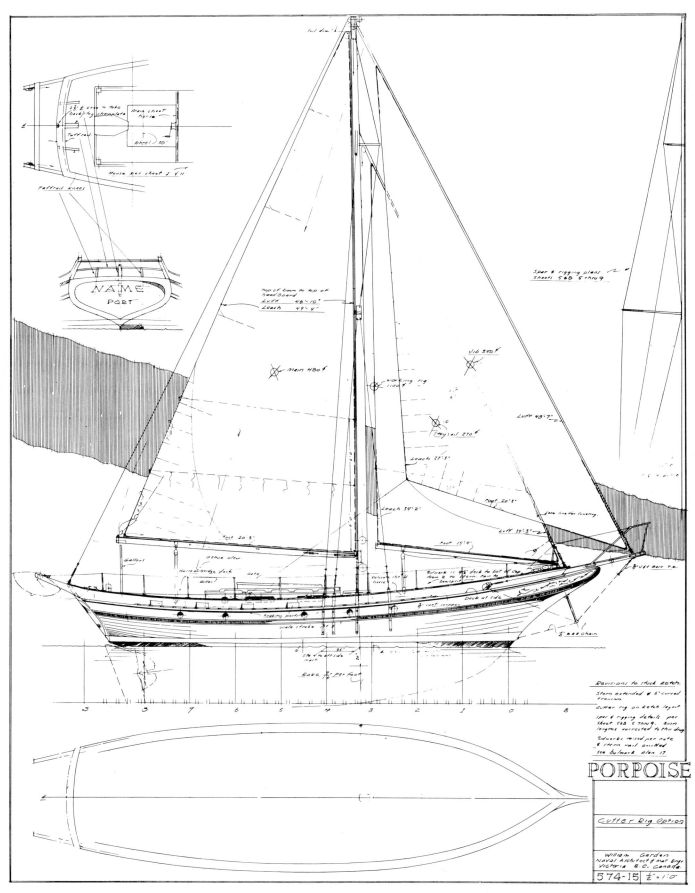

Jack Shacklock's cutter version. The bulwarks are 12 inches high, providing a feeling of shelter on deck.

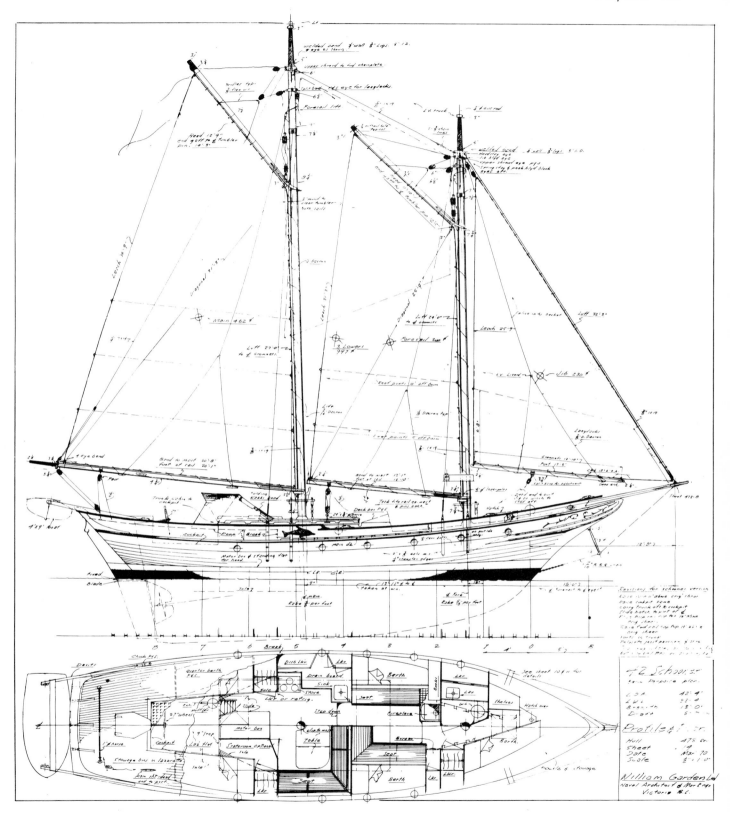

Tom Rigby's *Salty Dog,* a schooner version.

binations can be carried: from the mizzen, main, and large genoa in light weather to the reefed main or trysail and staysail under adverse conditions. The trysail and mizzen are interchangeable to simplify the sail outfit.

There is a tremendous amount of room on *Porpoise*'s deck, with her ample breadth of over 13 feet and the flush-deck arrangement. From the forecastle head, the deck sweeps aft to the transom without a break other than the small cabin trunk and cockpit footwell. An Edson steerer is fitted aft, and the cockpit extends forward to the trunk bulkhead, with a raised threshold at the cabin access.

The cabin plan is extremely flexible and allows four made-up berths — two amidships and two aft. For most ocean passages, the forward cabin can be used for stowage, and the crew can turn in amidships and aft where the motion is minimized. Another endearing feature will be found in the dinette area, directly opposite the galley. It is a place where a meal can be served without disturbing crew members sleeping in the forward cabin. The quarter berths aft are well outboard port and starboard, and the engine box sides hinge away for complete access to the entire engine, making inspection or maintenance a relatively simple matter.

She's built ruggedly but without excessive weight; the frames are 1¾-inch by 2¼-inch bent oak on 12-inch centerlines, and the planking is 1 3/8-inch yellow cedar or mahogany, with a 1 5/8-inch wale strake that fairs into the clipper bow and is banded by double bronze half-rounds.

The station 4 section drawing shows the typical framing details through the dinette on the starboard side looking forward; the curved bulkhead is the separation between the dinette and main saloon. The construction section shows a typical mold with ribbands. Ballast can be reinforced concrete with scrap iron, cast iron, or lead, depending on the pocketbook or whim of the builder. Several of this model are presently in the pre-construction or construction stage as home projects, and the majority of the builders are fitting the reinforced concrete ballast keel in view of the rising cost of cast iron.

Construction is straightforward carvel planking on a bent-oak frame. The keel is shaped and bolted up while lying on its side on the shop floor, then it is hoisted up onto the keel blocks to the proper height to accommodate the ballast. The transom is fitted, the molds are placed at intervals along the keel, and then the ribbands, which are usually of flat-grained green fir, are bent around the molds and spiked to them. The steamed oak frames are bent around the ribbands. The frames can be either in one piece or laminated of two layers. In the latter case, the pieces must be separated after cooling and taking shape in order to dry for gluing or bedding. For a laminated frame the bending is somewhat easier than for a solid frame, but the time required to glue up the layers or to get mastic between them makes the job more time-consuming than for a solid frame. Glue will make the layers essentially one again, and the plank and stringer fastenings extending through each layer will tie everything together, perhaps equally well even if the pieces are set up with plain paint between.

Once the hull is framed, the floor timbers may be fitted, and the deck beams and carlins put in place. I usually proceed then with the sheer strakes, decking, cabin trunk, etc., while with a shop crew the interior bulkheads and joinerwork can go ahead.

One or two frames can be cut for easy crew access from the shop floor; these are replaced and sister-framed alongside only when things are well completed inside. Meanwhile, rubbish can conveniently fall through the unplanked hull, though I must admit some tools escape, too; but access from outside seems to be a great help in piping, bulkhead fitting, and similar tasks.

Planking will be well seasoned by now, and one of the last jobs will be to close her in.

As mentioned previously, ballast may be concrete, cast iron, or lead. Concrete might be the best for the home builder and can be cast after the keel is upright. This ballast requires a broad keel to get in enough volume for the relatively light material, since concrete by itself is close to the weight of aluminum and satisfactory only if packed with scrap iron. The iron must be well insulated from the sea, so about two inches of waterproofed concrete shell is required. The usual practice is to tack-weld or form-wire the metal to the keel bolts prior to

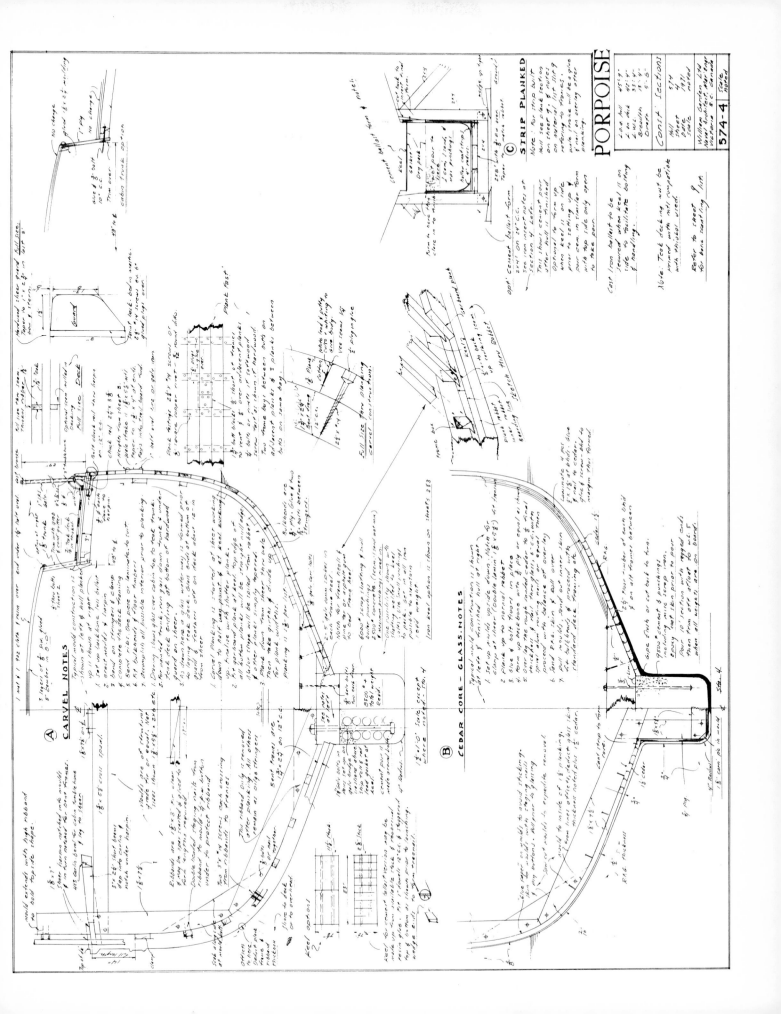

pouring the concrete. The keel detail shows this and indicates the sequence of pouring.

Iron is my choice because of its resistance to impact when grounding and its ability to bounce or slide over rock or coral. Corrosion prevention is a chore to be attended to at haul-out time, but a good epoxy tar coating prior to painting will do much to alleviate rust. Lead is number one in density, lovely to cast, drill, shape, and smooth, but not recommended for a cruiser of out-of-the-way places as it forms over rock or coral upon impact and you stop with a shuddering jolt. But for a competitive boat around the buoys, lead is it. No contest.

The most economical fastening plan is to use hot-dipped galvanized bolts through the backbone, counterboring and plugging each one to insulate it from sea water. Plank fastenings may be hot-dipped galvanized-iron boat nails counterbored and with glued plugs, or, best of all, silicon bronze screws, Everdur screws, or copper rivets, which are more difficult to get. The latter three types of fastening leave no eventual rust stains as do bleeding iron fastenings, and they are clean and a pleasure to handle. For an old boat with rusty fastenings, the only answer is to paint her the same rust color.

So we get to the deck of *Porpoise*, which is shipshape and has plenty of room to work the rig. The sweep of the deck planking is noted on the plan and will look very well if you can manage enough teak to do the job. Painted fir is equally shipshape, and red cedar is a safer bet from the standpoint of rot, but it is soft and requires a flow coat of polyurethane to harden the surface. Teak should be layed in Thiokol rubber, and the fir or cedar should be hard-glued to the plywood or to the diagonal cedar sub-deck.

Spars are best of hollow spruce or fir and painted or given first a covering of fiberglass cloth set in resin. Tangs and terminals are all simple sheet-metal work, but in total constitute a pile of metal. A lot of jobs, such as making tangs, can be let out to unsuspecting friends who have specialized skills, but the long, hard days of patient boatbuilding will be yours, and yours alone.

Porpoise is a fine little ship, able to stow the immense supply of stores required for distant waters without appearing half sunk. She's a real home on the ocean, designed to carry her crew in comfort wherever they may wish to wander.

18 *Tillie Howard*, a Sharpie Ketch

LOA — 46' 0"
LWL — 41' 6"
Beam — 8' 0"
Draft — Keel up, 2' 0"; keel down, 5' 0"
Displacement — 7,515 pounds
Ballast — 3,600 pounds drop keel
Sil Area — 555 square feet in working rig

Tillie Howard is a more fanciful animal than the usual bottoms-up sharpie. She might be best classified as a king-sized Texas canoe-ketch. Frank Davis had her built in El Paso for sailing and weekending on the Texas lakes where a trailer is required for access. The highway's total length limit is 65 feet, so by deducting the length of the tow truck we ended up with 46 feet available for the boat. A chine breadth of 6 feet 7 inches proved best. Besides the length requirement, the boat needed to be of extreme simplicity in construction, one well within the limits of a reasonably competent home craftsman, so we worked up a plain plywood double-ender based on stock lumberyard dimension-material utilizing a straightforward nail-and-glue approach.

You will notice that the basic structure is similar in theme to *Tlingit*, the 60-foot power sharpie described later, and this construction approach seems to result in a very simple form for reasonable performance. The long, flat-bottomed hull is in the traditional sharpie style, but here we've given her external ballast for sail-carrying power, something that all sharpies need. You have a choice: this sort of fin keel or

14-foot hiking boards with a crew of 400-pound orangutans as live ballast to keep her upright. Most of the historical sharpies whose lines we have seen in print are virtually worthless under sail due to a lack of stability or power to carry sail. Fill them up with rock or oysters and they are sluggish; sail them light, the big ones, and your weight is far from adequate to keep them upright and give them any drive. But hang a fin keel on most any of them and away they go.

I've included a stability diagram of *Tillie* with and without the ballast as an indication of what it takes to gain sail-carrying power in the narrow sharpie form. The lightest puff will dump her if a fin is not fitted, and this applies to any of the slim sharpie hulls — the owners are due for a wetting or a sad disappointment with the first real breeze.

Breadth in a flat-bottomed boat makes it a miserable, pounding affair until it is heeled and sailing on a chine, at which point it needs shifting ballast, such as a trapeze or hiking boards, requiring more active hopping around than most of us will put up with. The solution, of course, is a ballasted fin, fitted for ultimate stability and to give the drive and go of a proper

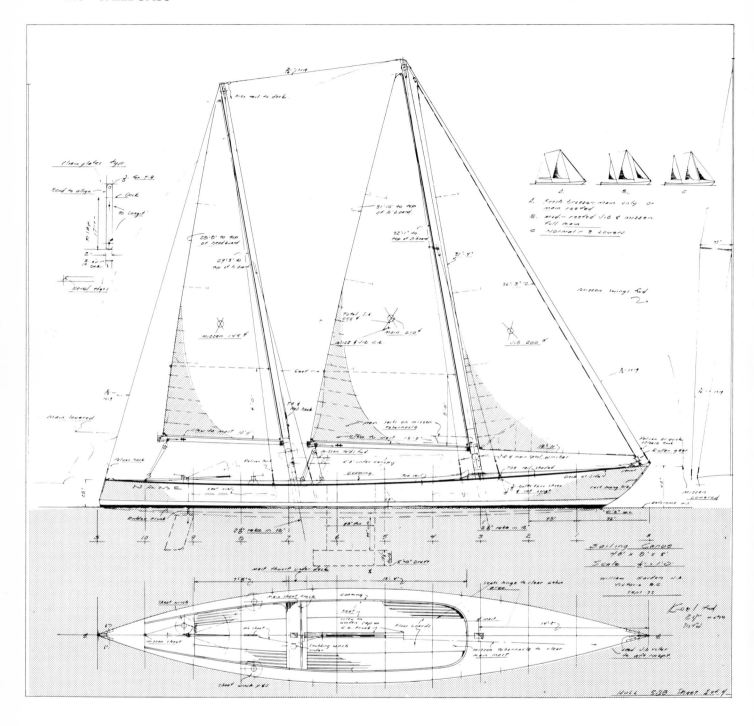

sailing boat. The fin is the only way to handle a large boat of the sharpie form. Build a long, lean canoe hull, hang a fin under it, have the bottom narrow forward to minimize pounding in a chop and light airs, and the results will be worth the lumber pile. But the big, inside-ballasted sharpie is trouble if competitive performance is required.

Many of the published plans of historical sharpies can make reasonable boats, but some reconstruction plans, many times based on the most nebulous data, produce beautiful boats that probably resemble the original about as closely as Burl Ives's polished folk tunes resemble the original dishpan-accompanied hill songs. The performance of these reconstructions is oc-

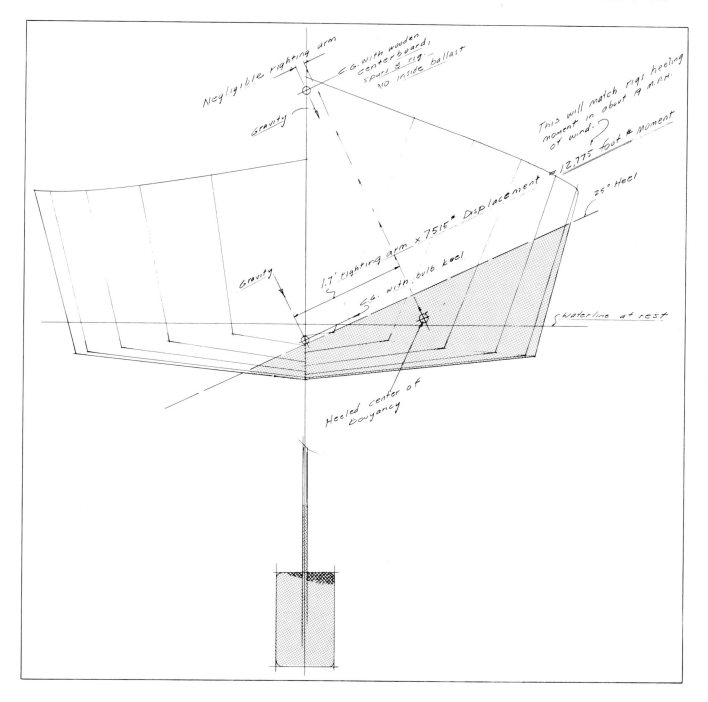

casionally noted as excellent — the *Saucy Bess* weathered the Great Gale of '96, etc. — but the enthusiast has perhaps never sailed anything that will really go, so it's performance as compared to *what* that is needed for a measure.

The lifting device to raise *Tillie*'s drop keel is of interest; it converts her from a deep water boat to one capable of being beached bow on for a shore picnic or brought up the beach on a trailer. The removable rudder is in a simple trunk with a retaining wedge.

Raising devices for drop keels have been awkward at times. One of the worst, perhaps, was a hydraulic truck crane seen mounted on deck over the keel of an English yacht. *Tillie*'s arrangement is comparatively simple and easily

Station #6 Showing completed
frame construction.
3" = 1'0" Scale

Station #6 Showing layout
from lines drwg.
3" = 1'0" Scale

Note
Lumber dim'n noted are nominal
2×4 = 1⅝ × 3⅝ net etc.

Sailing Range
40' × 6 × 5'
Scale 3" = 1'0"

William Garden N.A.
Victoria B.C.
Sept. 73

handles the heavy fin, either manually with a crank or by an electric motor with limit switches. The plan shown is of a simple Sprague keel hoist utilizing a Joyce screw jack with a long shaft. Brinton Sprague, mechanical engineer, Winslow, Washington, can furnish components and plans to match any installation.

A few words about the rig: to allocate centers I went through the usual calculations, meditations, and adjustments, but, upon sailing the boat, Frank reported a lee helm, the keel being too far aft — by about 19 inches I would say as a second guess. This gave me much worry until Frank Davis found that, by raising the keel

partway up in normal sailing weather, she would balance perfectly with the three lowers set. In a hard breeze, when maximum stability is needed, the board is cranked down and the jib taken in, giving her a handy cat-ketch rig all on travelers and with the same proper balance. This is a very simple way of maintaining balance as the wind makes up, though we didn't plan it that way. We lucked out on this one, and it is the sort of accident that we should really take credit for as a piece of exotic planning to make up for some of the blame we occasionally have to take that we don't fully deserve.

For the boat to balance with the keel all the way down and under three lowers, I would

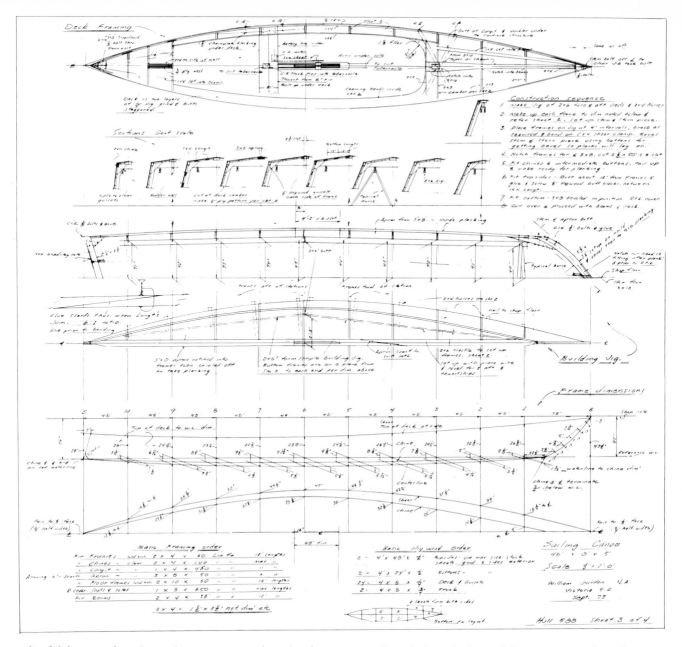

build her with a board 19 to 22 inches farther forward. The plans show the "as built" original arrangement, which suits the sail-shortening philosophy noted above. The rig is pleasing to the eye and about as simple as one can make it, with plenty of room here for a mizzen without cluttering up what would normally be a ketch's tight cockpit area. There are no go-fast gadgets to get wet and short circuit or to take your mind off the luff of the jib. She's just a nice, plain, sailing boat with a low, efficient rig, aluminum stock spars, good sails, and maximum enjoyment.

In layout on deck, she is basically a dayboat; however, in this length, a good cruising arrangement can be fitted with sleeping bags, air mattresses, a portable head, and a canvas hood for shelter. I have a couple of nice color photos of her, one with her on the trailer prior to launching and one with her under sail with more crew heads showing than I can count. A wonderful picnic boat.

The general arrangement is on the plans. The framing is indicated, and you'll note the camber or rounding that's cut in the deep floor frames to help channel the bilge water and to ease the thump of a slop and light air. Normally, the forefoot is immersed to keep things quiet, and, in any sort of a breeze, with an angle of heel, the sharp chine slides through with a nice vee'd cutting edge.

A boat of this sort — hull and deck a soft gray with a wide, white boot top, red bottom, and the sheer set off with a bright teak guard —

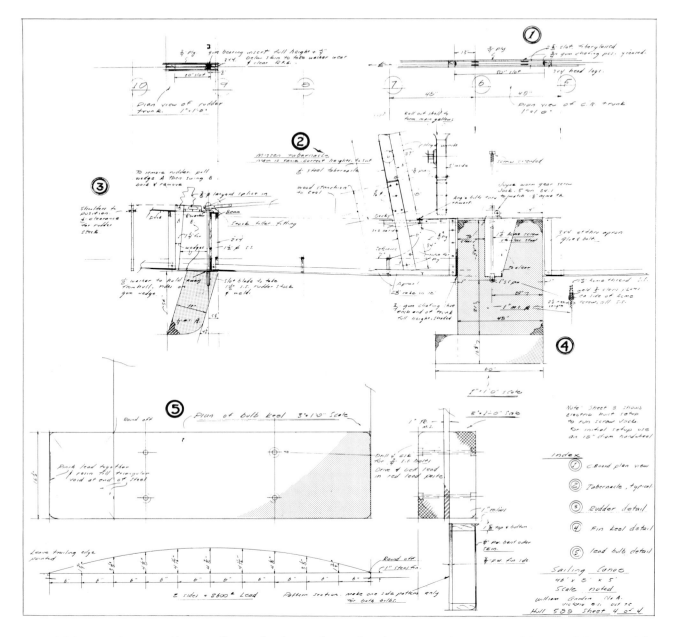

would be an elegant affair. *Tillie* as built, with her black hull, sand-buff decks, and red bottom, has a more piratical look about her and better matches her namesake, Tillie Howard, who I'm told ran an elegant El Paso cat-house. The paint job's significance just struck me. I'll have to check on this.

To wind up *Tillie*'s story on a note of caution: a centerboard is a forgiving thing in shallow water, with its bump and rise giving you a warning should you touch shoaling water at speed. A fixed drop keel, however, is like any fin keel and will bring you up all standing with a terrible thud if you hit a reef. For continuous

shoal-water sailing, I would use a lift assembly in a trunk that is longer than needed, fit the short, deep fin, and arrange a hinged stop at the forward top end of the trunk so the assembly would hinge there and relieve a grounding shock by swinging back into the after part of the long trunk. And since she's an open boat as designed, it's best to fit her with air tanks in case she swamps, as *Tillie* has done.

And a final note: I see that *Toadstool* and *Tillie* by coincidence both carry the same 555 square feet of sail. That is a vast spread in type and size, but nearly the same amount of effort to sail.

19   *Windstar III*, an Auxiliary Ketch

LOA — 56' 0"
LWL — 47' 6"
Beam — 15' 6"
Draft — 7' 0"
Displacement — 71,000 pounds
Ballast — 23,000 pounds
Sail Area — 1,809 square feet in 4 working sails
Power — Volvo diesel 130 hp

Windstar III is about the maximum size for a family cruising boat that is still able to be handled without the mixed blessings of a hired crew. Within the dimensions of 56 feet overall and 15 feet 6 inches of breadth, she has excellent cruising or live-on-board space incorporating three double staterooms and one good single, the doubles having adjacent baths and the single a basin.

The plans fail to indicate the wonderful feeling of space on board a boat of this breadth, and she makes up for a dozen or so compromises we've done when, upon completion, we've thought what an improvement another 20 percent in internal volume would have made. *Windstar's* accommodations afford the room and privacy so important on a long cruise plus a handy layout for the cook and the engineer.

The galley is along the starboard side under the cockpit and on the general sole level. The framing plan indicates the cabin soles and elevations. An oil-burning range is located aft opposite the refrigerator, with an electric cooking top adjacent to it for hot-weather meals. Opposite the double sink and along the engine room bulkhead is a serving counter. Directly forward of the galley is a dinette that looks small on the plan but is full size. It's a handy place for off-watch coffee or for use as a serving bar when in port. Forward of the dinette is a roomy chart table and navigating area; radio gear is along the forward bulkhead, with book racks outboard and chart drawers under.

To starboard of the stateroom passage is a fireplace, and the port side of the saloon is taken up with an L-shaped settee, sideboard, and the main dining table. The aft bulkhead has the companionway to the cockpit and a door to the engine room. The elevation at station 7 shows this bulkhead looking aft from the saloon. The locker between the ladder and engine-room door is for wet clothes and is fitted with engine-room heat louvres for drying.

The section drawings indicate a finish of varnished, red-cedar, vee-edge staving set off with teak moldings, jambs, fiddle rails, and

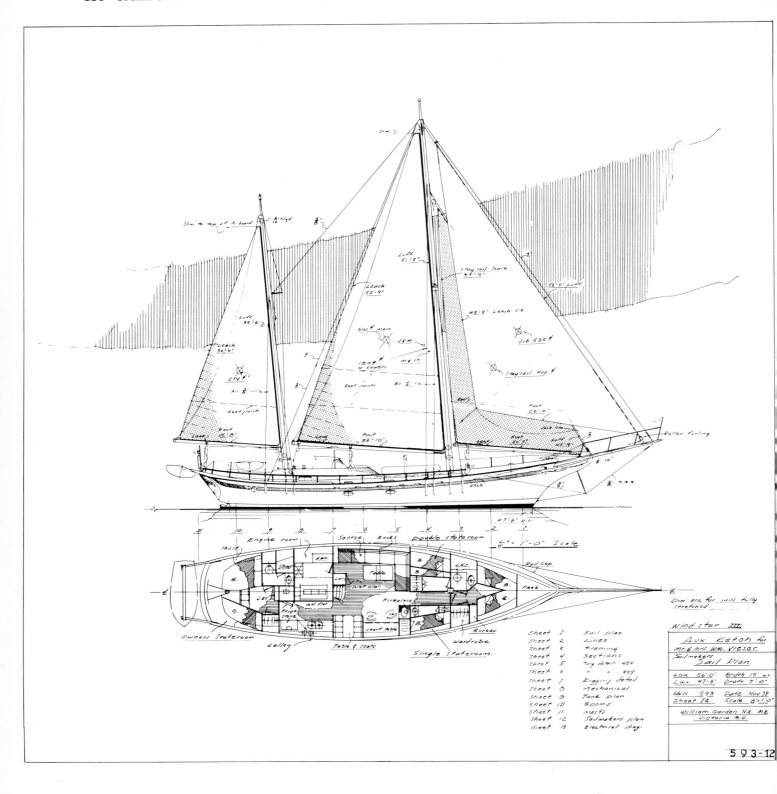

trim. The deckhead is bone white with teak beam soles. The cabin soles throughout are of teak with maple seam feathers. The staterooms port and starboard foreward of amidships are painted bone white over the staving; with teak trim they look very shipshape and pleasant. Each of these rooms has a skylight-vent-escape, which adds much to the light and airy feeling.

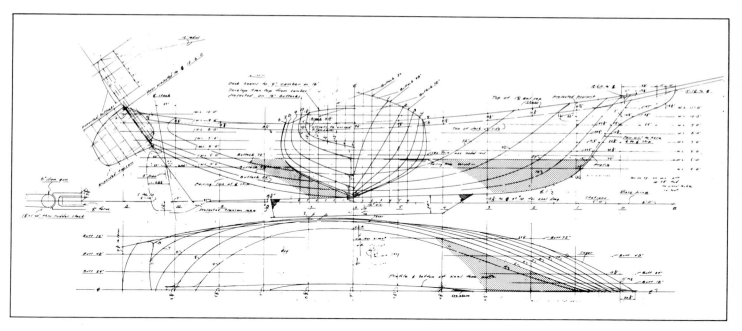

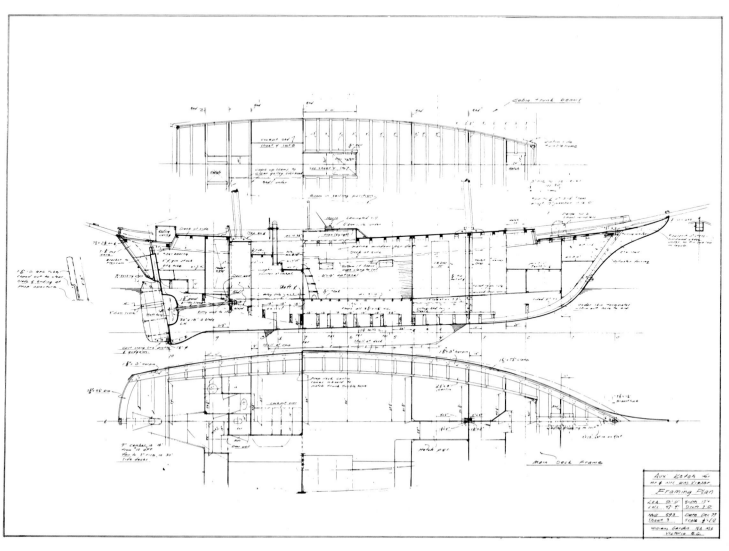

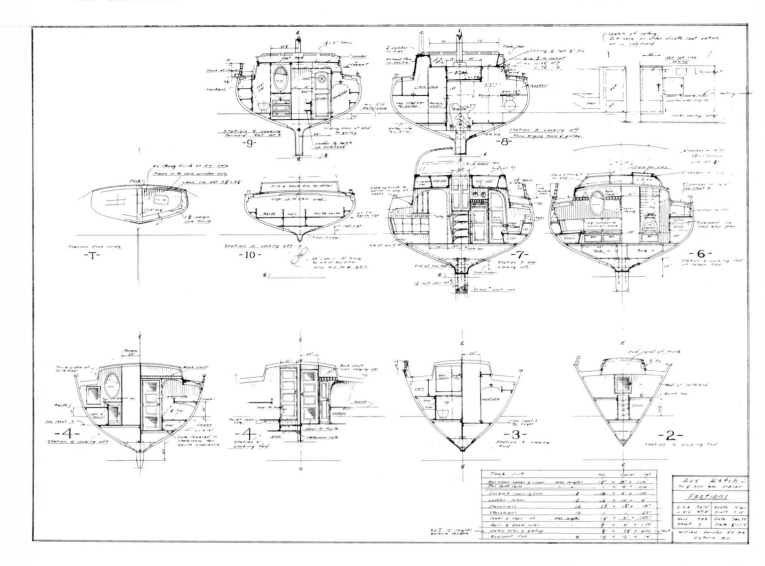

In this size hull, either a flush-deck or a trunk-cabin layout will fit. In *Windstar*, we chose a trunk cabin for better portlight ventilation, deeper bulwarks, and maximum cabin sole width. Tanks fit under the sole, and the deep bilges are a real bonus in gaining space for cruising stores, holding tank, fuel, water, and piping. A flush-decker's deck area seems to be taken up eventually with boats and deck boxes, so the trunk cabin configuration usually seems to be the best choice all around.

On deck, *Windstar* has a deep bulwark supplemented with a teak taffrail running through the waist and ending at the running light towers; a solid rail runs from the lights to the bow. The cockpit has a shelter over the forward end, big deck boxes flanking the companionway, and a steering console directly over the motor space. The entire cockpit sole can be removed for major engine repairs. Power is a Volvo diesel turning a two-bladed propeller with a sailing shaft brake. In the engine room, the generator set and batteries are to port along with tools and other engine room accumulation; all this is trimmed off with 2,000 pounds of inside lead ballast stowed to starboard at station 4. The boat's electrical system is 12-volt, with a 110-volt standby generator for cooking, hot-water, auxiliary heating to supplement the engine loop, and area heaters.

Let's go back on deck for a moment, then we'll get at the general form. The small boats are noted on the sail plan. A dinghy can be carried athwartships on the aft trunk, and a nice little

11-foot Hiram-Lowell-type, double-chine rowing dory is stowed on the stern davits. Amidships is an inflatable rubber boat with an outboard motor of about 600 advertised horsepower for use in scuba diving and exploring. The windlass is a Delta No. 2 rope-or-wire-on-drum model. Aft is a big freezer box abaft the trunk cabin with a roomy deck box opposite.

The lines will outline her basic form — a round-bilged model without "S" section and with strong tumblehome amidships. The 21,000-pound iron keel is bolted under her after the hull fiberglassing is completed. With the outside iron plus the little bit inside to trim the mechanical layout, plus a heavy engine and low tanks, she has a normal ballast-to-displacement ratio and great sail-carrying power.

The rig is designed to balance with a light helm up to a breeze of about 20 knots. As the wind and heel increase, the mizzen is taken in, and at about 30 to 35 knots, the jib is rolled up, leaving her under a snug, all-inboard rig of main and staysail. I had best mention that the wind speeds are actual and should be multiplied by the standard 1.5 for yacht club bar discussions. The three centers are noted on the sail plan. A total of 1,809 square feet of sail is carried in the four lowers, and the center of effort under jib and mizzen or under main and staysail are all at nearly the same spot, giving good balance under several combinations. The lead of the center of effort of the sails forward of the center of lateral resistance is 20 percent, which we've found to be required for the type.

Windstar was strip-planked: 1½-inch plank thickness, glued and edge-nailed, with a simple, formed-up, box-keel section above the iron added while she was in the upside-down position. Garboards were coved with a 12 inch radius using a dry-wall approach, then the shell was given a heavy glass skin and rolled over.

The cedar lining was left in for insulation and a point for securing joinerwork. The keel forms were then stripped out, leaving a clean bilge ready for the wooden floor timbers, which are required to hang the iron ballast. The cedar liner is a blessing for ease of completion, since it simplifies the tedious attachment problem of a normal glass hull when bulkheads and joinerwork must be fitted. From the standpoint of time expended for a "one only" hull, there may be some slight saving over a simple carvel bent-frame hull, but I believe that the latter would be my choice. Glass forms a seamless structure, but otherwise I don't like to work with the material. The smell is offensive, and one day it may be that the industrial insurance people will be confronted with a generation of lungs damaged from the dust. We're building the little schooner *Toadstool* now, and what a pleasure it is to get out in a wooden boatshop on a nice spring day and work with the proper materials — pine tar, varnish, red cedar, oak, and teak.

Mike Handford of the English Cranfield sails was in last month and told me that he's even back to furnishing flax sails with Italian hemp boltrope. To take new delivery of a hard-earned flax or cotton sail with fragrant steam-tarred Italian hemp boltropes was once the ultimate. Night number one after delivery the sail was draped over the bed as a regal spread for a slumber fit for the gods. I'm going to order a flax trysail and a small jib for the *Toadstool* just to smell them. Maybe even a hat would be nice with a neatly sewn quarter-inch diameter Italian hemp boltrope.

Windstar III was built by Philbrooks Shipyard in Sidney, British Columbia, for former Downeasters, and the boat is the traditional bottle green with black bulwarks, a white boot, red copper bottom paint, and sand colored decks and spars.

20 *Sand Lark*, a Traditional Schooner

LOA — 60'
LWL — 51'
Beam — 19' 4"
Draft — 7' 8"
Sail Area — 4 lowers, 1,780 square feet

Sixty by nineteen is a big chunk of boat, perhaps the practical limit for ease of handling by an amateur crew, yet with enough weight to give the feeling of a real ship when under sail. Nineteen feet of breadth is impressive when the area is relatively unbroken — the deck space is a real pleasure at sea or alongside the dock. The *Sand Lark* has all this and more. The surrounding bulwarks rise forward to the well-steeved bowsprit and sweep aft to a broad transom stern flanked by timber boat davits and lapped with a low taffrail. She's a fine little ship under foot, and the schooner rig is a happy workhouse for four or five stalwarts.

Sand Lark has been built in wood and steel. The wooden construction is perhaps the better choice, since it suits the era when a small commercial schooner could be made to pay. The construction plan for wood shows the general details of framing and scantlings, with the rugged sawn frames, backbone, beams, and skin taking a fair bite out of a good-sized wood lot.

To build her today, I would haunt the building wreckers for seasoned fir that would outlast all of us twice over. Details of the framing can be followed on the drawings. The frames are of double 2 5/8-inch flitch on 18-inch centers, molded 7 inches at the heel, and tapering to 5 inches at the deck and top timbers, which take the bulwarks. The total frame size then is 5¼ inches by 7 inches at the keel running on up to 5¼ inches by 5 inches at the sheer, so, with these on 18-inch centers, we have a rugged framework.

Sawn frames are interesting to make up, and what looks tedious at a glance is an interesting and absorbing job. Each frame is laid down on the floor, and a full template is made from the centerline to the sheer. A template has to be made for only one-half of a frame since it can be flopped over for the other half. The template, once made, is placed over available 2 5/8-inch stock, and the straight-grained pieces are cut to utilize best width. Butts are staggered in each frame half to maintain strength, and bevels are noted on each piece so the sawyer can carefully bandsaw the material to the varying bevels and minimize the fairing up after the framework is set up. Careful layout work with accurate sawing and running of the bevels will result in a frame requiring an absolute minimum

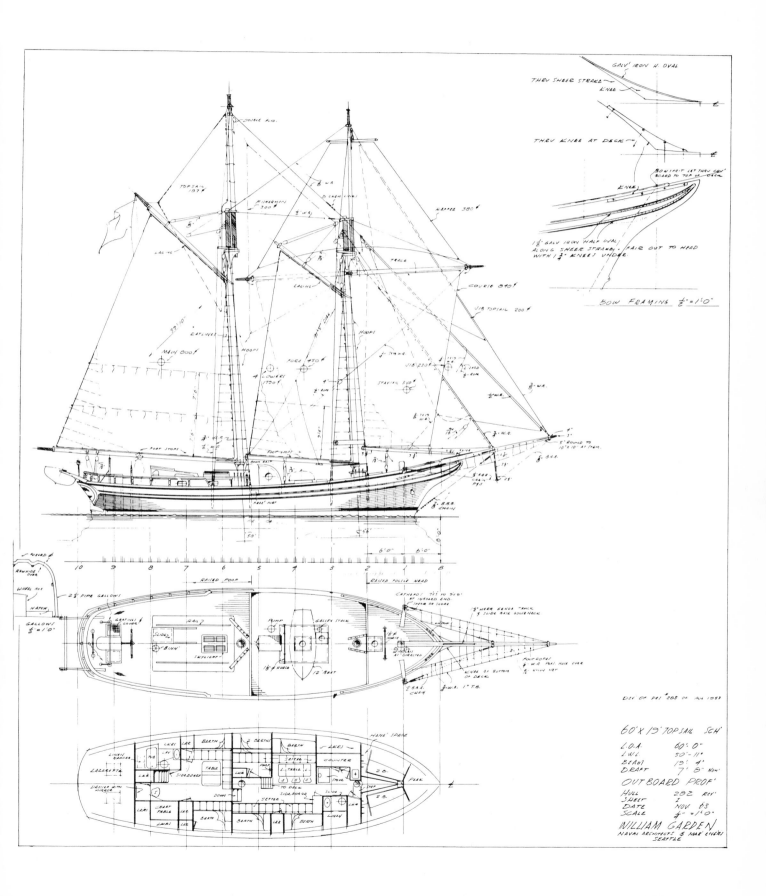

BOW FRAMING ⅛"=1'0"

DEV OF DES #253 OF AUG 1953

60' X 19' TOPSAIL SCH'
L.O.A.   60': 0"
L.W.L.   50'- 11"
BEAM   19' 4"
DRAFT   7' 5" NOM'
OUTBOARD PROF'
HULL   282 REV'
SHEET   I
DATE   NOV 63
SCALE   ⅜" = 1'0"
WILLIAM GARDEN
NAVAL ARCHITECTS & MAR' ENG'RS
SEATTLE

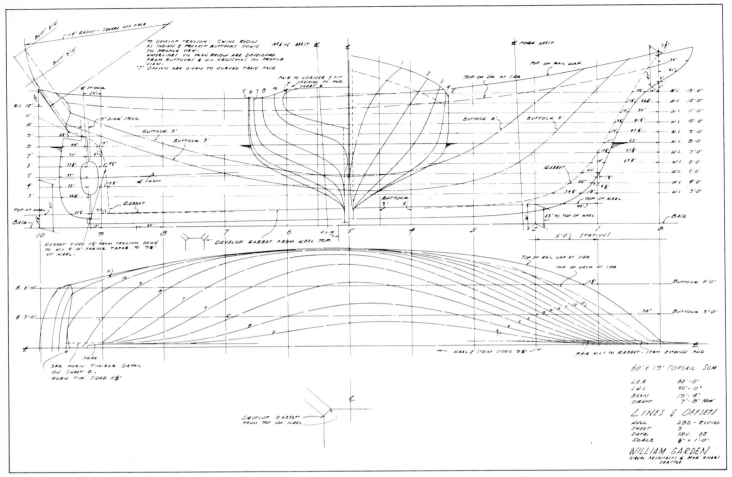

60' X 19' TOPSAIL SCH

LOA	60'-0"
LWL	50'-11"
BEAM	19'-6"
DRAFT	7'-8" NOM'

LINES & OFFSETS

HULL	282 - REVISED
SHEET	3
DATE	NOV. 63
SCALE	¼" = 1'0"

WILLIAM GARDEN
NAVAL ARCHITECTS & MAR. ENG'RS
SEATTLE

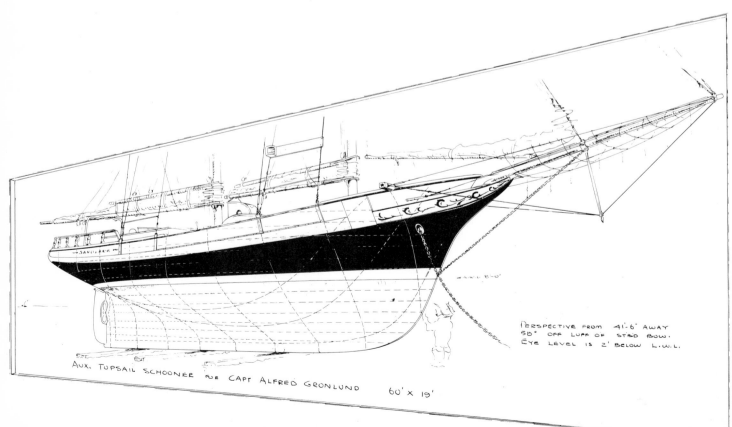

AUX. TOPSAIL SCHOONER FOR CAPT. ALFRED GRONLUND   60' X 19'

PERSPECTIVE FROM 41'-6" AWAY
58° OFF LUFF OF STB'D BOW.
EYE LEVEL IS 2' BELOW L.W.L.

of dressing off. You'll soon find a few whacks at each frame with an adz as planking progresses will suffice to land the strakes. I've always felt that a saw offends the wood and that a few clean-up strokes with an adz and plane are worthwhile to pacify things and to leave a slick fungus-free faying surface. The frame flitches are spiked or bolted together, or, best of all, glued up with the plank fastenings tying the halves together mechanically. The frame fastenings are simple, square, galvanized-iron ship spikes, countersunk and plugged. Beams are sturdy, few in number, and spaced to take the 2¼-inch by 3½-inch caulked deck. Seasoned decking of this weight, given a thread of cotton, oakum, and payed with hot pitch after setting down the caulking with a hawsing iron and beetle will be absolutely tight for a long, long time.

The planking is 1 3/4-inches net, and the ceiling, or inner skin, is 1 5/8-inch material. The stem and backbone members can be followed on the inboard profile. The rudder stock is made of Australian gum, a hardwood; it swings through a wooden rudder trunk and is connected by a worm-screw gear to a 36-inch diameter wheel.

The sail plan shows the character and features of a traditional schooner of the last century. She is something on the theme of a small coaster, or, if revised with a leg-of-mutton main sail and a full-width trade-goods cabin abaft the mainmast, she might be a South Sea Island trader of the 1870s. This latter arrangement could be an interesting way to build such a schooner, and the full-width deckhouse would afford a tremendous space for airy accommodations plus a raised poop deck that would honor a 130-footer. These early South Sea traders were a mixed lot — schooners, brigs, and ketches of varied tonnage — but from the mid 1870s on, the schooner with a full-width, aft deckhouse and leg-of-mutton mainsail seems to have predominated. The old-time trading schooners are all gone now, but as recently as the late 1930s one, such as the *Lanakai*, could still be found touching at the West Coast; the rig in the 1930s, however, was usually supplemented by a good, big Atlas or Union diesel.

Clifford Hawkins, in *Out of Auckland*, quotes a shipshape description of a California Schooner of long ago from a Rarotonga source:

The California vessel carries her beam well forward and well aft, consequently she is much broader and shallower than the New Zealander. From main-mast aft to cockpit are not deck beams, but cabin beams run from bulwark rail to rail. While this gives a large roomy cabin and trade room, the vessel is to some extent weakened. She is better finished but not nearly so strong as the New Zealand vessel. Built of wood, more or less green and unseasoned, she is, as a carrier, much inferior. Fore and aft rigged, setting five, or at the most six sails, the mainsail being triangular, she is without doubt the faster and handier of the two. Her rigging is lighter, and she carries patent appliances, such as the wheel and windlass. The wheel, known as the "Pilot Boat Patent," instead of a clumsy arrangement of blocks and chains, consists of a series of cog wheels, etc.

She is by her lightness, finish, cabin accommodation, handiness, and speed, better fitted for the Island trade than her New Zealand competitor. The New Zealander is longer, deeper and narrower. Built of well-seasoned material, she lasts more than twice as long and carries a much larger cargo. But there is a want of finish, and appearance of roughness about her quite unnecessary. She is of all rigs and carries any number of sails over six as fancy dictates. She sticks to the old-fashioned boom and gaff mainsail, which makes her more troublesome to wear quickly in off and on work, of which so much has to be done, and in sails, rigging and appliances is not so easily handled.

The book then goes on to outline the fate of the unseasoned softwood schooner in the tropics, an end matched today by the northern

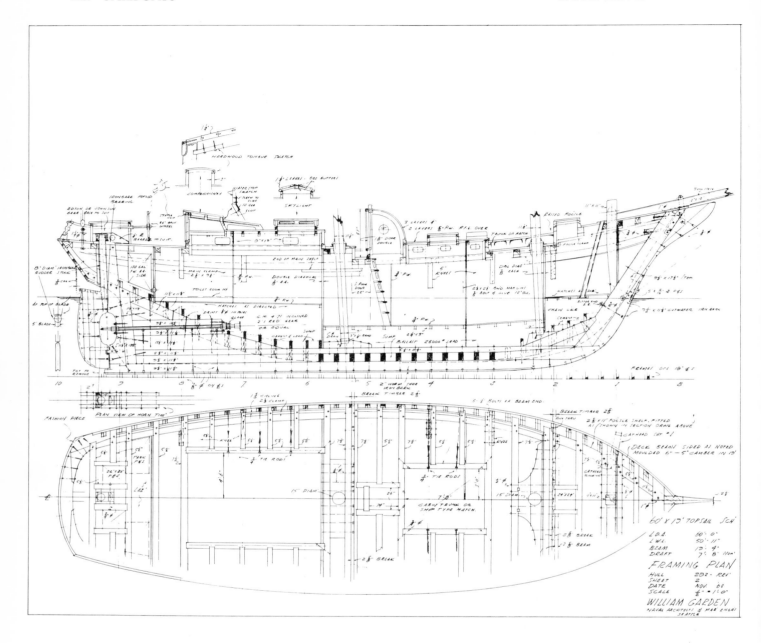

European softwood vessels when they end up in southern waters.

The California schooner for the first five years is perfection, but after that her decline is rapid. The chain plates begin to draw, her elliptical stern lets water through, and she begins to damage cargo. After ten years she goes downhill by the run, and is comparatively worthless. But she costs new little more than half a New Zealand vessel of the same tonnage. The New Zealand schooner costs more, lasts much longer, carries a larger cargo, sails duller, has no cabin or trade room accommodation,

and is in every respect stronger and heavier. For the timber trade she must suit as obviously only light work can be done by the Californian — anything else would soon use her up.

The softwood ship of semi-seasoned stock has always been a worry in the tropics, but in northern latitudes a softwood boat will probably outlast us. My daily run to the Island is made in a launch with a 70-year-old hull, so if we build carefully of seasoned stock and ventilate well, we're cranked up for a long run.

The perspective and line drawing of the *Sand Lark* give an idea of her form, indicating a

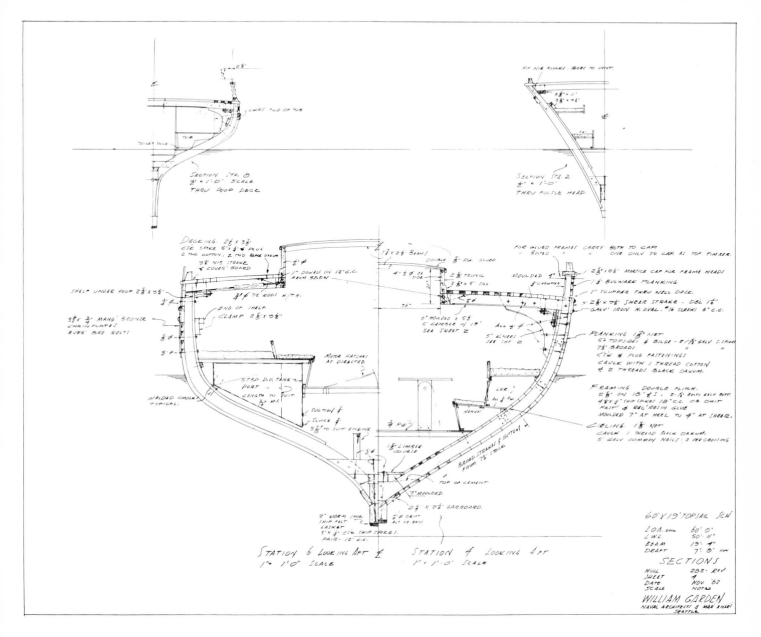

powerful model, easy lined and capable of carrying a real press of sail.

The schooner rig is supplemented with a fore course and raffee; the split course is similar to those used on the big Pacific barquentines. The little sketch shows her with foresail, forestaysail, and flying jib stowed as she broad-reaches along under full course and raffee. The windward course only is often set along with the foresail for an equally effective rig. The course furls up and down on the mast with an outhaul to fetch it out along the yard. To take in the sail, the outhaul is slacked and the inhaul and brails taken in to bring the course back to centerline, where it can be gasketed. The luff or center panel of each course is hanked to a pair of jackstays which run from the yard just outboard of the sling to eye bolts in the deck, port and starboard of the foremast. The brails dead-end to the jackstays and the brail lead-blocks secure to them also, while a simple ratline made up between the jackstays extends from the deck to the foretop. Handling the squaresails this way makes a nice rig for seagoing; it is fun to work and applicable to the smallest squaresail. The last rig of this type went on a 30-footer here at Toad's Landing last year, so romance and hard work will be with us for a long while yet.

21 *Oceanus* and *Claymore*, Fast Cruising Yachts

Oceanus (Sloop)
LOA — 60'
LWL — 48'
Beam — 12'
Draft — 6' 8"
Displacement — 36,000 pounds
Ballast — 13,500 pounds
Sail Area — Main and fore triangle, 1,145 square feet

Claymore (Express Cruiser)
LOA — 70'
Beam — 12'
Draft — 3' nominal
Displacement — 26,000 pounds
Power — Two Cummins diesels,
1½ : 1 reduction, V-8 370 model,
230 continuous hp
each at 2,600 rpm

These two boats, although one is sail and the other is power, are grouped together, since they represent the same theme — the development of a fast, cruising yacht. Maximum efficiency is achieved in each case, and both were a pleasure to cruise with or to sail. We had a 12-year love affair with *Oceanus*, a costly mistress but worth the expenditure tenfold. Her design as of 1976 is 22 years old. Thinking back on her, perhaps her most endearing quality was her simplicity, particularly when compared to many of today's electronic, oversexed, plastic hustlers.

Oceanus was designed as the ultimate in an easily driven cruising sloop that could be handled while cruising by a man and wife, have good accommodations, and be a boat that would perform equally well under sail or under power. Not much attention was paid to the racing rule, so her rating under the C.C.A. rule was 47. On the occasions when we raced her, it was with the outlook that, if you could see them astern as you crossed the finish line, you had lost the race on time. As a fast, cruising boat, however, she was a superb way to travel. Perhaps the nicest compliment of the hundreds that she received was: "She's pure vanilla." Simple, easy to handle, and reasonable under all conditions of wind and sea, she gave us much pleasure, and we always have been sorry that we couldn't find time for any serious voyaging while we had her. Her success for our use was symbolized best by the fact that she was the

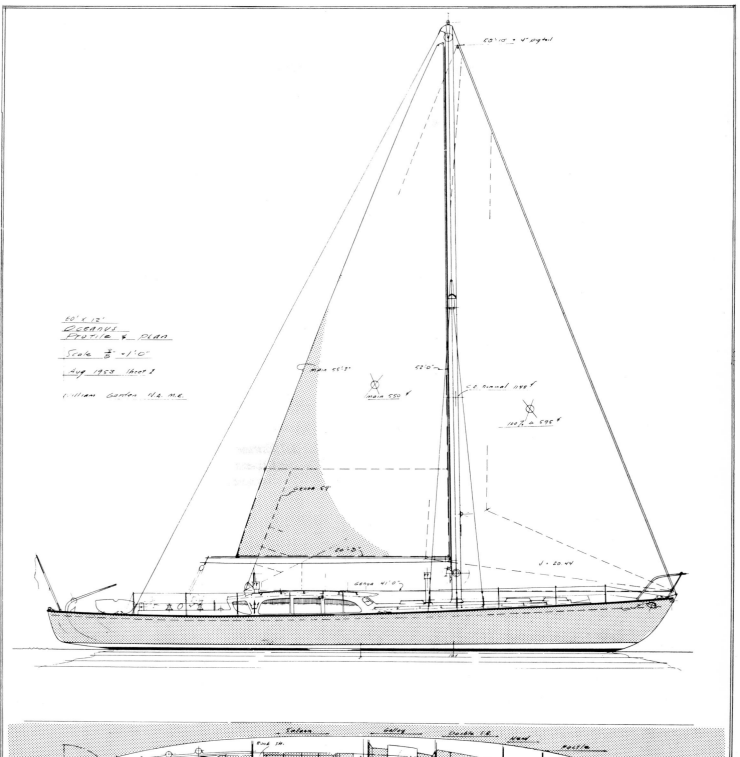

60' x 12'
Oceanus
Profile & plan
Scale ⅜" = 1'0"
Aug 1953 Sheet 1
William Garden N.A. M.E.

Oceanus under sail. She was a delight to handle.

arrived at a boat measuring 60 feet by 12 feet by 6 feet 8 inches, with a waterline length of 48 feet and a displacement in cruising trim of 36,000 pounds. A sail area of about 1,000 square feet was settled on as one of the first factors, and the gear was designed to be light, simple, and strong, so that I could sail her alone without undue exercise or inconvenience. The deep deckhouse windows dictated the long trunk cabin, which in turn allowed us to have fair bulwarks, 8 inches forward, without excessive freeboard. I have always liked a ship with bulwarks, so here we took advantage of the triple topsides and carried them up to form a smooth, strong bulwark without timberheads. The photo shows the clear expanse of deck; its fiberglass covering is coved up to form a seamless skin from rail cap to rail cap.

Under sail, *Oceanus*'s performance was up to expectations. She ghosted along in a lively manner, and in winds of 12 to 15 miles per hour, she was effortless to sail, with the big cockpit being a most pleasant spot to lounge in and to work from. In 19 to 20 miles per hour of wind, I would say her performance was superlative; one of our most memorable sails was across the Juan de Fuca Strait at night, with a hard westerly and a heavy overcast. The night was exceptionally black, and with the deck just down while close reaching, the speed of the lee bow wave sluicing past the cockpit gave the same effect as looking out of a fast steamer's low loading port when the back-light on the foam blocks out all but the rush of water.

Under power, *Oceanus* would slide along effortlessly at 1,600 revolutions, doing an easy seven nautical miles per hour. The 2:1 Chrysler Crown would turn 2,400 revolutions maximum with the propeller that was fitted, so the engine had a lot in reserve. At 1,750 revolutions, we could run with the average 10-knot, 40-foot powerboat, and almost keep up with the outboard cruisers of one motor who imagined they were doing about fifteen. Since short miles are the rule when discussing auto gas mileage and boat speeds, I probably should give you a sales speed of at least ten knots. At seven knots and 1,600 revolutions, she burned 1.85 gallons of gas per hour. We could steam about 330 miles on our 90-gallon capacity, and, with her long waterline and sharp bow, she bucked very well under power, maintaining close to six knots in

only boat I've built that didn't have a successor sailing around on paper before launching time.

Oceanus was first sketched out on the plywood subfloor of a house we were building, to the detriment of an afternoon that had been allotted to laying the oak flooring. The schooner *Rain Bird* was moored out in front at the time, and we were slowly struggling through the building of the house. Nothing becomes quite so stale as house-building over a long period of time, so the hundredth or so boat doodle evolved as a sketch of what we should have for our next ship. Anyone who has gone through the do-it-yourself house-building stage will understand, too, that the sketch was rapidly covered by flooring to prevent any worry at this point by my patient wife.

The rough idea was refined later in some sketches, and gradually the plans evolved at odd times during the next eighteen months. We

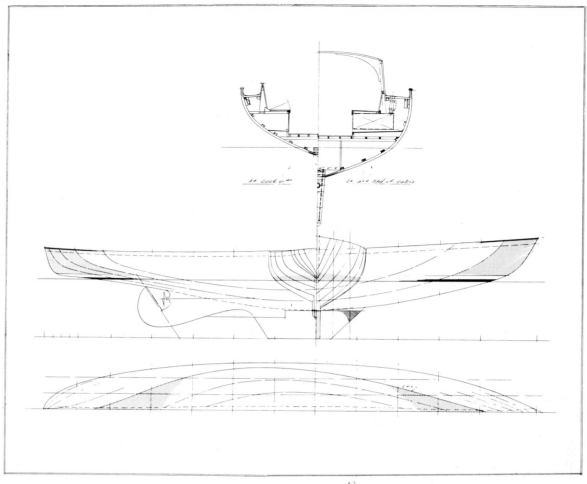

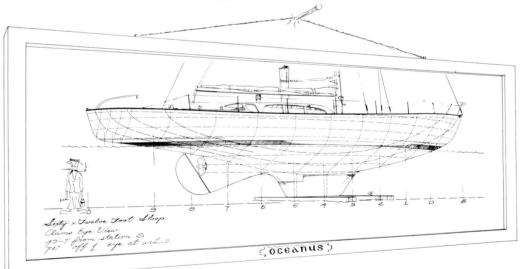

Sixty x Twelve Foot Sloop
Clams Eye View
42'-7 from station 3
72" off L eye at w.L. 2.

⟨OCEANUS⟩

open water against a 20-knot breeze and moderate sea.

Accommodation is spartan on *Oceanus*, with an underlying theme of minimum upkeep. The layout is indicated on the plans. The deckhouse in particular was a pleasant area. There was enough room to sit around, a big sliding window on each side to muzzle the spinnaker through, and reasonable visibility. After a good sail, and anchored for the night with a fresh-caught grilse browning over the fireplace coals, feet up, toes warming, plus a glass of hot rum at hand — nothing could be finer.

One of the all-time great boatbuilders, Marty Monson, laid up the cold-molded shell in his Lake Union, Seattle, shop, then we towed her up to Maritime Shipyards (now defunct), side-tracked her, and spent a year and a half of spare time in her completion. We had lots of steam in those days.

Claymore is a high-speed boat that can handle the sea.

Claymore was designed for running performance that combined high speed and seagoing ability with simple accommodations. A boat of this sort is a revelation to the average boatman, who is used to the pushwater characteristics of the usual fat-bowed, overloaded cruiser. *Claymore*'s angle of entry is very sharp and her deadrise is high. The rabbet along the centerline is almost level, then swings up about 6 inches in the last 25 feet to the transom, with the chines dropping as they run aft. The sections athwartships are straight lines in the underbody without concavity or convexity, with the deadrise decreasing toward the transom for running efficiency. A boat of this size and power seldom becomes airborne, certainly never on purpose. The form is straightforward to set up and has resulted in an excellent sea boat. She can be driven to windward in conditions that will stop most fast boats, and running in the trough or quartering the sea, she slides along equally well. Quartering into a big chop, she will occasionally catch one under the chine abreast of the wheelhouse, with a slight jar, and at anchor, the first chuckle of a rising breeze comes right under your head in the midships berth, similar to a lapstrake boat talking at anchor as the catspaws come up.

My old friend Ed Monk was on board one day and we had a good laugh about the chine or "spray-knocker" ending up at the waterline right under the owner's ear. He had just done it to himself on his own last boat.

Most power yachts are designed around accommodations, with performance taking last place after cost and practical mooring considerations have governed the boat's length. The number one consideration when designing the *Claymore* was to get the utmost performance from a pair of Cummins 370 turbocharged diesels, so we approached the task from an optimum-shape position, rather than from the position that the hull would be an envelope to contain 16 berths and a gold medallion galley. John Case, an old chum and former owner of a couple of other yachts that we had developed together and designed for him in the past, had always shared my interest in long, easily-driven hulls, and off and on for years we had discussed a modern version of the commuters and rum-runners of the 1920s. Things finally clicked when John was temporarily out of a boat, and when my Island shop was empty.

The late naval architect Leigh Coolidge, of Seattle, was one of the foremost rum-runner designers, and the old man, before he died, had given me the lines and data of his best boat — 65 feet on the water, 10 feet in breadth, and powered by a pair of Libertys. She was a lovely, round-bilged old-timer, with a double skin of teak, a bulletproof pilothouse, and all. I made a towing model of this Coolidge boat as a trial horse along with a model of a chine boat that looked like an ideal form for our use to test her against. Each full-scale boat would displace 26,000 pounds; the model scale was 3/4 inches equal 1 foot 0 inches, or one-sixteenth size, which gives, at this scale, a towing speed for the

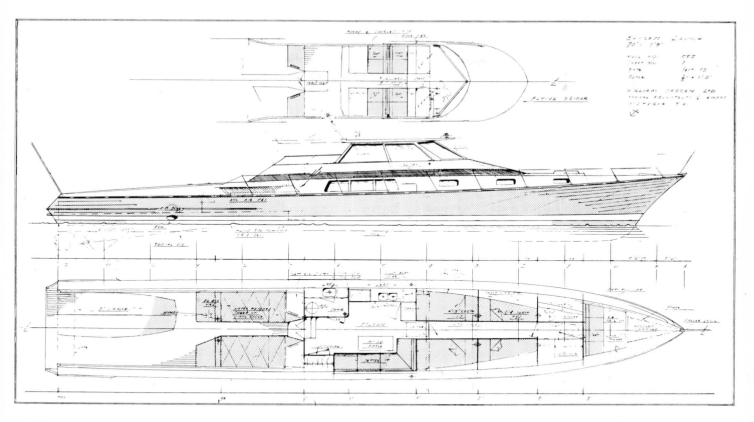

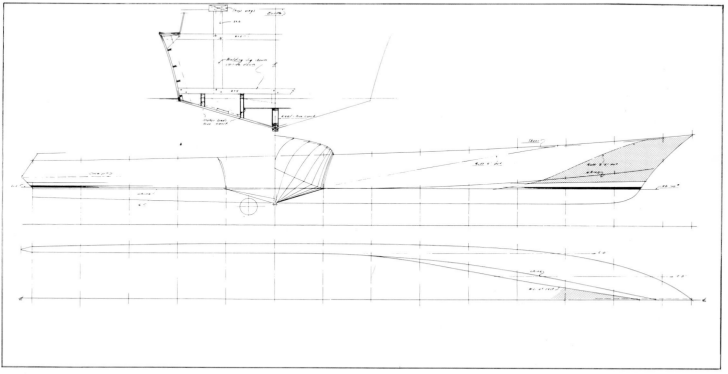

model of one-quarter the full-scale hull's speed. Six knots of speed for the model would equal 24 knots for the full-scale hull, making a practical towing speed range for simple equipment.

My towing gear is crude but accurate when working against a prototype, and we ended up with an interesting set of tests. John fell in the bay once, and the classic, textbook, speed-length ratio, optimum-hull-form rules were upheld. To about 22 knots, the round-bilged

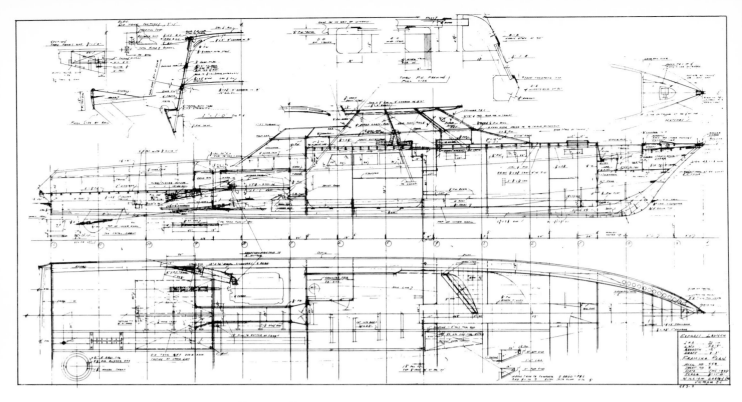

Coolidge model was most efficient. From 24 to about 34 knots, our *Claymore* hull was the most efficient, and from 34 to 70 knots, a stepped hydroplane version tested was best. At a V√L of 6 (close to 50 knots), the old rum-runner as built and without spray-knockers became unmanageable, while at slow speeds, 24 knots and under, the stepped boat, as expected, was directionally unstable and her resistance was high, but we were curious and ran the stepped version despite past experience. A step is of great value in minimizing wetted surface while maintaining fore-and-aft trim in a boat that is nearly airborne with only half the prop in the water, but doesn't fit in the operating speed of 95 percent of the small, fast boats.

So our tests bore out the textbook fact that a round bilge might be best for general economical running, but that the chine boat would be best at the 25-knot service speed and 30-knot top speed that the weight, horsepower, and form would achieve.

Claymore was the resulting hull, the length, breadth, and weight being dictated earlier in calculating the optimum proportions for the engines. Coolidge probably took the same course 50 years ago when he came up with his 65-footer. With spray-knockers added, the old Coolidge model would be hard to beat today. *Claymore* slides along at close to one nautical mile per hour for each 100 revolutions, and, although she was run for the first 200 hours at 2,600 revolutions and 25 knots plus, I notice that the usual speed is now 2,000 revolutions for

a pleasant, economical 20 knots. This speed takes about half the fuel consumption of 2,600 revolutions per minute, and 20 real nautical miles per hour with engines throttled to two-thirds rpms is a nice way to travel. For *Claymore* 3,000 rpm is nearly 30 knots, an easy match at this speed for the average 40-knot speedboat. When a sea makes up, the *Claymore*'s 25-knot speed carries on, and the little fellows quit after taking off a few times.

With this speed and weatherliness, *Claymore*'s cruising range during a holiday will cover an impressive amount of coastline; she's gone around Vancouver Island in an easy four days elapsed time and little over one day's continuous running time. Summer sea conditions can be taken as they come, but until a person experiences the seagoing qualities of such a boat, any discussion of them is just conversation.

As in *Oceanus*, *Claymore*'s accommodations are spartan, but comfortable, with reasonable privacy. The bridge seats form berths to supplement the cabins, giving six berths in all, about the limit for a boat of this volume. The long afterdeck carries a whaler and a canoe, with the original plan being to swing a float plane up over the boats via a hydraulic lift. The plane enthusiasm passed, but with such a setup a coastline and adjacent lakes and territory could be explored during one summer in detail that would take a lifetime with my little 70-year-old launch *Merlin*, but what an arrogant use it would be of the poor old earth's evaporating pot of oil!

Part Two

POWERBOATS

22 *Blister Boat* and *Queen's Gig,* Two Pulling Boats

Blister Boat
LOA — 17'
Beam — 2'
Draft — 9"

Queen's Gig
LOA — 18'
Beam — 2' 10"
Draft — 1'

Two little pulling boats begin the power-boat section of this book and illustrate one of the most pleasant ways to go miniature voyaging. They are boats that utilize the full power of backs, arms, and legs and without doubt would be the ultimate way to explore along the shoreline if only we had owl necks fitted with a tireless 180-degree swivel. Each year we hold nearby the Great Sidney Rowing Review with a four-mile course around my place and back to the Sidney Wharf. Reasonably flat water prevails in mid-summer, and the fleet of 17-footers has proven to be the most interesting, since they can be rowed at good speed and are still handy on deck or on a beach, a feature that makes them superior to a standard wherry or shell.

John Newman, a local farmer 69 years old last race, makes a clean sweep of the 17-foot class with a cedar dugout that he built in the early 1930s and has been rowing alternately with a slightly fuller boat all the year round as weather permits for these past 40 years. Our

lightest boat, the 17-foot Blister Boat, was designed to be built in fiberglass to beat Newman's boat, but to beat Newman himself in any boat will take some doing.

The race-course is four miles, not just a sprint, as the shells normally race. One mile full bore will take the starch out of most men. Four miles is deadly, and the finish line has seen some hollow-cheeked, bug-eyed oarsman who felt that the last mile was three miles long.

Newman's time with his dugout is shown as a mark to shoot at in a boat not over 17 feet long, and in checking your own speed, remember that a full-length nautical mile must be certified. Three timers must be on hand and accuracy stressed or your speed is just conversation. Until we shoot Newman, I feel that his record for the mile will be unbeaten. Lots of inaccurate data and nonsense is published about pulling boat speed, so bend your back and oars to an accurate nautical mile and see what John Newman has done, and this without the aid of a sliding seat.

TIME TRIALS — 16-foot Pulling Boat

Date:	October 16, 1973
Course:	1 nautical mile (6,080 feet)
Conditions:	Calm, 50°, sunny — minor swell due to wakes from distant passing boats. Open water.
Observers and Timers:	Gen. R. C. Weston, RCAF ret. G. D. Anderson, boatbuilder William Garden, naval architect and marine engineer
Boat:	Fixed seat cedar dugout, about ½″ average thickness. No deck.

16′ 4-1/4″	LOA
15′ 1″	LWL
21-1/8″	Breadth
9-7/8″	Depth amidships
10-1/4″	Depth bow
10″	Depth stern
63#	Weight total
6′ 6″	Oars, 6# total
41-1/2″	Center to center locks, 3# weight
2#	Seat

Builder:	J. Newman
Designer:	J. Newman
Oarsman:	J. Newman
Age:	68
Weight:	145#
Height:	5′ 8″
Time:	Average of 2 watches, 1/2 second variation: 8 minutes, 47 seconds
Speed:	6.831 nautical miles per hour

The Blister Boat was designed as an ultimate, stock, glass, 17-foot racer or afternoon single. Bendt Jesperson did the tooling and Philbrooks shipyard builds the boats for Ashby & White, Ltd., Sidney, British Columbia. On an overall length of 17 feet, the Blister Boats are 24 inches wide on deck, about 18 inches wide on the waterline, depending upon the rower's weight, and the depth of hull amidships is 9 inches. The boat's weight varies from 45 to 60 pounds, depending upon the layup.

In hull form, a nearly circular section is maintained for minimum wetted surface. The centerline is given a slight rocker, which I would perhaps delete from amidships aft in doing it again, and, although the round bow loses waterline length, it gains weed deflecting ability and seems about right.

A wale strake is molded into the shell to form a flat for the seat assembly and also to form an additional spray deflector. The wide rail cap forms the final spray-knocker for choppy water. Fixed or sliding seats are available. The photo shows a sliding-seat model with seat

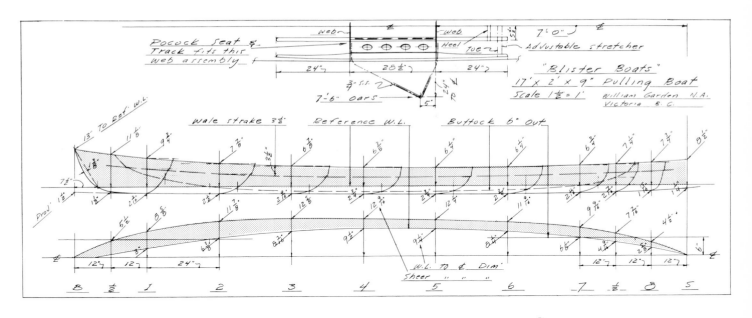

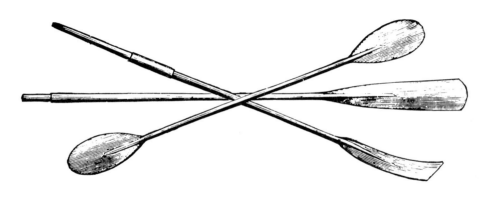

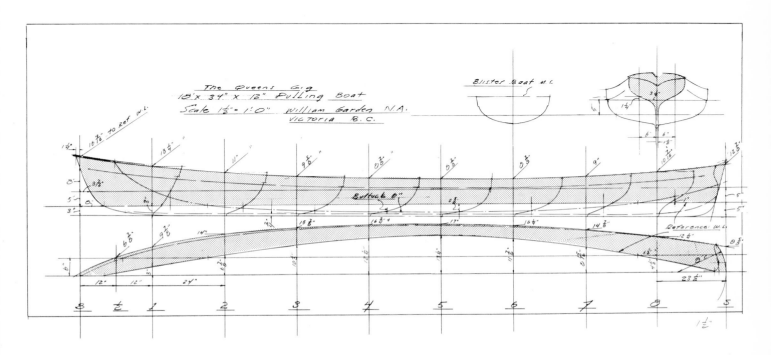

and runners from stock units from Pocock Shells, University Station, Seattle, Washington. The vee outriggers of stainless tubing are an option, a simple removable outrigger is furnished as standard, and 7½-foot oars are the usual length. Nine-foot seven-inch oars and stock shell or wherry rigging seem to be overdoing it for a 17-foot boat, and the shorter oars, as furnished, along with 48-inch, center-to-center oarlocks, appear close to optimum for an all-around, open-water pulling boat, but each year generates some new ideas, and next year will probably change our minds again.

Meanwhile, Newman gets older and some time he's going to start running out of steam. For the four-mile course, he gives us a mark of 42.50 minutes to try for, nearly six nautical miles per hour for four miles, which is just about the cruising speed of my harbor launch. Newman's time in the Blister Boat illustrated is 34 minutes flat for a 3.5 nautical-mile course, or slightly over 6 knots for his first go at a new boat with sliding seat and strange oars. One of the young oarsmen who have the boats might give him a pull next year, but from all

calculations, his time for the mile seems about the limit for a 17-foot boat.

For speed, open water ability, and the sheer pleasure of rowing, the illustrated 17-footer is close to ideal.

The Queen's Gig might be likened to a logical double, or rower and passenger version of the single shell, or could be likened to a highly refined two-man Whitehall boat. The lines of a Whitehall are shown in the *Toadstool* schooner chapter, and a comparison of the Whitehall with the Queen's Gig will show what a slim little packet the gig really is.

The old Whitehall boats were built as workboats in the pre-engine era. They were able to handle the rough-and-tumble action around the docks and alongside ships with proportions combining reasonable rowing ease with good carrying capacity, since they hauled, on occasion, sails, men, light goods, and miscellaneous cargo, which dictated a reasonably burdensome model.

The Whitehall ancestor mentioned is 17 feet long overall, 54 inches breadth, and 19 inches depth amidships, with an all-up weight of about 275 pounds, which is over twice the weight and volume of the Queen's Gig. This is typical of Whitehall dimensions and would fit within the old Whitehall racing rules of 17 to 20 feet in length, not under 4 feet in breadth, 19 inches minimum depth, and a minimum weight limitation of 265 pounds.

Some good data for the researcher can be found in *Building Small Boats for Oar and Sail* (International Marine Publishing Company, Camden, Maine), which has some good Whitehall photos and data, while *Rudder* of August, 1943, has perhaps the best information on the type by an old-timer who was there.

In selecting a rowboat, remember that a 265-pound Whitehall is too much for pleasure rowing and will require real muscle and two men to make any time. About 100 pounds is the limit for enjoyable rowing, and a double of the Queen's Gig proportions will be close to ideal. A hull 18 feet overall, 34 inches breadth, and 12 inches depth amidships will produce a boat lovely to row, easy on the beach, and nearly the size of a canoe, although much easier to propel with oars and short, folding outriggers. In midsection you will note that the Queen's Gig is about twice the Blister Boat's size and weight. A

Blister boat with Pockock sliding seat and spoon-blade oars (photo by Studio West).

wineglass transom has been fitted to open out the stern sheets for a passenger aft when three are on board, and the skeg is eased off in a light radius to facilitate pushing the boat off the beach. The load waterline shape is shown, and the offsets to the outside of the skin are noted on the drawings of each boat. The freeboard and proportions of both boats allow them to be driven hard in a fair chop, but for extended rowing I would fit a light canvas spray hood forward to protect my stores and to turn back the occasional cupful of spray that slops over the rail.

If the Queen's Gig is run under power, the lightest outboard will suffice. One boat is planned to carry a tiny, single-cylinder Easthope, another to carry a light canoe steam engine, but, for either of these powerplants, a true Whitehall would be far superior due to its greater load-carrying ability.

The Blister Boat and the Queen's Gig are outrigger boats and require folding or fixed outrigger gear for the rowlocks. Folding outriggers were once a stock item in very limited patterns, but standard outriggers or on-the-gunwale rowlocks seemed to be produced in nearly unlimited variations. Some of these old rowlocks are collector's items. The more beautiful patterns combined utility and form to a high degree. Many shapes can still be found in second hand shops along the coast, and occasionally one can come across a real find of unusual type from away back. Most rowlocks that I have are in bronze, which was the preferred material, but in either bronze or galvanized, the shapes are all interesting and a reminder of the gas engine's short span and of the time when we'll probably all have to row again. We've included here some rowlocks from old ship chandler's catalogs.

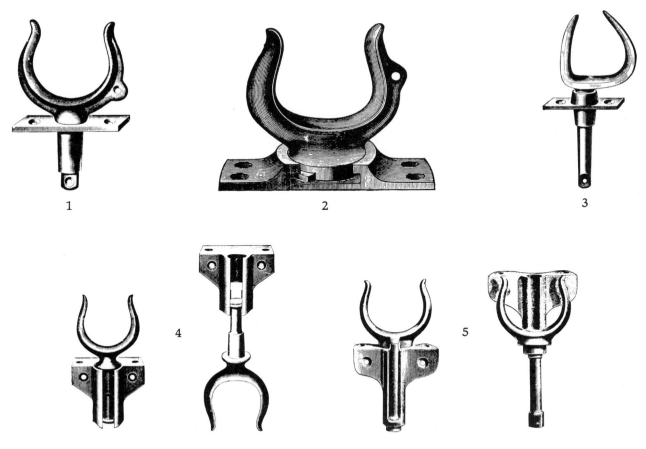

1
2
3

4
5

1. Ribbed socket, available in side plate or top socket patterns.
2. Patent swivel.
3. The beautifully proportioned Victoria pattern.
4. Davis Standard of 1890. The Robertson Patent is of the same design, which makes one wonder.
5. Acme Patent or drop pattern.

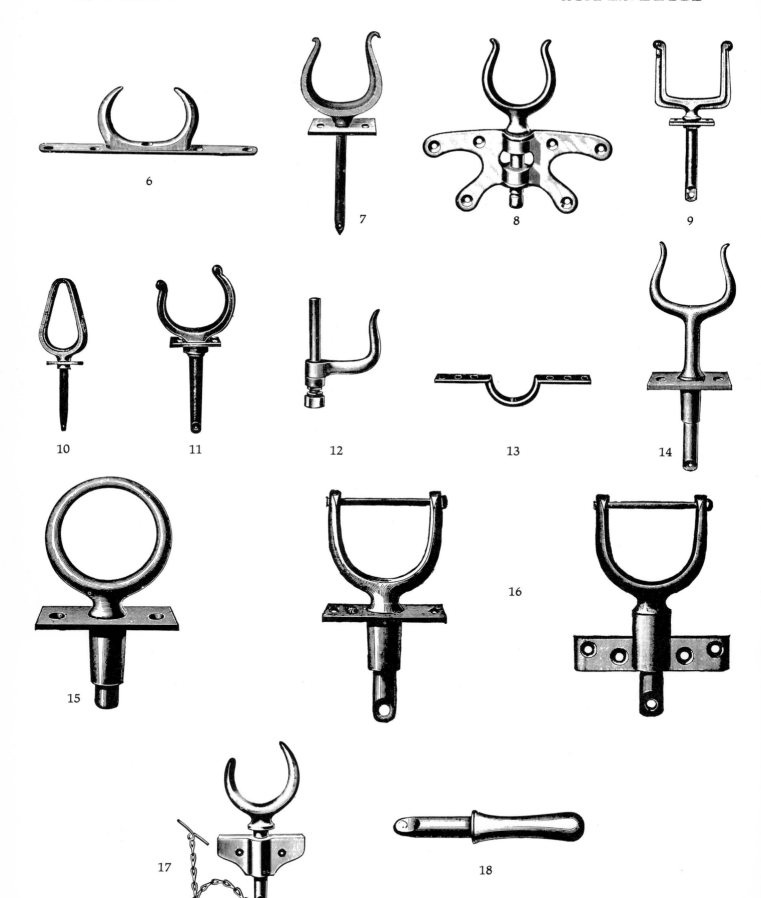

6

7

8

9

10

11

12

13

14

15

16

17

18

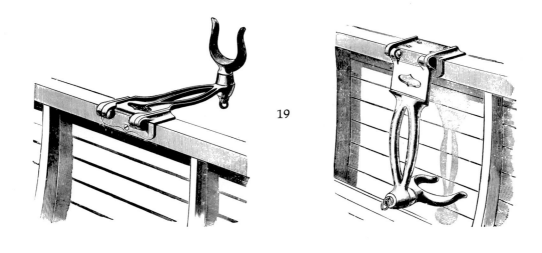

19

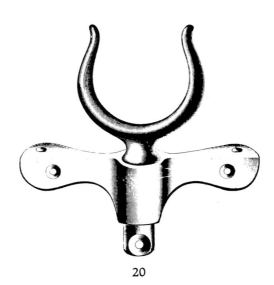

20

6. The fixed Blackburn, perhaps 3,000 years old.
7. The elegant Vancouver. This and the Victoria must have been executed by a patternmaker with a soul.
8. Moline side plate.
9. Square pattern, a good businesslike appearance.
10. Steering rowlock. The egg shape is to allow the oar blade to be withdrawn.
11. Government pattern, which is of the heavy type fitted on gigs and workboats.
12. The unusual Windemere.
13. Bulwark sculling chock.
14. Connecticut River extended pattern. For stand-up use or for raising the loom above the coaming or rail.
15. The round closed pattern, the common dinghy oarlock fitted to the oar, contained by the leather. Available in side plate or socket patterns.
16. North River, both side plate and gunwale plate.
17. Strong pattern, side socket with safety chain.
18. Thole pins, here in galvanized wrought iron but also made of locust and oak.
19. Outrigger rowlock. My old 1895 pulling boat *Wild Oats* has a pair of these that, over the past 75 years, must have transmitted an impressive amount of energy.
20. Standard side plate pattern.

23   *Gulf 32*, a Sailing Motorsailer

LOA — 32' 0"
LWL — 23' 4"
Beam — 10' 0"
Draft — 5' 2"
Displacement — 16,000 pounds
Sail Area — 506 square feet, 100% fore triangle
Ballast — 6,500 pounds

The Gulf 32 was designed as a sailing motorsailer and unfortunately came out some years prior to the motorsailer cruising-yacht era of popularity, so only three dozen were built. She is a nice size, and the combination of fairly easy sailing lines and relatively heavy displacement results in an easy boat at sea.

We have done several glass boats over the years with this inside-ballasted hull configuration and it is so logical to drop the weight down into a completed keel trough that, from a structural viewpoint, the fin-keelers seem illogical. The ballast in the keel trough is a controlled pour of cement, sand, rock, and boiler punchings to total 6,500 pounds. This is about a 220 pounds-per-cubic-foot density, about the limit usually achieved with a concrete and scrap-iron mix. Another interesting possibility is a ferrophosphorus mix, which will allow a 300 pounds-per-cubic-foot density without rust or loss of strength.

Polyester resin with Stauffer Chemical Company's ferrophosphorus is a third approach and can result in about 300 pounds-per-cubic-foot density. Ferrophosphorus was once cheap, but I suppose that by now the price of anything, even that of plain concrete, will be greatly increased. The 6,500 pounds of cement and punchings ballast in the Gulf 32 takes up about a cubic yard in volume when using the 220 pounds-per-cubic-foot mix.

Compared to polyester resin/ferrophosphorus, ferrophosphorus alone would require proportionally less volume at 300 pounds per cubic foot, cast iron less again at 440, and lead the smallest volume at 710.

Controlling the pour is the greatest difficulty of the inside-ballasted boat, and, once the mix has set up, the results can be tragic if a mistake is made. A uniform mix is difficult to maintain in a stock boat program, but, for a careful home builder, it can result in a good job at a major saving.

Notice here that a centerline gutter is formed in the cement top to carry water along under the tanks and dump it aft in the sump. The tanks are up on sleepers and held down by the husky cabin sole. A chain locker drain can be seen from the peak almost to station 1, then the bilge runs aft via the gutter to the sump.

The hull sections indicate a model that is full through the garboards in order to ac-

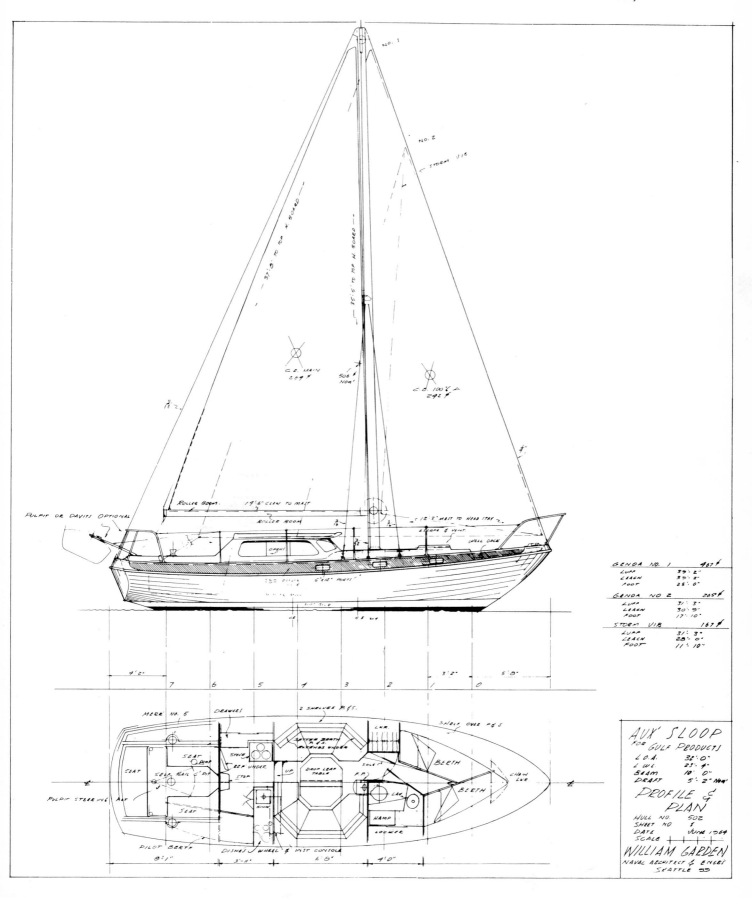

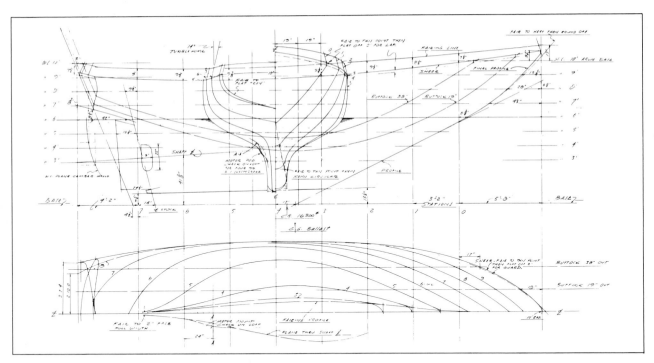

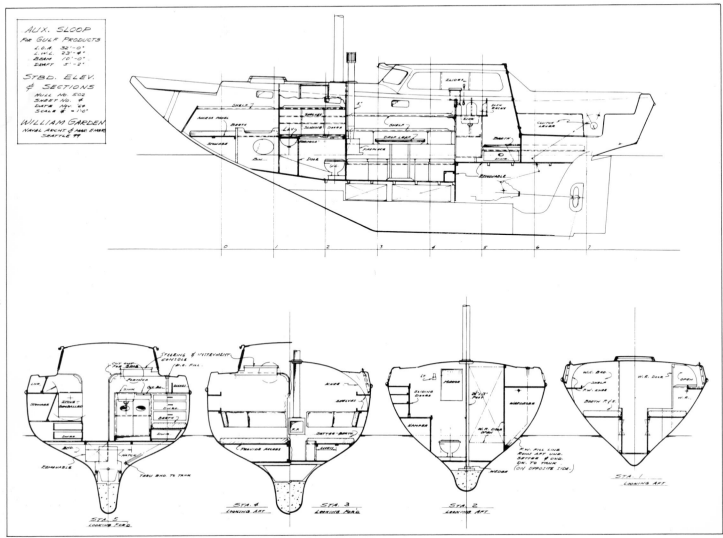

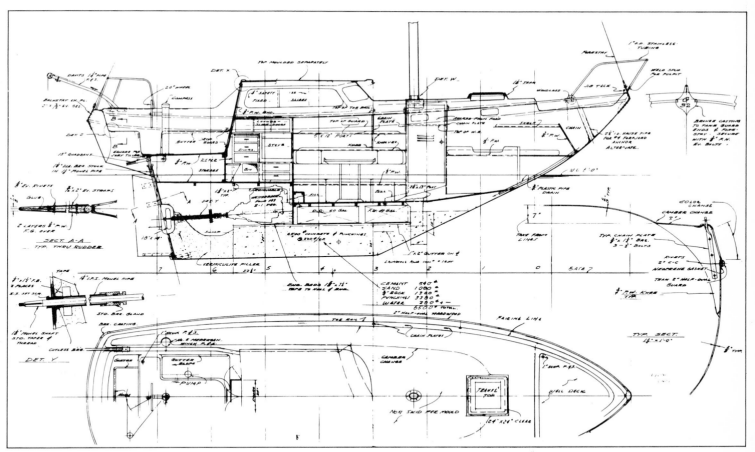

commodate the ballast, and the hull has a faired-in swelling at station 5½ to accommodate the motor mounts. This allows the motor to be well aft and low without impairing the basic form of the run, an easy feature to incorporate when working with fiberglass.

The cabin layout is a reasonable compromise, allowing an orthodox forward cabin, head, and locker, followed by a circular-effect saloon with fireplace, bookshelves, and stowage. The galley is two steps above the saloon and large hatches give engine access. The bulkhead is cut away between the galley and the saloon to give an open effect so pleasant in a small yacht's cabin.

Over the drainboard on the starboard side you will note a steering station for running in bad weather under power, which gives the deckhouse a dual purpose. For northern areas, an enclosed steering station within talking distance of the saloon and in a warm, dry spot can make off-season cruising much more pleasant. A jump seat is located on the after bulkhead for the helmsman.

George Quinlan made the molds and prototype of this one in his barn in Seattle, so we were able to check out all features during construction. If I were building something this size for myself today, I believe I would ease out the forebody to sharpen the entry; the waterline length would then be about 23 feet 6 inches and the length overall perhaps 34 feet. The rig would be a cutter with a roller jib and a staysail extending to 80 percent of the masthead height. I would retain the existing mast position. The sail-area-to-wetted-surface ratio would be slightly improved, and the larger fore triangle would balance the new forefoot, but when you start dreaming, the choice of form, rig, and layout is endless. With the outlined revision and after a few voyages, I am sure we would decide that happiness would be another four inches of breadth or a foot more length in the main saloon, but so it goes. Perfection is never static. In the mind's eye, the proportions can be adjusted instantly to any configuration, but, short of some sort of instantly adjustable rubber boat, the perfect ship will always be just over the horizon.

As built, the Gulf 32 is an excellent sailer and most pleasant to cruise on board.

24   Power Launches

On the ways back of the shop today, Don Miller is painting up a restored 16-foot by 5-foot open launch, a nice, little, carvel boat of unknown ancestry whose near downfall came when she was left in a Brentwood chicken house for several years. To clinch her pastoral sojourn, a lamb was born in the 20 minutes while we were inspecting the boat, so she'll probably be renamed *Spring Lamb*.

The first good launch that I had was a dandy, double-chine, 17-foot dory that was taken as part payment on the sale of the little yawl, *Pelican*. The dory was nearly new, an excellent model, and was powered by a one-cylinder, four cycle, five horsepower, direct-connected, gas engine built around a Ford piston and rod, as so many were in those days. We painted her up, named her the *Omar K*, and used her for transportation from the end of the harbor to a shop that I had then where we were building a schooner. That is the only way to go to work on a nice morning. In wet weather, a raincoat was draped over the engine with the valves pushing up and down like a bag of cats as she thumped up the bay. The yawl sold for $325.00 and the *Omar* was turned in as a $125.00 credit. Lovely days of a real dollar.

We had many power seine skiffs and miscellaneous workboats built during the next few years, but I didn't have need of a launch for myself again until we required a tender for a summer camp on the west coast of Vancouver Island. With unfailing good luck an old, seagoing, Canadian dredge was towed along past the office window one morning en route to the shipwreckers across the canal, and on deck were four nice lapstrake boats, two with transoms and two double-enders. After a colorful go-around, I ended up with everything on deck, and *Mary Anne*, as we subsequently named her, was one of them. Built by Turner in Vancouver, I believe, the *Mary Anne* is 17-feet by 5-feet 4-inches, and originally was of low freeboard, powered with a lovely, old, two-cylinder, 8-12 Vivian and used on the dredge for line handling or as a crew boat. The engine looked like a write-off and the hull looked good, but after striking our bargain, the opposite proved to be the case. With the little fleet swung overboard alongside the ship, we dumped a gallon of fresh gas in *Mary Anne*'s tank, barred the engine over a couple of times, and away she went, kerchunking home, the flywheel throwing spray and my old shipmate, Ellis Provine, bailing like no 75-year-old has bailed before or since, while the little fleet astern, full of floating oars, floorboards, and gear, steadily settled lower in the water. The shaftlog had rotted out after the outside stuffing box held water in the hole when she was on the dredge's deck, so a new shaftlog, deadwood, and lower transom came first on the list. Then we built up a wale strake nine-inches high to give adequate freeboard, fitted towing bitts, a motor casing, fenders, and a short, sloop rig to change her from an overpowered skiff to a proper, little, sea boat. The old Vivian was a jewel, and after 12 years I still haven't pulled a head. Ignition is by a Bosch magneto — no bat-

(Top left) Mary Anne, our towboat. *(Top right) Merlin*, our daily transport (photos by Studio West). *(Center)* 16-foot fiberglass launch built by Philbrooks Shipyard as a stock boat. Her simple, traditional form provides 6 knots.

teries to worry about — and the mag has an impulse coupling for a hot spark when starting. I've been on the lookout ever since for a spare 8-12 Vivian, but no luck. We've come up with two 3-cylinder, 18-horsepower models and a single-cylinder, 6 horsepower; one of the 18's and the single are still squirrelled away in the shop, but, alas, not a twin.

For some time, we kept *Mary Anne* at Ostrom's machine shop in Bamfield, Vancouver Island, for use in Barklay Sound where we had many good times with her, exploring and sea fishing. For the last seven years, she's been our standby launch in Canoe Cove. She lies alongside the float now, in her fortieth year, looking ready for anything: red bottom, orange boot-top, black wale strake, white rail cap, and

a neat, tan dodger. At the present time, the *Mary Anne* is our tow boat, with the 26-foot by 7-foot, double-ended cabin-launch, *Merlin*, used as daily transport.

Merlin was a backyard acquisition of four years ago; we spotted her propped up in a Sidney lot, well submerged into the last downhill slide. A year's spare time work put her back in seagoing trim, but at her first launching time after purchase, she looked old and sad. Snuffy Rourke, an Aleutian Island shipmate and old friend, signed on for the inaugural two-mile pumping voyage back to Toad's Landing, and we must have lightened her up by at least 1,000 pounds en route by heaving overboard a great accumulation of rock ballast and junk. So the work began; eventually, the 4-cylinder Univer-

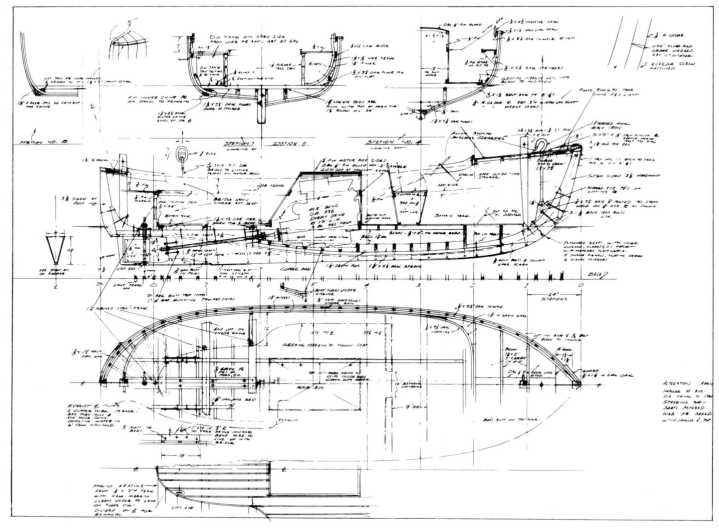

A nice little double-ended launch.

sal was replaced by one of the 3-cylinder, 18 horsepower Vivians, one resurrected in Tahsis of 1926 vintage and rebuilt to be *Merlin*'s fifth power plant since she was launched originally in 1905. Number one I'm told was a single-cylinder Lozier; number two was a 2-cylinder Scripps; and numbers 3 and 4 were Universal utility fours, both with 2½:1 reduction gears. Number 5 seems a better match for the boat, with plenty of reserve power and an easy service speed of 450 revolutions per minute; she's pleasant to live with and has lots of interesting parts flopping back and forth: push rods, rocker arms, pumps, a nice spoked flywheel — things to oil.

If the Rover Boys had had such an engine, they never would have looked back.

A little lapstrake launch with an Arnolt Sea Mite came and went, and a nicely done, glass, outdrive boat, plagued by the usual highstrung outdrive problems, emptied our pockets a couple of times, but the ones that seem to stick are the thumpers.

Last week, my old boatbuilding partner, Black Dave, sent up a wad of money and a lovely two pound planking maul for old times' sake, along with a note for the plans of a 16-foot launch, able to take a one-cylinder diesel. A simple, carvel-planked, bent-frame boat seemed

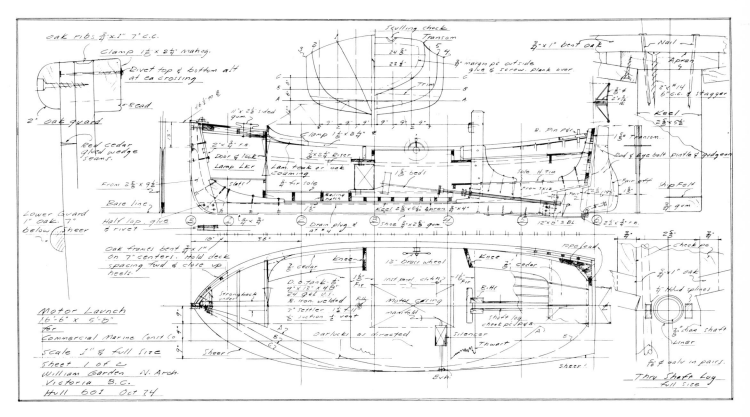

A 16-foot 6-inch launch for Black Dave to use around his boatshop in Seattle.

suitable for short trips and for the miscellaneous jobs required around Dave's boatshop in Seattle, so the launch illustrated was drawn up and returned. A rugged, useful, and economical boat that, like *Mary Anne*, will be good for years of hard service and would look right as a coasting schooner's push boat or on the deck of a yacht.

Everything is piled on one sheet, but the details can be followed on the reduced drawing. Notice the heavy keel, solid stem, hollow waterlines forward for slicing through a chop, the tow bitt, the nicely rounded transom, and the good sheer. Run some iron-bark sheathing along the waterline — but the glass-boat world is starting to shudder.

25 *Katherine*, a Modern Express Commuter

LOA — 36' 0"
LWL — 29' 3"
Breadth at deck — 10' 0"
Breadth at waterline — 9' 2"
Draft of hull at rest — 1' 9"
Displacement — 12,500 pounds
Power — Twin 427-cubic-inch Mercruiser 2:1
outdrives. 290 continuous hp at
3,200 rpms service speed
Speed — 32 knots service speed
40 knots flank speed
Fuel capacity — 200 gallons U.S.
Water capacity — 40 gallons U.S.

Katherine might be considered a 1970 counterpart of the classic express commuters of the 1920s, since she was designed for high-speed, private transportation. In this case the run is through the San Juan Islands from Anacortes, Washington, on the mainland, to the owners', Jack and Kay Hughes, home in Roche Harbor, a run requiring an able boat that would eat up a sea condition in the off-season and a boat that would give trouble to the usual small express cruiser.

A length of 36 feet was decided on for the boat as optimum for the service, and a contract was let with Philbrooks Shipyard in Sidney, British Columbia, for her construction. The method of building and the scantlings are indicated on the plans. She is longitudinally framed on bulkheads and molds and has a plywood shell covered in turn by fiberglass mat and cloth for a light, strong surface. The photos indicate her appearance afloat and also the rugged framework required to withstand the loads of the owners' hard-driving schedule.

The hull form is a developed shape to take the plywood skin, so the long, cutaway bow is dictated by material use as well as by running efficiency. The chine forms a spray-knocker, and the run of the water can be seen in the photo. The form is designed to eliminate the need for the pound-producing spray strips required on a normal hard-pushing, deep-vee hull, and the deadrise plus chine-immersion aft make her an easy platform when either lying at rest or running slowly.

(Left) Katherine underway. Note how the chine knocks the spray down. *(Right) Katherine* in frame. She's built for a tough commuting schedule.

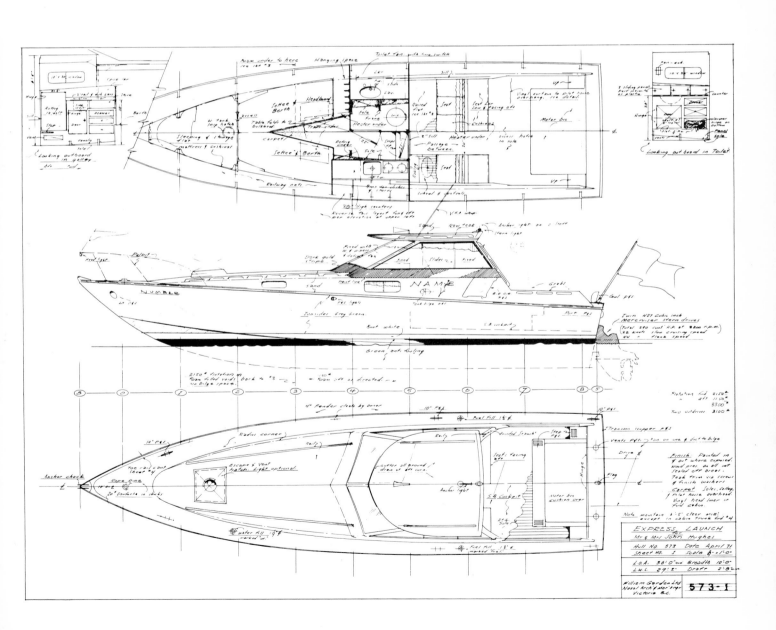

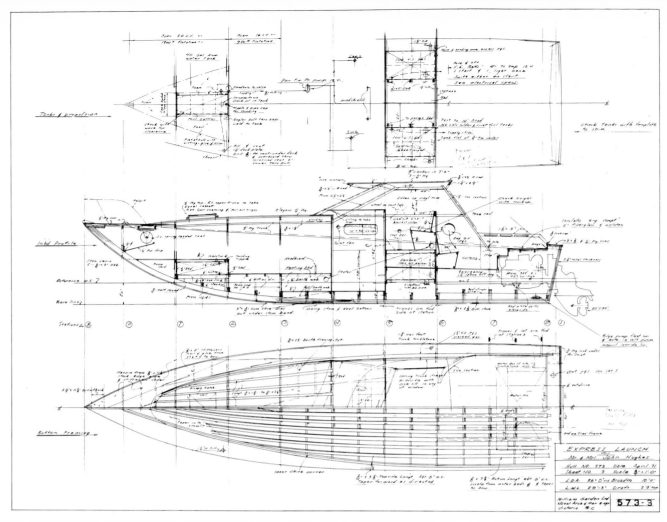

EXPRESS LAUNCH
for
Mr & Mrs. John Hughes

Hull No. 573	Date	April 71
Sheet No. 3	Scale	3/8" = 1'-0"

L.O.A. 36'-0" on Breadth 10'-0"
L.W.L. 28'-3" Draft 2'8" Min

William Garden Ltd
Naval Arch & Mar Engr
Victoria B.C.

573-3

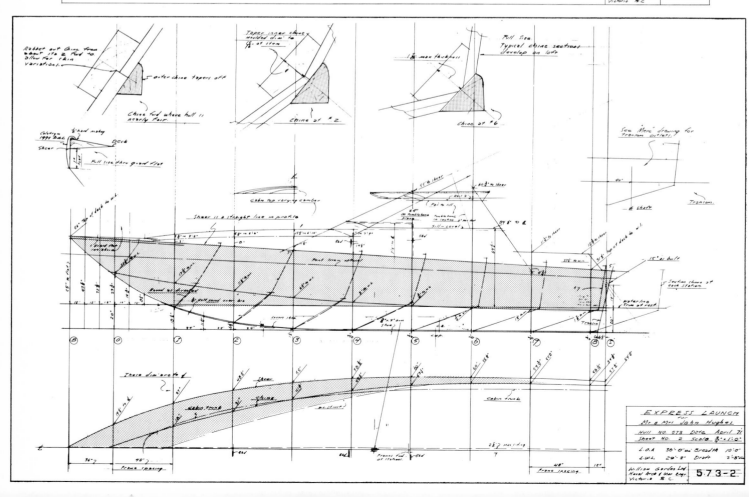

EXPRESS LAUNCH
for
Mr & Mrs. John Hughes

Hull No. 573	Date	April 71
Sheet No. 2	Scale	3/8" = 1'-0"

L.O.A. 36'-0" on Breadth 10'-0"
L.W.L. 28'-3" Draft 2'8" Min

William Garden Ltd
Naval Arch & Mar Engr
Victoria B.C.

573-2

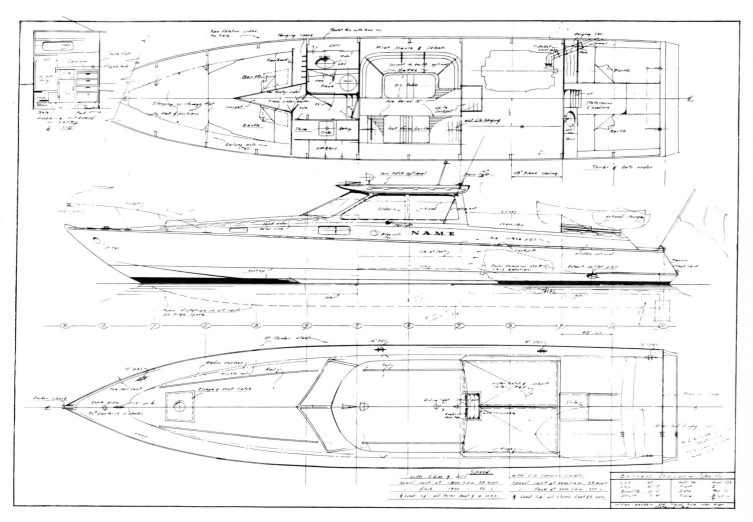

A 47-foot jumbo version of *Katherine*.

At this speed-length ratio, the center of buoyancy must be well aft, combined with a long, sharp entry for bucking ability with minimum shock. *Katherine* is about as able a high-speed boat as one could desire. A rough-water run in her is a revelation to a boatman who feels that weight and depth are the only answers to seagoing ability.

Outdrives seem ideally suited for a boat of this sort but are an endless source of upkeep and worry in salt water. The next boat completed in this series, an aluminum 42-footer, has a pair of diesels with vee drives; this power plant delivers five knots less speed at the top than *Katherine*, but is a longer-lived, more economical power package that comes into its own with the larger hull.

The ultimate development of *Katherine*'s type, and my choice for sheer go, is a 47-footer powered by twin 370 turbo-charged Cummins engines. This would be a jumbo version of *Katherine*, with a 29-knot continuous speed and the elegance that always seems to come with the king-sized model of anything.

Her flank speed would be 33.5 knots at 3,000 rpms. Using Italian CRM-9 diesels rather than the Cummins, she would set a flank speed of 42 knots at 1,900 rpms.

Each performance figure is with two-thirds of the liquids, all stores, the dinghy, and six men on board.

Gas turbines will about match the CRM diesels' performance, the lighter turbine weight being lost in the greater fuel load required for

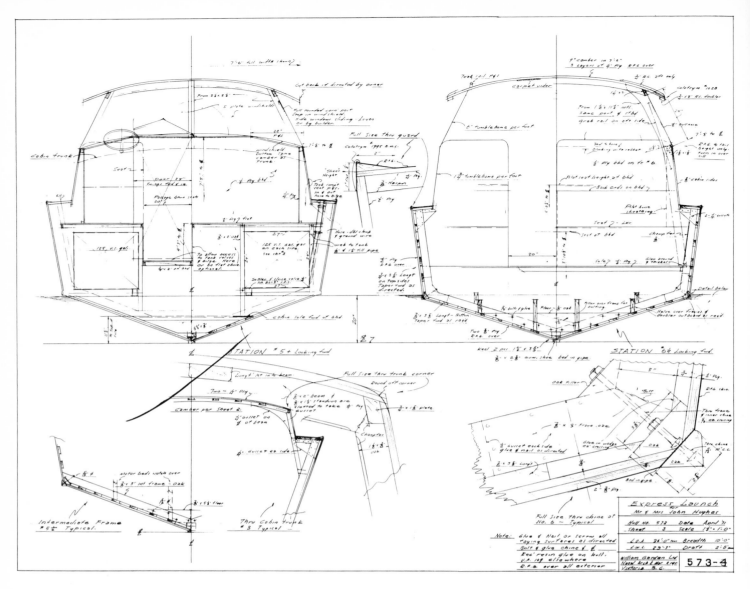

equal endurance. During the last 15 or 20 years, we have worked with several turbines and find that lack of fuel economy means a heavier fuel load for equal endurance, which neutralizes some of the turbine's weight saving. Unfortunately, the turbine afloat, unlike the aircraft installation, replaces only the short block of the diesel, and the reverse and reduction gear weights, major factors, remain constant. But turbine is an exotic word with the free-wheeling hardware lovers, and we see continuing interest, with many takers — and some taken.

Engine life is another factor usually overlooked by the turbine enthusiast. The last manufacturer's guarantee of turbine life between major overhauls was less than half that of comparable diesels, and overhaul costs of turbines or diesels are about the same. This isn't a big factor for a yacht's service life, but is of real concern to the more realistic commercial operator who can get two to three times the proven operating time with diesels. On the plus side for turbines is wonderfully smooth operation, and their initial costs are getting closer to diesels. The last turbines we installed, however, were about double the cost of comparable diesels — $100,000 all up and installed as against $50,000 for the diesels. Prices and fuel economy will improve with today's push for better power plants, and the state of the art has come a long way from the marine gas turbine exhibited at the 1924 Motor Boat Show.

Up to the *Katherine*'s size, the gasoline engine will give best performance. The diesel comes into its own at about 40 feet in a boat of this sort and is ideally suited to the 47-footer. Double the 47-footer to 94 feet by 20 feet, fit three 12-71 turbo-charged GMs in the stern, and it would take quite a sea state to slow her down.

26 *We'll Sea*, an Express Cruiser

LOA — 40'
Beam — 14' 4"
Draft — 4' 2"
Power — Twin Perkins turbo 354 diesels, 2:1 reduction
Speed — 21 knots tops at 2,650 rpm, 17 knots continuous
Displacement — 17,500 pounds when 2 years old

Philbrook's Shipyard built *We'll Sea* as a proposed stock boat that incorporated what we both felt would be practical in a "big boat/little boat" express cruiser. I believe that she's hard to beat, but, unfortunately, she was never put into production. I've watched her many times go sliding by the usual hard-driving, pushwater, stock motor-cruiser with what always seems to be an effortless rush.

Three things are going for *We'll Sea*: the center of buoyancy is well aft in the optimum position for her velocity, which in turn dictates a long, sharp entry; the tight, double-diagonal, glued skin over bulkheads and longitudinal framing has resulted in a light, strong structure with a waterplane loading able to get up on top easily; and the gull-wing sections seem to add the last bit of lift for best performance. We have had boats built with straight, convex, and concave sections, with and without spray strips, and with lapstrake, smooth, inverted vee, and step skins, but for some reason the deadrise and frame curve of this little boat seem the best for her speed range. The chines aft are just immersed at rest in order to give the hull initial stability and to avoid the flop-over feel of a deep

vee at anchor or lying to. The usual deep vee is excellent for a runabout but totally unsuitable for the usual high-center-of-gravity cruising yacht. While the deep-vee form runs smoothly but uneconomically through its speed range, it is an uneasy platform at slow speed or at anchor, where a motor yacht spends so much of its time.

The photo illustrates *We'll Sea*'s trim when underway, pushed along by the twin 354 turbocharged Perkins diesel engines. You can see her running trim, low wake, and nice entry. A top speed of 21 knots at 2,650 revolutions, and an easy, backed-off, continuous cruising speed of 17 knots is attained.

We'll Sea's cruising speed is accompanied by a low sound level, since the engines are out of the cabin. The monotonous rumble of high-speed diesel engines can best be cut by an airtight, leakproof closure between the engine and the quarters, with the engines located, whenever possible, out from underfoot. In the past 30 years we've spent a lot of time and money on sound-proofing, have had many learned opinions, have tried endless options of foam on lead, acoustical tiles, carpeting, baffles, rubber

We'll Sea shows her fine form underway (photo by Studio West).

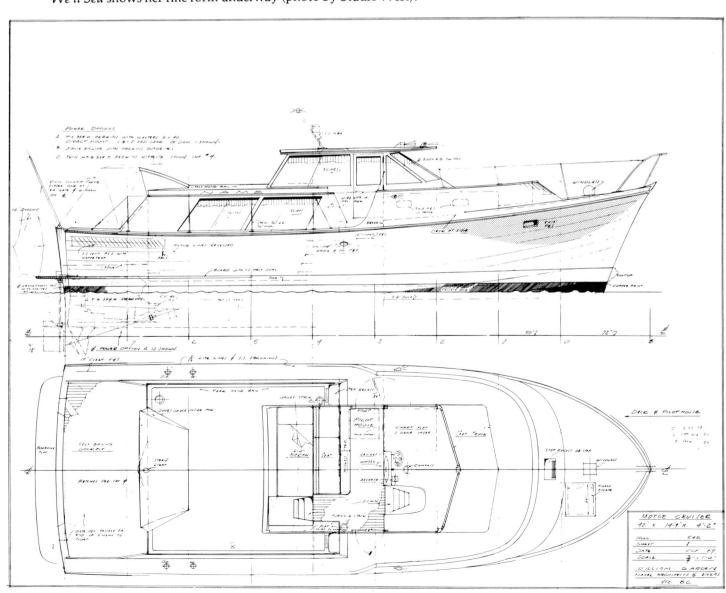

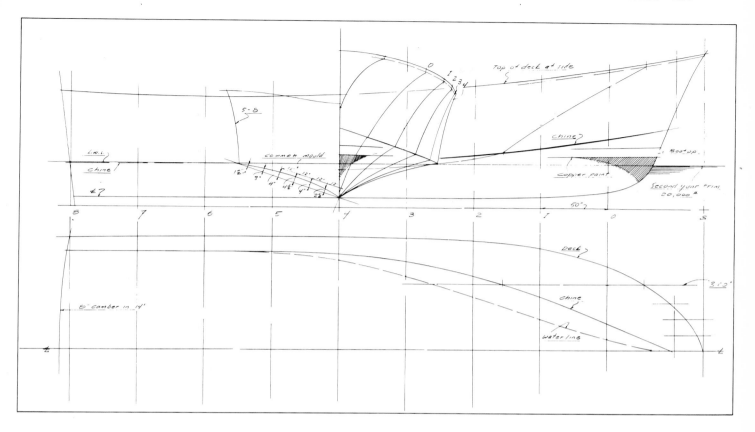

mounts, double bulkheads, and six-inch rein-forced-concrete bulkheads, and have read end-less decible charts: but a hairline crack in my auto manifold brought the light.

With a cold motor, the crack was barely visible, just a scratch, but the noise upon start-ing was a teenager's delight. Three blocks down the road, the engine heat pinched the crack off as the manifold got hot, and the noise was ab-solutely gone. So, if we contain the sound or keep it out, the battle is practically won. Gasket all hatches, pull combustion air from outside, close every possible sound-leak hole in the fire wall, and any almost-solid casing seems suitable for a motor box. Diesel generator sound shields are good examples of efficient closure when coupled with an effective muffler system.

A "work-in" engine room needs the same seal-off with gasketted doors, but here a man will spend some time inside and every effort has to be made to prevent echo or bounce back within the space; fire retardant carpet, navy board, and acoustical tile all help. The engine can also be given a hood or a complete soft-foam blanket on a light, pipe frame, with in-dustrial zippers for access; the blanket will con-tain the noise at the source.

For water-knock or propeller noise, a moderate propeller speed and the maximum possible hull-propeller blade-tip clearance will also help. One of the smoothest running boats that we've designed has a pair of 370 Cummins with vee drives and four-bladed propellers with a tip clearance of about half the propeller's diameter. The four-bladed propellers were spares, but performance was so close to top efficiency that the smoothness made them the final choice.

The shaft angle of *We'll Sea* is about the limit, but I feel that efficiency or thrust doesn't seem to vary between level and 15 degrees. Oc-casionally, an advertising claim is made for an increased efficiency with horizontal thrust, but I have found that the opposite is true, except possibly when the propellers are tucked under the boat as with a pod drive, such as a hydrofoil requires when the horizontal thrust is deeply im-mersed. We have used units well under the hull with a horizontal thrustline on United Aircraft gas turbines yet the speed worked out exactly as

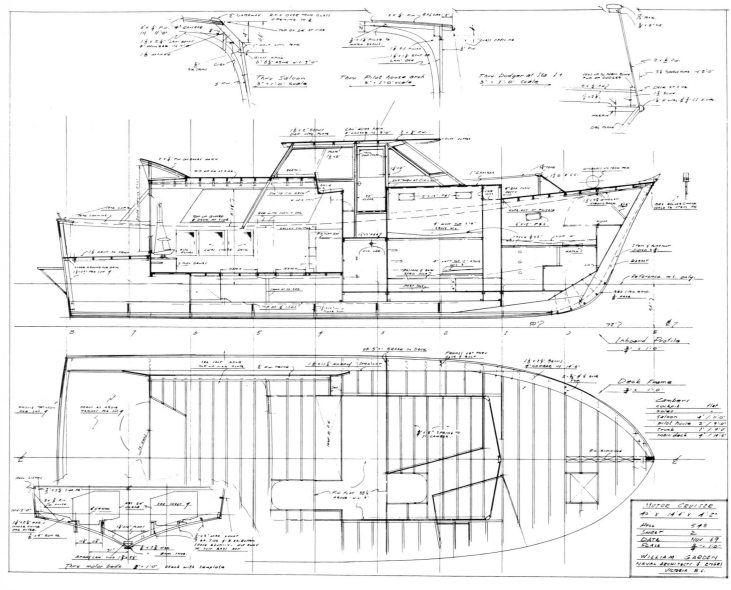

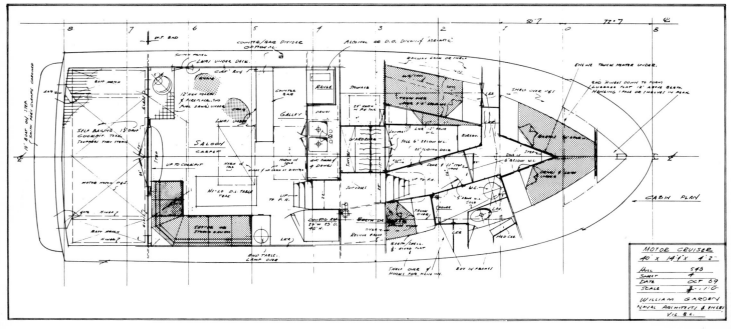

calculated for a normal 12-degree angle. So *We'll Sea*'s angle of shaft, although appearing excessive, still works efficiently. From performance figures, improvement would be difficult to accomplish.

Tanks, you will notice, are generally on the center of the waterplane, so the hull goes up and down bodily with fuel and water load variations. The weight of the liquids is in the best fore-and-aft position for rough-water travel.

The accommodation plan seems to be a reasonably good solution for summer cruising, with the saloon opening onto a cockpit with a boarding platform able to take a dinghy stowed on edge. In the Northwest, a dinghy is a necessity, along with good ground tackle. Here on the transom, the dinghy may be put afloat quickly and, if desired, another boat can be carried on the cabin top. The layout with the saloon aft and a sunken deckhouse has real charm but puts the sleeping cabins all in the forward end of the ship, where privacy is lacking. For summer cruising, perhaps the compromise is worthwhile, since we're up and about 70 percent of the time during a cruise, and the saloon with the galley across the forward end is a pleasant spot either underway or at anchor, when one has a 180-degree view with eye level well above the sill to command a fairly unobstructed outlook.

The pilothouse access from below is on the starboard side, with observation seating abaft the wheel. The companionway down forward opens up on a quarter berth to starboard for an extra hand or for stowage, and under the pilothouse is a good suitcase hold or galley stores space. The two staterooms are a good size, and the accommodations indicated seem to be an efficient use of space.

On deck, *We'll Sea* has the dodger that we have used on so many boats to cut height and to form an outside bridge. There is a cushioned area over the trunk as the principal outdoor seating space. Boatbuilder Ted Hopkins, her owner, is a dedicated fisherman and finds the cockpit ample for his needs, but a flying-bridge lounge abaft the pilothouse could be a nice feature for sun-bathing or for another set of controls; however, the existing pilothouse visibility is excellent, although it does lack the open-air feeling so pleasant in fair weather.

So that's about it for the *We'll Sea* — close to an ideal little express-cruiser for Northwest waters.

27 *Snow Goose*, a Production Diesel Cruiser

LOA — 41' 0"
LWL — 37' 6"
Breadth — 13' 6"
Draft — 4' 0"
Displacement — 38,200 pounds
Power — Twin Perkins 354 diesels
Speed — 8.3 knots

This design is for a series of 41-footers for Bob and Dick Alley and built by Howard Roberts in La Conner, Washington, during the 1963 season. Howard built the original four, and since they came out it seems that about half of the Northwest's diesel cruisers built since are look-alikes, which is a sincere form of flattery but doesn't do much for the stew pot.

The breadth of *Snow Goose* is 13-feet 6-inches, draft is 4-feet 0-inches, and waterline length is 37-feet 6-inches. The displacement of the twin-screw version is 38,200 pounds. The tank capacity is 540 gallons of diesel oil and 240 gallons of water, giving her a good coastal range with the twin Perkins 354 diesels throttled back to an easy endurance speed of 7 knots. Maximum speed is about 8.3 knots. An optional tank plan providing 775 gallons of oil was also designed.

The general form of *Snow Goose* can be visualized from the lines and the construction sections. A quick "S" section is worked in along

the garboard, and ballast is located here and in the wings directly outboard of the motor stringers. The centerline concrete forms an engine-room sole, and a low duck-board is also fitted for the same purpose. With this arrangement, there is stooping headroom between the engines, which provides an excellent working space for such a small boat. The engine-room plan and elevation will give an idea of the seating for the tanks and engine.

The profile and plan show two cabins forward, each with a bath, which have proved quite roomy in practice, but this basic layout favors the saloon and walk-around deck areas. The latter is perhaps a shippy feature that we can't afford on such a small cruiser; however, it has great visual appeal for the sailor and affords excellent security when working alongside floats and docks. Even though big freeing ports are fitted, I wouldn't want to take a boat with this much well-deck around Cape Horn, yet it is quite practical for summer coastal yachting.

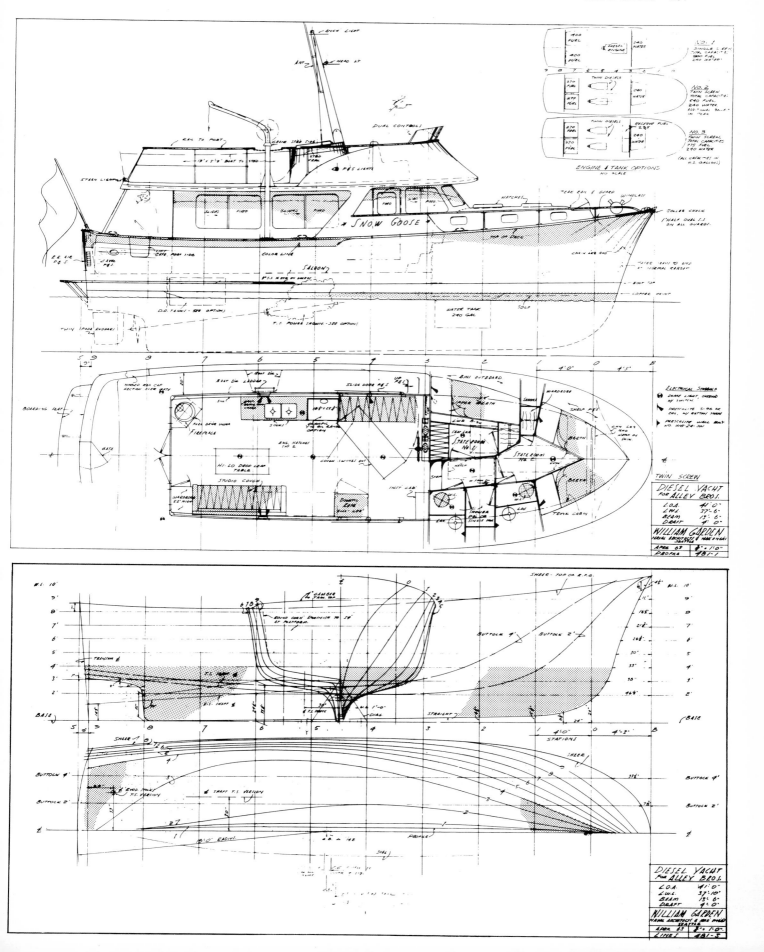

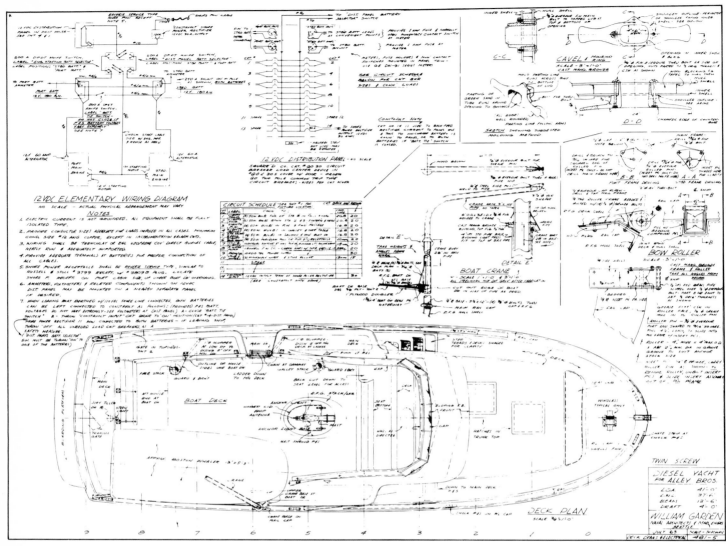

12 VDC ELEMENTARY WIRING DIAGRAM
NO SCALE · ACTUAL PHYSICAL ARRANGEMENT MAY VARY

NOTES

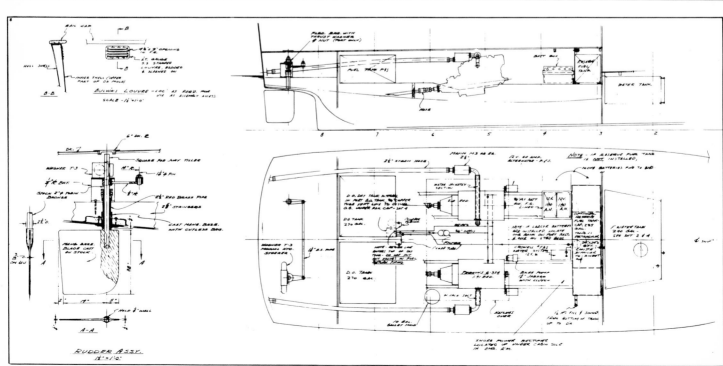

DECK PLAN

TWIN SCREW

DIESEL YACHT
FOR ALLEY BROS.

L.O.A.	41'-0"
L.W.L.	37'-6"
BEAM	13'-6"
DRAFT	4'-0"

WILLIAM GARDEN
NAVAL ARCHITECTS & MAR. ENGRS.
SEATTLE

JULY '63

RUDDER ASSY.

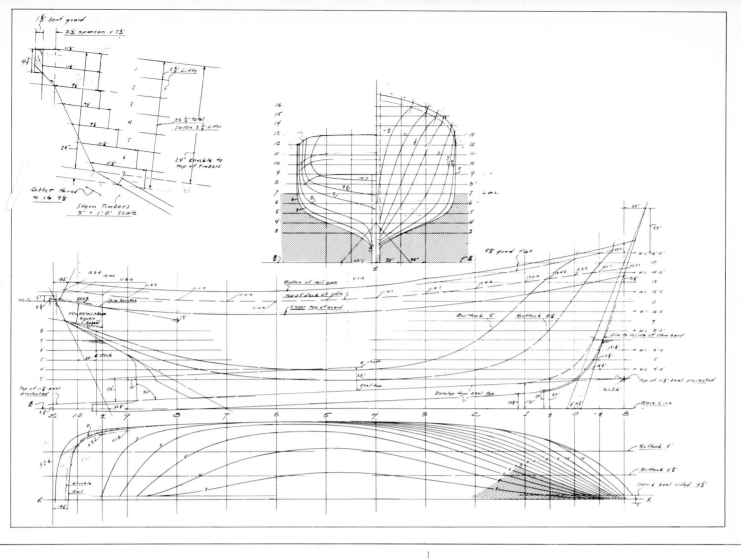

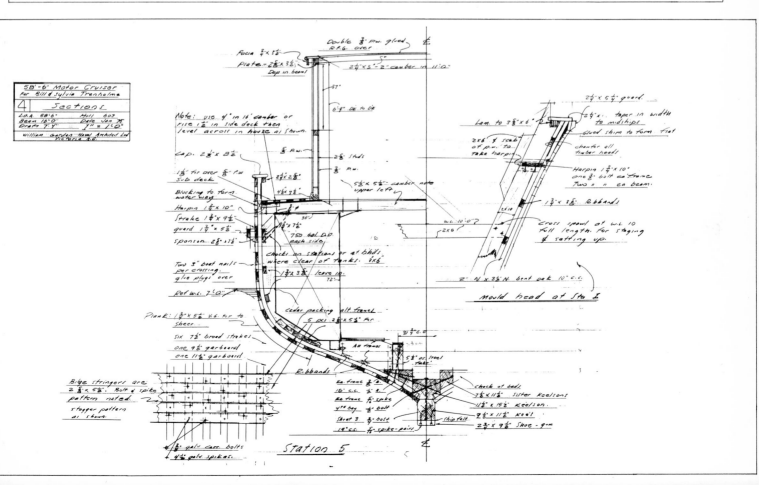

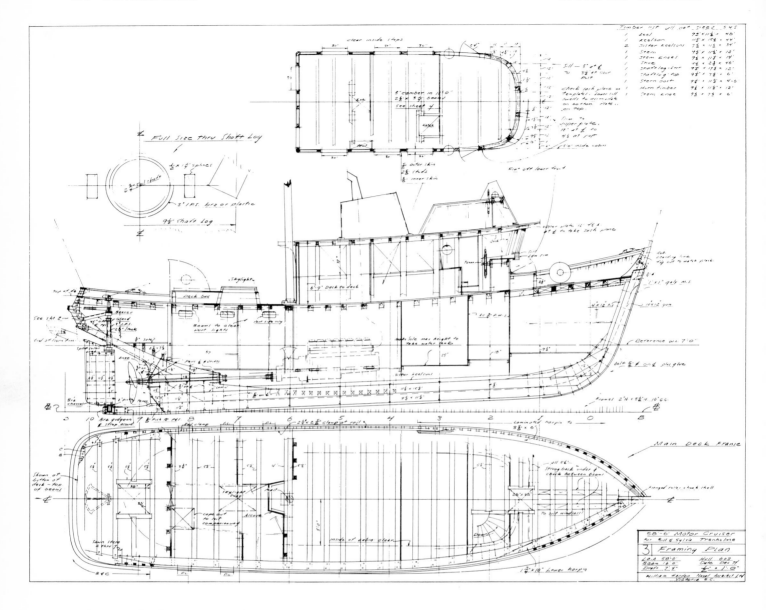

indicates the live-on-board arrangement. Each boat is developed around an owner's needs and ideas of aesthetics. Bill Trenholme's early background was with towboats, so the theme is on the rugged side.

The engine, you will notice, is about 11 feet long. It is an eight-cylinder Gardner developing 150 horsepower at 900 revolutions per minute. It is connected through a 3:1 reduction gear to a propeller of 56-inch diameter and 48-inch pitch that turns over at 300 revolutions per minute for a normal continuous speed of 9 knots. The engine sits on blocks alongside the boatshed now, with fuel, water, and exhaust lines hooked up, and it is used as a morale builder. Push the button and the elegant thing quietly starts turn-ing over as a prelude to the effortless power it will furnish.

The equipment throughout Bill Tren-holme's boat will be to simple commercial stan-dards — strong, heavy, and cranked up for a long run.

The next ship, *Grime*, is about the same over-all length as Trenholme's vessel, and she is near, but short of, the practical limit in strength and weight of construction for the heaviest boats designed to work in ice. Originally, she was designed with a timbered-up horseshoe stern, similar to that on many of the nineteenth-century Pacific Coast steam schooners, and I believe that such a stern would be a better device for the hull than the double-ender finally

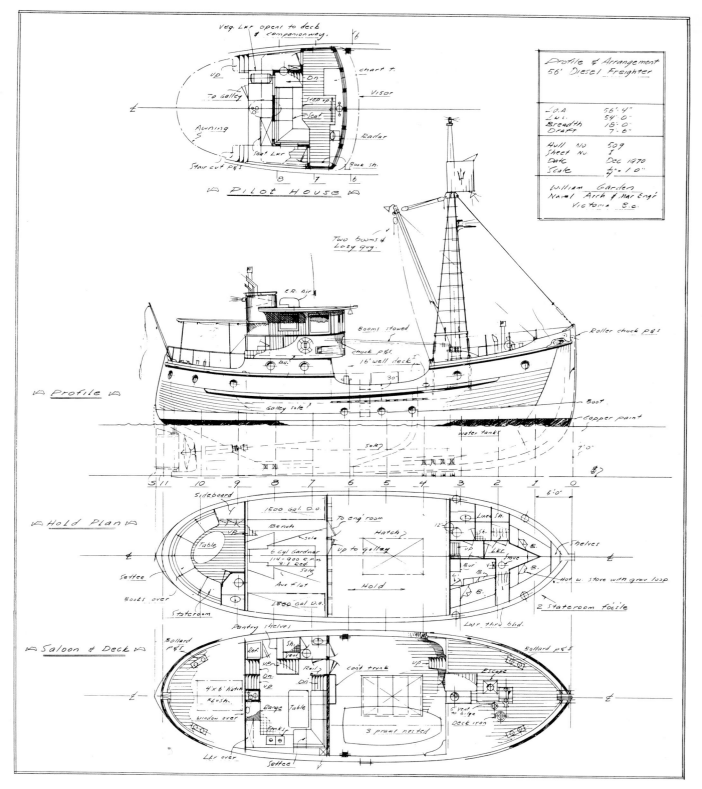

decided on. Either termination, however, gives nearly the same room.

Grime's 18 feet of breadth and 56 feet of length make a deck area of impressive proportions. The deck plan can be a good starting point, so let's go on board at the amidships, starboard, gangway, the owner's side — five steps up and a swing over the 12-inch wide rail cap. We're faced first with three little nested prams, originally designed for a 75-foot ketch

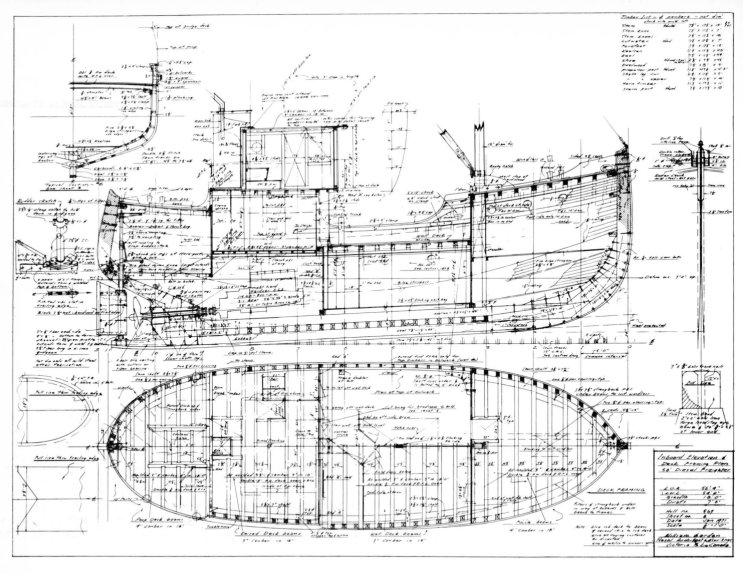

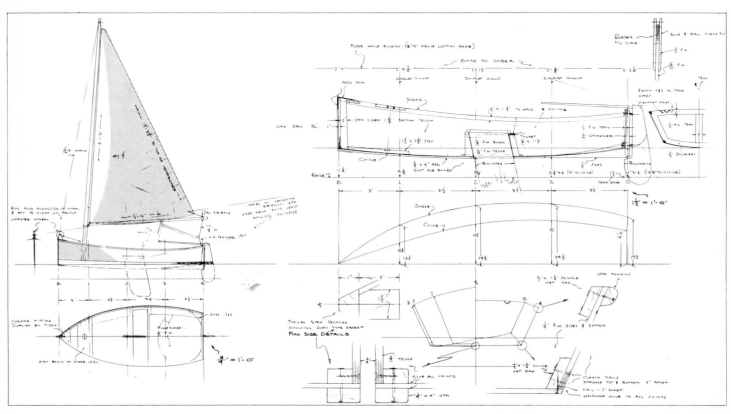

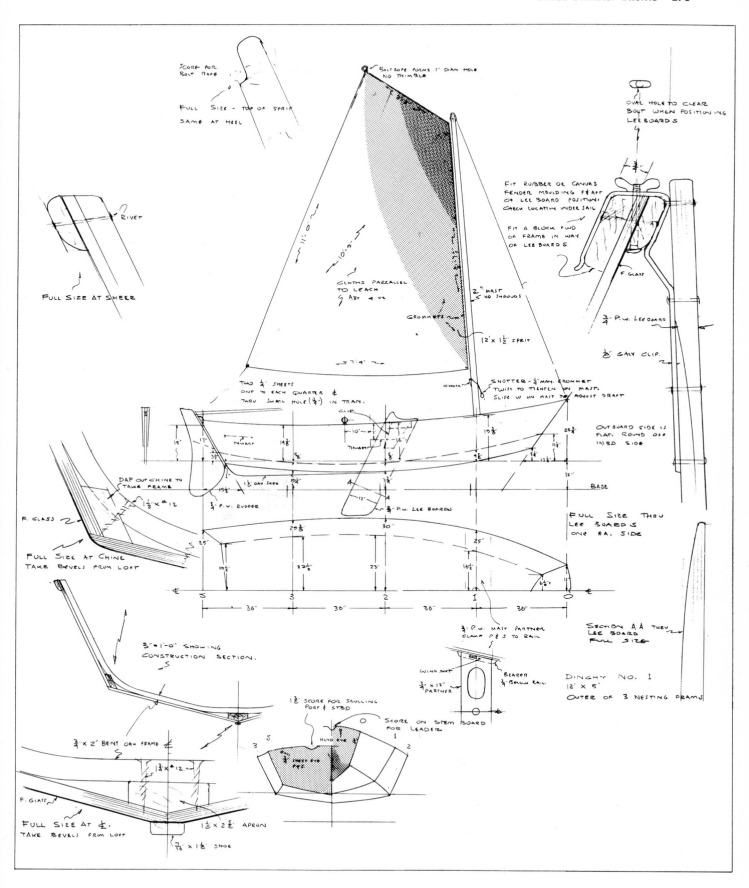

SCORE FOR BOLT ROPE

FULL SIZE - TOP OF SPRIT SAME AT HEEL

RIVET

FULL SIZE AT SHEER

BOLTROPE FORMS 1" DIAM HOLE NO THIMBLE

OVAL HOLE TO CLEAR BOLT WHEN POSITIONING LEEBOARDS

FIT RUBBER OR CANVAS FENDER MOULDING F&AFF OF LEE BOARD POSITION CHECK LOCATION UNDER SAIL

FIT A BLOCK FWD OF FRAME IN WAY OF LEE BOARDS

F. GLASS

CLOTHS PARALLEL TO LEACH Abt 4 oz

2" MAST NO SHROUDS

GROMMETS

12' x 1½" SPRIT

¾" P.W. LEEBOARD

⅛" GALV CLIP.

SNOTTER - ¼" MAN. GROMMET TWIST TO TIGHTEN ON MAST SLIDE UP ON MAST TO ADJUST DRAFT

OUTBOARD SIDE IS FLAT. ROUND OFF INBD SIDE

TWO ¼" SHEETS ONE TO EACH QUARTER & THRU SMALL HOLE (¼") IN TRAN.

DAP OUT CHINE TO TAKE FRAME

1½" x #12

F. CLASS

FULL SIZE AT CHINE TAKE BEVELS FROM LOFT

¾" P.W. RUDDER

1½" OAK SHEE

¾" P.W. LEE BOARDS

BASE

FULL SIZE THRU LEE BOARDS ONE EA. SIDE

SECTION AA THRU LEE BOARD FULL SIZE

3" = 1'-0" SHOWING CONSTRUCTION SECTION.

¾" x 2" BENT OAK FRAME

1½" x #12

F. GLASS

FULL SIZE AT ℄ TAKE BEVELS FROM LOFT

1½" x 2⅝" APRON

⅞" x 1½" SHOE

1½" SCORE FOR SCULLING PORT & STBD

SCORE ON STEM BOARD FOR LEADER

WING NUT

¾" x 12" PARTNER

BEARER ¾" BELOW RAIL

¾" P.W. MAST PARTNER CLAMP P & S TO RAIL

DINGHY NO. 1
12' x 5'
OUTER OF 3 NESTING PRAMS

and built in plywood. These are handy boats; they nest well and solve the dinghy problem with a crowd on board and limited deck space. Take the little one so yours won't be on the bottom. Over to port is a nice little sailing dinghy, so here is a regular fleet.

Looking over the nested boats, we can see a cargo hatch with battens, staples, and wedges; the high coamings lead into a hold about 15-feet square, serviced by a pair of sturdy cargo booms. The booms stow port and starboard on the bridge wing chocks and are amply strong to swing a car on board or to load her up with all sorts of interesting loot. Forward on the port side of the well-deck is a short, sturdy ladder leading up to the forecastle deck. Directly alongside this ladder is the Dutch-doored booby hatch entrance to the forecastle.

Going on up the steps, we have about 15-feet of rising deck ahead with mooring bollards port and starboard, a pair of heavy bow rollers on the stemhead, and, at station two just forward of the mast, a hydraulic, spool, anchor windlass carrying 60 fathoms of half-inch wire rope swiveled to two shots of three-quarter inch stud-link chain and a 300 pound Forfjord anchor. The extra roller is a standby to take a 60 pound kedge, one shot of half-inch chain, and 600-feet of three-quarter inch nylon. A 24-inch chock rail backs up the stem and dies out at the break, and, along with the pipe stanchions, which carry a half-inch wire rope rail, gives real security when working forward. The smoke stack vents a forecastle hot-water heater, and the cowl vents lead below.

Let's stroll aft now, down the ladder and along the port well-deck to the two-inch teak, three-plank, edge-bolted, gasketed Dutch-door and look in the top half. Here is a galley with room for a 300-pound cook, pots, pans, and

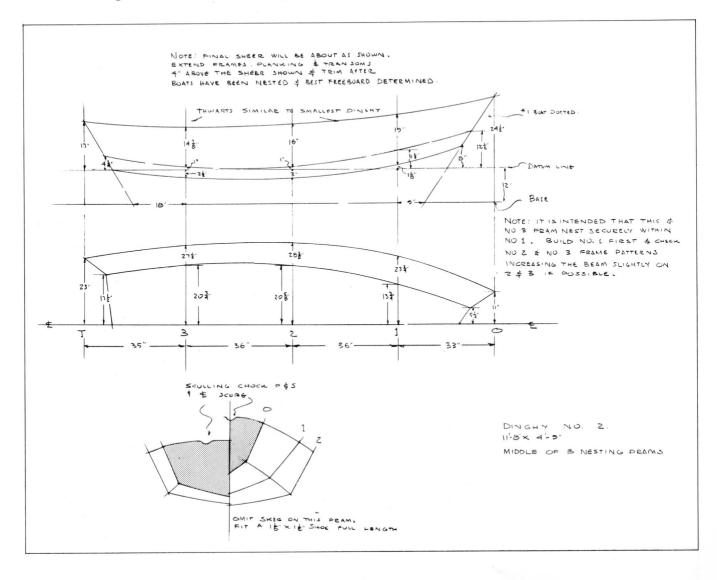

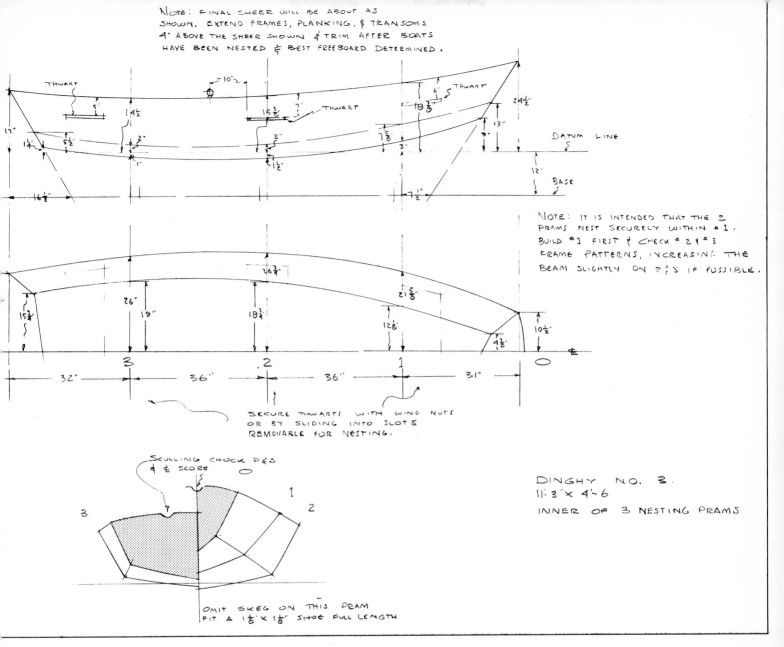

Note: Final sheer will be about as shown. Extend frames, planking, & transoms 4" above the sheer shown & trim after boats have been nested & best freeboard determined.

Note: It is intended that the 2 prams nest securely within #1. Build #1 first & check #2 & #3 frame patterns, increasing the beam slightly on #2's if possible.

Secure thwarts with wing nuts or by sliding into slots removable for nesting.

Sculling chock P & S & E score

Dinghy No. 3.
11'-3" × 4'-6
Inner of 3 nesting prams

Omit skeg on this pram
Fit a 1½" × 1½" shoe full length

lockers galore. Slip in and sit behind the big table; directly across from you is a 600-pound "marine comfort" oil range, with a coal or garbage burner alongside, a nice oven, warming bins, and some pleasant nickel-plated filigree to set off the dull-black stove polish.

Along the starboard side of the galley is a double sink with lockers under the drainboard and along the aft bulkhead. The drainboard is two-foot ash properly grooved to drain into the sinks and scrubbed bone white to match the heavy table that we're leaning on. Amidships the galley is split with the exhaust uptake and stove flue, then to port is the stairway up via another booby hatch with Dutch-doors to a broad poop deck, with bollards, hatch, and all surrounded by a stout rail with a rain and sun

awning over — an ideal place for the afterguard to enjoy a quiet nip and watch the sun go down.

Directly below the poop deck is a nice cabin with bath, curved settee berths, a sideboard bar, and six brass portlights looking out astern. This cabin can be quickly cleared to make way for kegs of ambergris, rum, or other priority cargo, but as a snug gathering and moderate boozing place, it will be cherished.

Back in the galley now: directly facing the aft stair is a brass-treaded teak stair leading up to the tee-headed pilothouse, which extends the width of the ship, almost 16-feet inside measure. There's excellent visibility here; the house is watertight and has doors port and starboard leading aft to sheltered outside wings. Across the after end is a raised, L-shaped settee, ideal to sit on and watch the miles slide by. There are charts to port, a radar to starboard, and amidships a 42-inch brassbound teak wheel with "God Save The King" on the hub. The windows outboard and port and starboard drop in pockets, the Dutch-doors lead out to the wing bridges, and the whole thing is finished in narrow, vee-edge varnished staving. The stack is aft on the centerline, and across the forward curve of the pilothouse, on a thick, teak nameboard, is carved and picked out in gilt the ship's name, *Grime*, escorted by dolphins port and starboard. Running lamps are recessed in the wings, followed by life rings chocked off with water lights.

One flight below is the galley and a stair down forward leads to the hold. Around the corner, through the engine-room door, and we're faced with a lovely Gardner, a 6L3 developing 114 horsepower at 900 revolutions per minute. It has a 3:1 reduction gear turning a propeller of 52-inch diameter by 48-inch pitch at 300 revolutions per minute. There are real horses here. The engine is almost 10-feet long; it's the six-cylinder version of Bill Trenholme's eight. There's ample power here for the *Grime*, and the eight is more than Bill will need, but a reasonable match in either case.

So there you have it: three husky boats suitable for pleasure voyaging or for hard work.

29 *Kingfisher*, a Diesel Boat

LOA — 42′ 0″
LWL — 39′ 6″
Beam — 14′ 6″
Draft — 5′ 3″
Displacement — 57,000 pounds
Ballast — 10,000 pounds

A. J. Fisher's diesel boat at 42 feet by 14 feet 6 inches is a close relative of the *Grime*, with a generally similar ratio of large midsection to length and some of the feel of the old West Coast steam schooners in outboard appearance.

The plans show an all-wooden boat of traditional heavy construction, but the final decision was to build *Kingfisher* in one-off fiberglass, using a male, strip-planked plug or core with a formed-in keel. The mahogany core is heavily fiberglassed to the weight of a normal glass-only boat. The keel forms are removed, but the mahogany shell is retained, forming a permanent, insulating liner. The glass-over-wood core works out quite well as long as the glass is of sufficient thickness to withstand any wood movement. This method has proven itself with thousands of boats of the glass-skin, wood-hull era. The main variation is that, after glassing is completed and she's right side up, the deadwood forms are pulled out, leaving a clean, level, keel trough to take bilge lines, sump, ballast, or whatever is required for the particular model. The strip-built core terminates about a foot from what would be the garboard seam. Bulkheads are erected prior to planking and are used as molds, supplemented by ad-ditional molds as intermediates. *Windstar*, discussed earlier, was also built by this method, and a review of her plans will be more revealing as to method. The drawings illustrating *Kingfisher* will suffice for layout and major features and give the heavy-wood man some enjoyment.

After *Kingfisher*'s hull is right side up, the beams, deck, and superstructure will go on, as with a wooden construction plan. The beams are bolted and glued below the sheer harpin, which is sandwiched between the beams and deck. The decks are wood set in Thiokol rubber over a ply subdeck.

I've made a little sketch of her chugging along on some sort of brave voyage. The poke-stick boom forward is to put a skiff on the forward deck, and one pipe davit is fitted aft to put another athwartships abaft the stack. Nothing like lots of dinghies for a cruising boat in the Northwest and Alaska. With one dinghy for each two people, we gain true flexibility when at anchor; the three little nested prams shown with the *Grime* make good sense here, too. Your own dinghy to explore with or go visiting in is most relaxing when cruising in another's boat.

Here we have room for a nine-footer to

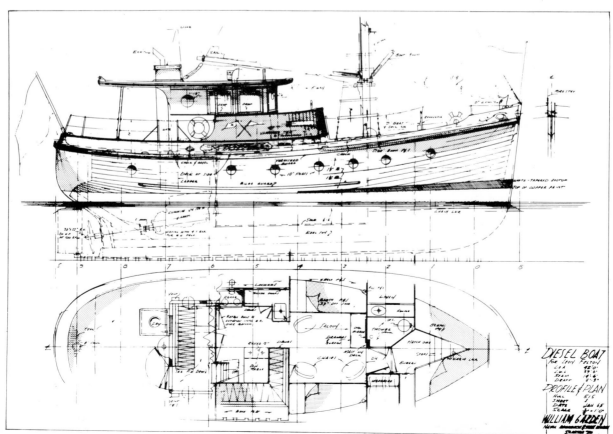

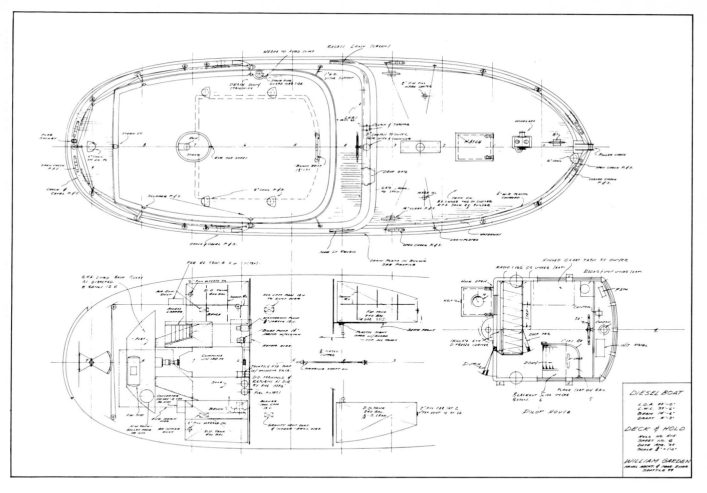

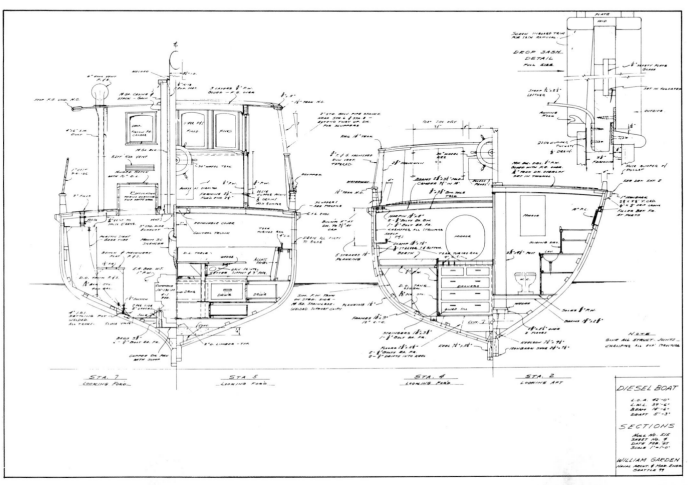

DIESEL BOAT

L.O.A. 42'-0"
L.W.L. 39'-6"
BEAM 14'-6"
DRAFT 5'-3"

DECK & HOLD

HULL NO. 515
SHEET NO. 6
DATE APR. 65
SCALE ⅜"=1'-0"

WILLIAM GARDEN
NAVAL ARCH'T & MAR. ENGR.
SEATTLE 99

PILOT HOUSE

DROP SASH DETAIL
FULL SIZE

STA. 7
LOOKING FORD.

STA. 5
LOOKING FORD.

STA. 4
LOOKING FORD.

STA. 2
LOOKING AFT.

DIESEL BOAT

L.O.A. 42'-0"
L.W.L. 39'-6"
BEAM 14'-6"
DRAFT 5'-3"

SECTIONS

HULL NO. 515
SHEET NO. 4
DATE FEB. 65
SCALE 1"=1'-0"

WILLIAM GARDEN
NAVAL ARCH'T & MAR. ENGR.
SEATTLE 99

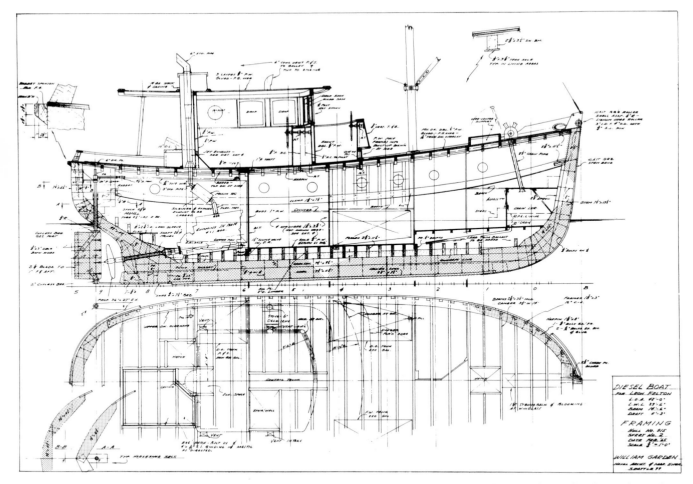

starboard forward and a canoe to port. The canoe, in particular, is a wonderful exploring boat. For rough knocking around, I've packed an aluminum canoe for several years and find it to be the first boat overboard in most anchorages. Come to think of it, it's the top one, but anyway, fit plenty of boats. And learn to row. Only seven percent of all boatmen today can row properly, and a mere half of one percent can scull. My old friend Harry Hardaway came up with these figures and they certainly seem accurate. More competent sailors and powerboatmen are afloat today than at any other time, but put most of them in a rowboat and it looks like a thing propelled by fans. A nice, clean, feathered stroke — standing, sitting, facing forward or backward — is a pleasant way to get across the water. There are many foredeck specialists today, or those who excel at making a sailboat go, but there are few all-around natural watermen.

I like a proper bridge on a boat, and here we have a space with about four feet from the pilothouse to the dodger with a wheel inside and out. There is shelter port and starboard alongside the wheelhouse. Around the poop deck there is a lifeline, with the option of a tan canvas weathercloth around the rail. Here we have room for steamer chairs and Hudson Bay lap robes.

The wheelhouse plan shown below the deck layout indicates a Spartan control station with a nice observation settee along the aft bulkhead. A pilot chair not shown will be located abaft the wheel, and to starboard is the companionway leading below. Flanking this is a polished brass handrail, with teak seat plank on top of the rail. This is a nice flat place to perch on, and a middle rail will take your heels.

Diesel oil capacity is 1,500 gallons and the water capacity is 240 gallons. The diesel tanks are of black iron and the water tank is stainless steel.

A. J. and his crew are building *Kingfisher* in Michigan for extended cruising in the Lakes and on the Atlantic seaboard.

30 *Crystal C* and *Ding Ho*, Two Diesel Cruisers

Crystal C
LOA — 53' 10"
Beam — 16' 6"
Draft — 3' 5"
Displacement — 41,700 pounds
Power — Twin 370 Cummins V-8 turbo-charged diesels,
2:1 reduction, 230 continuous hp
Speed — 18.75 knots at 2,600 rpm

Ding Ho
LOA — 58' 0"
Beam — 17' 0"
Draft — 3' 5"
Displacement — 46,760 pounds
Power — Same as *Crystal C*
Speed — See power curve

Crystal C is 53 feet 10 inches overall and 48 feet on the waterline, and has 16 feet 6 inches of breadth. She is powered by twin 370 Cummins through vee drives, and her cruising speed is about 18 knots. Philbrooks Shipyard built her for Art Christopher in 1968.

The arrangement was developed originally with Vic Franck for his *Viboco II* and gives three reasonably roomy double staterooms, one with a private bath. The pilothouse is above the galley and the main stateroom, which took some juggling to fit but which has proven most pleasant in service. The layout gives the feeling of one-level living from the transom to the forward cabin. Big windows let in good light and

air, and she has a feeling of roominess throughout.

The profile and plan illustrate the galley-saloon arrangement. With teak woodwork, the galley theme is that of a study-bar rather than a kitchen, so the areas seem to blend very well. Both an oil stove and an electric stove are fitted; the refrigerator is located forward and the sink with lockers is aft. Oil stoves are favored in the Northwest because of the damp weather. A pleasant bar faces the main saloon, and hatches in the saloon sole give access to a large storage area for case goods and spare gear.

These big locker spaces give us lots of trouble in a fast boat, since invariably the

Crystal C, a stylish diesel cruiser (photo by Dane Campbell).

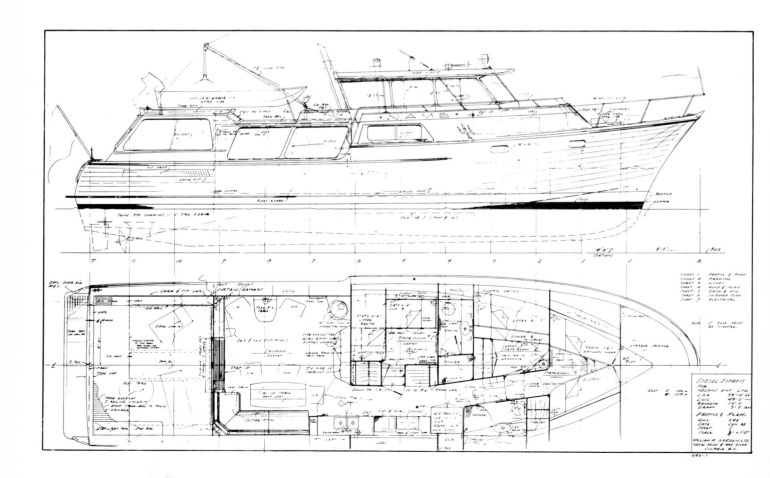

owner will accumulate a couple of tons of stuff that raise hell with speed. "As built" and new on trials, she should run continuously at close to 20 knots at 2,600 turns, with an upper limit of 3,000 revolutions. Weight and horsepower are the principal items entering into the speed calculations for a planing boat, and a disciplined owner can keep dumping things overboard and maintain reasonable performance, but invisible accumulation, such as another 75-pound coat of paint, heavier carpets, 20 cases of beer, and a bigger deck boat, causes a reduction in speed.

It is worth questioning whether stylish powerboats and competitive sailboats should be included in a hardcover book, since styles change rapidly in these fields. When you read this years hence and this design and others have become antiques, you must blame them on Roger Taylor, president of International Marine Publishing Company, who asked that powerboats be included in what was originally to be a book of sailing boats. Forgive me if some look

dated when you see this, but when they came out, some were widely admired.

The framing plan shown is for a 58-foot version of *Crystal C*, and basically she has the same structure as the 53-foot 10-inch model. We did about 30 express cruisers of this general construction theme, which consists of a cold-molded, double skin with sawn frames and bulkheads supporting longitudinal framing. The 58-footer herewith is Harold Walling's *Ding Ho*. The power package is the same as for the smaller boat. You will notice the engine and tanks are well aft for an ideal distribution of weights.

The hull form has worked out well; from the photo you can see her trim at speed. Each bottom section is the same arc. The after underbody is twisted, with the chine dropping and the centerline or rabbet rising for a good fast running release. A fixed wedge, which is 5/8-inch thick at the trailing edge, is fitted across the transom to a point 12-inches forward. For this weight and velocity of hull, the size of the wedge

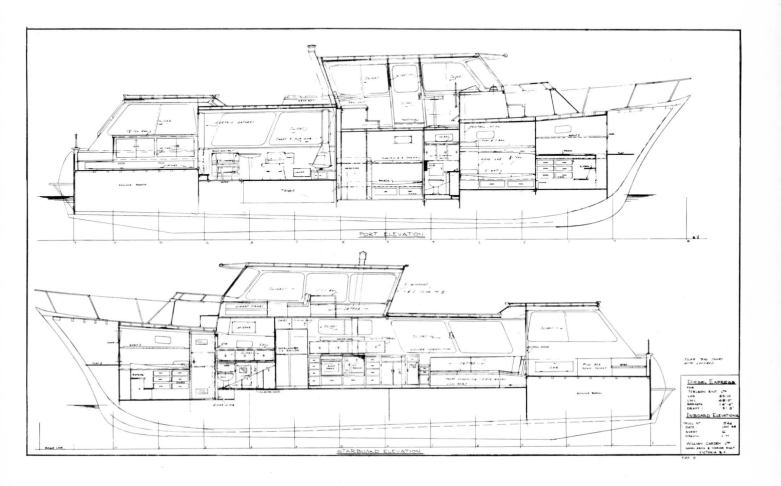

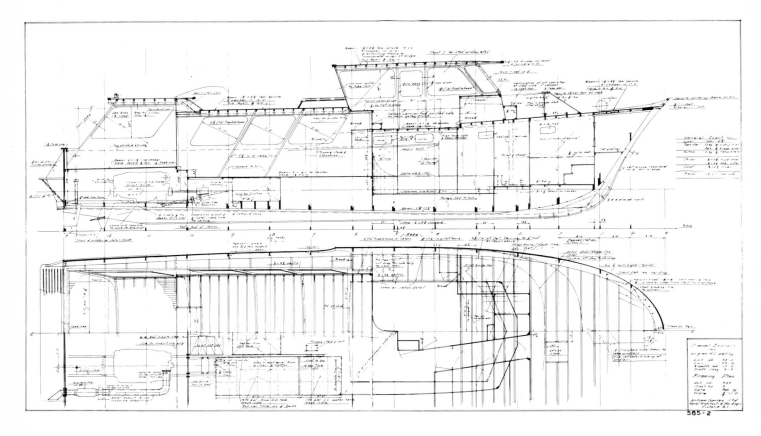

seems ideal. Wedges are difficult things to calculate and seem to require minor adjustment with each new model. We've built nearly identical hulls, one with wedges and one with a deeper transom immersion and greater angle of attack to the afterbody and found that the wedged model was the better running boat. So what seems to be an add-on afterthought is like the cupped propeller — where applicable, it is an efficient termination of the plane. In the case of the wedge, the boat's trim is improved, speed is increased, and, if not overdone, the performance is better in every way. Anyone having adjustable tabs on a fast boat will know the effectiveness of a small foil in a high-velocity flow. On boats of this size, where athwartships crew shifting and weight is relatively unimportant, we've found that the fixed wedge is the best solution to ideal longitudinal trim.

A long, straight keel for strength, directional stability, and ease of drydocking has been fitted. Aft, the keel is nipped up for quick maneuvering. Good, big rudders assure positive control under one engine or when running slowly before a bad sea. The little, inexpensive, pie plates under most boats work fine at speed,

but a real pair of blades will make most operations a vast improvement. The rudder stock, glands, and ports all have to be about twice their normal size to handle the increased moment of large blades, but their cost is well worth it.

The elevation drawings of *Crystal C* are shown to give a better idea of the pilothouse heights. The seat and settees to starboard are over the passageway or galley, while to port, where floor space in the pilothouse is shown, we have 6-feet 2-inches of headroom. The main stateroom is a step below the galley level to gain this headroom.

These are nice boats, but they are a terrible jolt to the pocketbook in building cost and yearly upkeep. Remember that, after trading lost interest on the invested capital for the pleasure of having the boat, we're still faced with the initial cost being duplicated every 6 to 10 years in operating cost, moorage, upkeep, fuel, insurance, crew, and the hundred and one leaky-pocket items. Tonight, as I was chugging in with the *Merlin*, the *We'll Sea*, discussed earlier, went sliding past, outward bound with a load of styrofoam on deck to raise a sunken

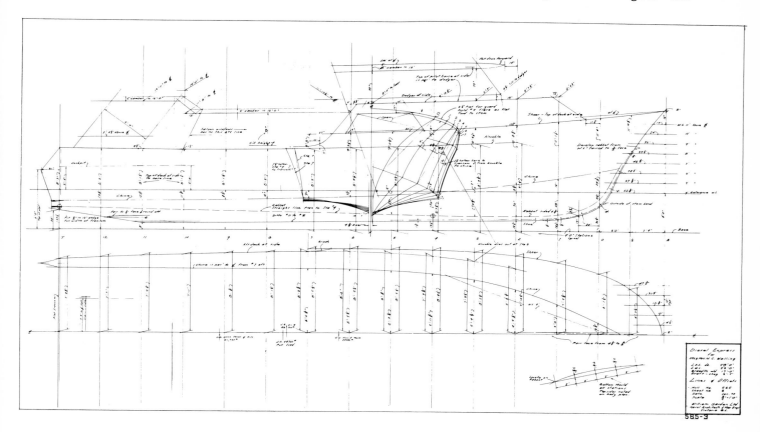

wreck. She looked like a real little ship, but even at 40-feet, she's a big investment unless you can put her to work occasionally as Ted Hopkins does. A 32-foot powerboat seems to be closer to an ideal size — you'll have lots of loose change left to jingle around in your pocket as you worry about where to camp the extra guests, and there will be ample room for almost any summer boating alongshore.

31 *Kaprice*, a Diesel Yacht

LOA — 60'
Beam — 17'
Draft — 5' 0"
Displacement — 84,000 pounds
Ballast — 10,000 pounds
Power — Caterpillar D.337 T diesel
Propeller — 36" diameter × 30" pitch
Speed — 10 knots

In these days when people seem to shed boats as often as wives, it's a privilege to do a boat for someone who thoroughly enjoys a boat and keeps her for a long time. Vic Franck built *Kaprice* in the winter of 1960-61 for Nat and Kay Paschall, who have enjoyed her and cruised extensively in her in northwestern coastal waters for the last several years.

Some boats seem to end up that way as a good member of the family; some seem destined never to go anyplace; while others, occasionally the most improbable ones, end up with a hundred thousand sea miles past their keels. There's no telling what the future holds for each. A lot goes into all of these small ships — time, thought, and effort. After that it's a disappointment to get through the construction only to find that the owner really hasn't the time to use her, plans have changed, etc., and she's put on the market. *Kaprice* is one of the blessed, with one owner and one skipper — that grizzled old sea-dog, Krist Martinsen.

Construction is of wood, carvel planked of 1½-inch yellow cedar on oak frames sided 2½-inches, molded 1¾-inches, and 10 inches center-to-center. Decks are of double plywood with a glass overlay. The basic structural details may be followed on the drawings.

Perhaps nothing is like a good, wooden boat. A neat brass plaque in the Canoe Cove Ltd. office reads, "If God wanted us to have fiberglass boats, he would have made fiberglass trees."

The plans show the steering gear, propeller, machinery, and piping layout, along with some sections to give a general idea of the below-decks arrangement. Outboard, the profile indicates a motorship type with passage decks alongside the saloon and a break in the deck. There are steps at the galley-pilothouse bulkhead and a single step at the pilothouse console inside the bridge dodger. This seems to be a practical, shipshape plan for a family boat. The galley-saloon can be combined or a sliding panel over the serving bar can be used to shut the galley off for clean-up privacy.

Two double staterooms are forward of amidships; the forecastle is entered through a hatch forward of the dodger. The saloon of *Kaprice* is in particular a most pleasant area. The colors are good and the traffic flow seems close to ideal for a pleasant cruising boat.

For the size, this layout and theme forms an interesting cruising yacht of relative simplicity and reasonable performance.

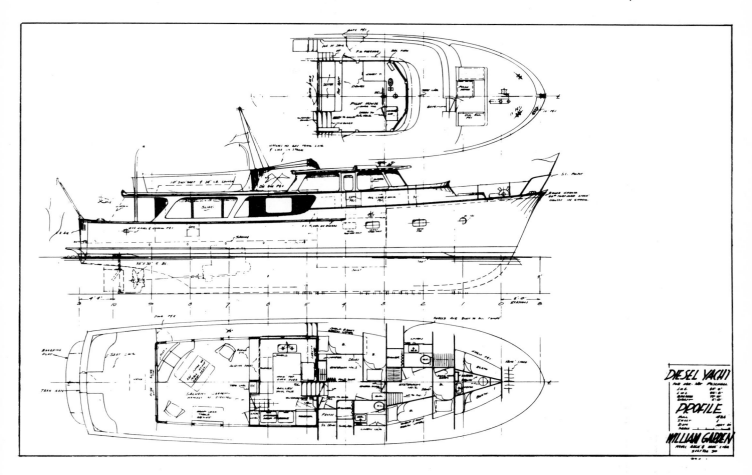

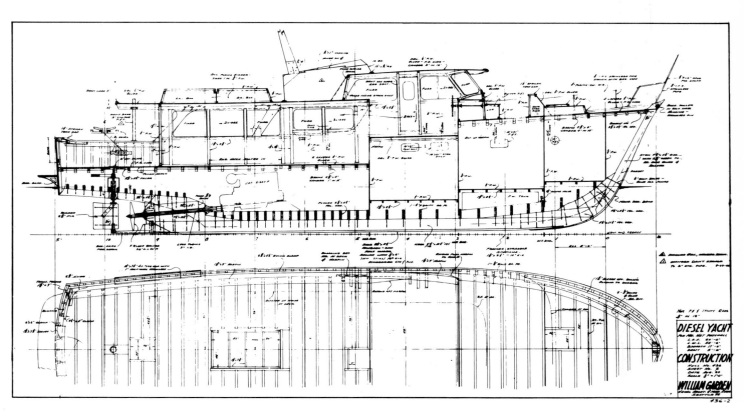

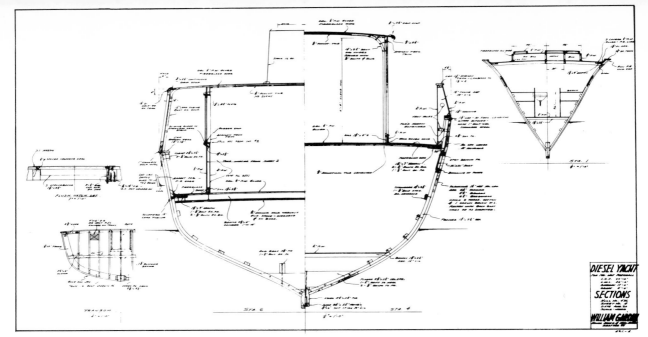

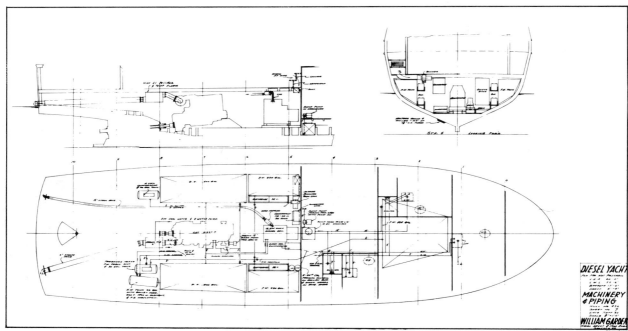

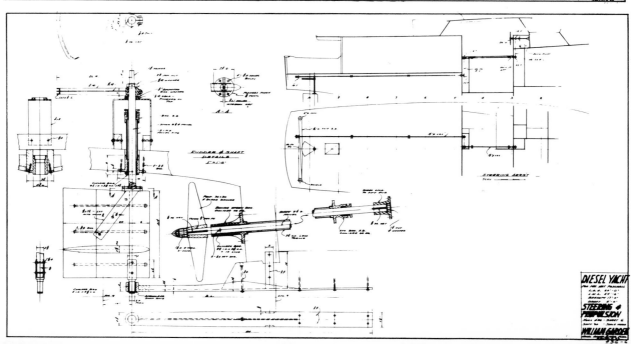

32 *Tlingit*, an Economy Commuter

LOA — 62' 0"
Beam — 7' 6"
Beam at WL — 4' 6"
Draft — 3' 6"
Power — Easthope 3-cylinder 30, gasoline,
463 cubic inch piston displacement
Speed — 10.2 knots continuous

Tlingit was designed as a maximum-velocity, minimum power, lumber, and material, "doomsday" boat, able to run effortlessly at 10 knots on about two gallons per hour fuel consumption or 20 hp net. With a 30-year-old rebuilt 3-cylinder Easthope gasoline engine, she slides along at an easy 10.2 knots continuous speed, accompanied by the reassuring boogeldy, boogeldy of the old-time engine, every part visibly busy with its appointed task, a pleasant revelation to many of today's boatmen who aren't quite sure that engines are hollow.

A tape of one of these old engine's pleasant running sound would be good to drown out the tiring hum of today's 2,000-rpm-plus machine. Plug it in to a speaker on the dash or to earphones and enjoy a day chugging along while your engine, particularly if it is one of today's two-cycles, drives everyone else around the bend. Sound is a deadly thing, and I've often wondered why the resonance of a kitchen fan doesn't move more noise-sensitive housewives to take midday nips.

The reasoning behind *Tlingit* was dictated by a nice, old Easthope that we had rebuilt and available in the shop, plus the need of my nearby island-neighbor, Dick Stewart, for a fast, interesting, ferry launch that would be able to pack a good load and also be capable of a steady 10 knots in any normal conditions here on the Gulf of Georgia. Dick is a completely open-minded boatman of long experience in everything from light-displacement, ocean racers to tugboats and claims that the only thing that confuses him is logic. We first thought of how a 60-foot Indian dugout canoe would go with the Easthope; we decided to go with the maximum structure and economy that could be achieved with a given pile of 2 × 4's and plywood. Before she was built, her design was tow-tested with a one-inch-scale model. We first tried a plumb-bowed model for maximum waterline length but found the model with the dory forebody far superior in rolling down the bow wave and in sliding over a chop.

I have included a couple of photos to show how shapely a motor canoe can be with straight

Tlingit might have straight frames, but that doesn't stop her from looking slick.

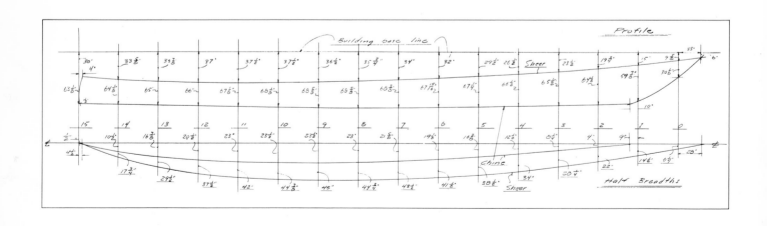

35 *Captain Teach*, an Economy Cruiser

LOA — 80'
Beam — 11'
Draft — 5' 0" nominal
Displacement — 47,000 pounds cruising trim
Power — Cummins 903 diesel
Speed — 12.5 knots continuous

Captain Teach was built as a cruising version of Dick Stewart's *Tlingit* by the same crew at George Fryatt's Bel Aire shipyard in Vancouver. This larger edition on the same, simple, plywood theme has belied her somewhat rough and cutthroat name by being a most pleasant boat to cruise on board. She is the perfect vehicle for Dick Stewart's easy-going way of getting places afloat. To achieve a given cubic content, *Teach*, like *Tlingit*, has a relatively small midsection and long length in order to slide along with modest power at maximum efficiency. She is powered by a V-8 Cummins of 903 cubic inch piston displacement, which isn't much power when compared with the usual 80 footer's engine, but it's a good match for the *Teach*'s easy lines. The engine is fitted with a 2.14-to-1 reduction gear and a 28-inch diameter by 26-inch pitch propeller on a 2-inch diameter shaft. The propulsion group plan outlines the arrangement, and a good glass will help decipher the notes. *Teach* can attain a high average speed in nearly any coastwise summer weather.

A note from Dick in September, 1974, says: "Ran trials just before we came home, one-half fuel, one-third water, 625° exhaust temperature, 1,750 revolutions, almost 13 knots. Full fuel and water dropped about two-thirds knot. I feel most satisfactory." Earlier in the summer we had taken her out to sea and back. Around 12 knots is a pleasant cruising speed for relaxed travel, and 1,750 revolutions is about two-thirds of her top revolutions, which is more soothing than an engine putting out its limit and seemingly in danger of firing some of its costly parts through the pilothouse sole.

A designer gets to know an owner after a couple of boats, so with *Blue Heron* Casey or *Tlingit* Dick Stewart the first question you ask when entering the shop is, "What have you done to me today?" As *Teach* was built, the tanks indicated on the plan were enlarged to fill the after compartment, and the water tanks were proportionally increased. Every owner seems to add weights, and, in the case of increased tanks, the human sense of well-being

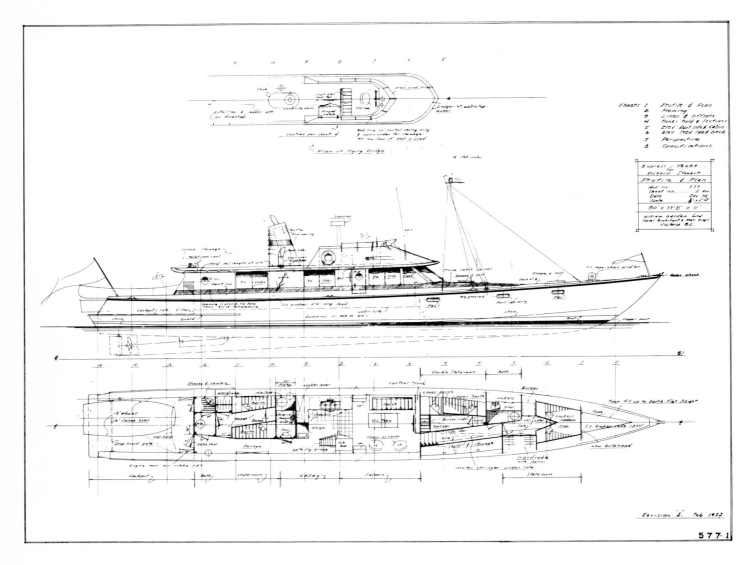

is best served by keeping them topped off full. The only way for the designer to fight that is to indicate a conservative speed estimate and a high waterline.

The tank plan shown indicates the general fuel arrangement with two tanks, the port one being subdivided at the forward baffle to form a separate, day tank. Either main tank can be valved by gravity to the day tank, which will then reflect the parent tank's level or, optionally, the port and starboard tanks may be left on the crossover and be drained at the same time. In either case, the fuel pump's return line continually dumps into the day tank, maintaining constant trim. Settling pots are fitted below the suction valves, and the tanks are well baffled for strength and to minimize free surface surge, and noise.

Steering is straightforward with a simple quadrant, cable, and sheaves, for ease of steering, trouble shooting, and pleasant control. This, I feel, is the best choice every time for a small boat as compared to manual hydraulic steering's mushy, no-feeling response. But you pay your money and take your choice; they both work.

Captain Teach's interior layout has proven to be a pleasant cruising arrangement, with the owner's stateroom on deck where he can sit up in bed to take a bearing or run around in his nightshirt resetting the anchor without bothering guests who are sleeping forward. Accommodations are at one level from the cockpit forward to the wheel, with a good oil-burning range about central for warmth. An engineroom entrance is between the stateroom and galley

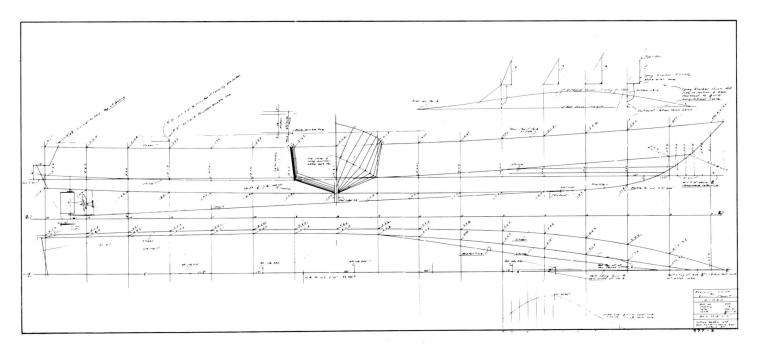

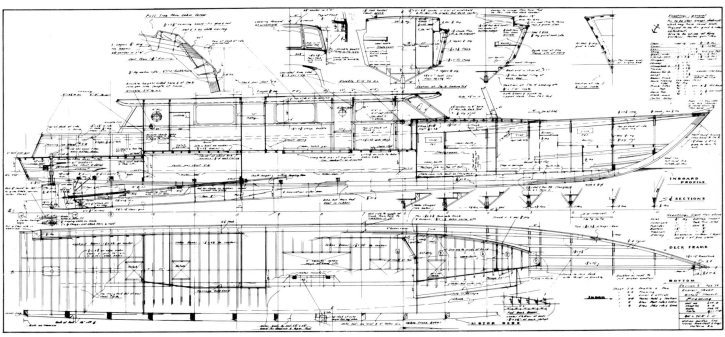

and is supplemented by big hatches in the sole for access to the engine for major work.

Forward, the accommodations consist of two double staterooms with one bath, plus a great array of storage bins. These staterooms are far removed from the deck accommodations, and no one can complain of a lack of two-couple privacy with this spread. On the *Teach*, it's quite a walk just to go aft to the galley for breakfast.

The hull form is that of a big, easy-lined sampan. For the designed speed, I've run the chines and buttock lines up aft, so in this way she differs from a hull designed for planing speeds. The sections are straight, and, in this elongated form, the plywood skin will wrap around without difficulty.

The topsides are formed with two layers of half-inch plywood, with the butts well staggered and glued. The bottom is three layers

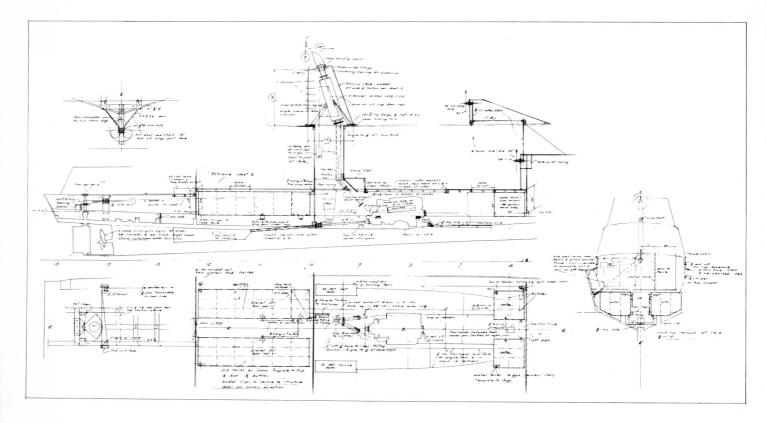

of half-inch plywood. The entire structure, with the exception of the keel, is covered with a heavy fiberglass skin. The longitudinals and frames are of 2 × 4's. She is designed to be built upside-down over the bulkheads, which are supplemented by station molds. The hull is framed out and planked as downhand work, then fiberglassed. The next step is to fit the keel assembly, which is through-bolted to the laminated inner keel as shown. The hull, which at the glassed stage looks like a beached whale, is then rolled over. When she is right-side up, the mechanical outfitting and deck work can proceed.

The deadwood aft is relieved for access to the tail-shaft bearings and to assist in maneuvering. She has proven to handle very well in close quarters, so the long drag of keel seems worthwhile for tracking or for directional stability plus ease of haulout.

The shipyard did their usual workmanlike job through the extent of the contract, which was to have the boat afloat, running, but stripped; although they did let a big-ship insulator do a magnificent lagging job on the exhaust uptake. He covered the little mouse pipe to the diameter of a garbage can. It is gorgeous workmanship, but unfortunately plugs the fidley entrance. Dick bows to it as he descends below, but I'd chain saw a great slab of it off or cut steps in the brute wide enough so that two could climb abreast.

Since the shipyard left off, she has been completed by tradesmen with two left hands and ten thumbs, with a few notable exceptions, so the *Teach* is not yacht style. But by careful scrutiny, you will see under the camouflage an interesting concept of simplicity, seagoing ability, and efficiency.

36 *Nereus*, a World Cruiser

LOA — 85'
LWL — 75'
Beam — 20' 6"
Draft — 8' 6" sea trim
Displacement — 320,000 pounds
Ballast — 40,000 pounds

The comfort, range, and ability of a yacht of *Nereus*'s size is interesting to contemplate, although much of the anticipated pleasure is neutralized by manning and upkeep problems. Perhaps a 32-foot waterline steel cutter, bone simple in equipment, would be the best choice for extended voyaging. But given the wherewithal, a background in boating to enable you to handle her yourself, and access to a couple of good men to keep her going, then a *Nereus* might come into focus.

The electrical and mechanical specialists required today have replaced the sailor crew of yesterday. Today, a couple of men well able to keep control over a wide range of equipment has replaced the services of half a dozen of the men required on board at the beginning of the power yacht era. So we replace a lot of people with a couple of people and a lot of equipment. Grief is just over the horizon in either case.

If this were the year 1887 and we were contemplating a vessel of the caliber of *Nereus*, in addition to the serious consideration of first cost, we would also have to consider the relatively massive cost of crew. From an accounting of that day, we would have to maintain and pay a crew as follows:

Captain or pilot —	$100 a month	
Engineer	—	$ 80 a month
Stoker	—	$ 40 a month
Cook	—	$ 40 a month (or any higher rate, as the proprietor might choose)
Steward	—	$ 50 a month
3 Deck Hands	—	$ 30 a month each

This makes a total outlay for wages of at least $400 a month. The commissary would cost at least as much more, the coal $200, and repairs and sundries, including men's uniforms, $540, making a total of $1,540 a month or $9,240 for the six-month season. The dollar then was solid gold.

In comparison to her 1887 counterpart, *Nereus* was designed to be operated by a competent owner and his friends, a skipper-engineer combination (which, incidentally, is a

Nereus has "passage-maker" written all over her (photo by Ray Krantz).

tough job to fill), and one or two hands, usually a seaman or two picked up for one voyage or transient dockside help to keep up with general maintenance.

Mechanically, however, the steamer of 1887 had it all over us for simplicity. Today the owner probably wants radar, loran, recording fathometer, high seas ship-to-shore phone, automatic pilot, electric lighting, central heat, air conditioning, intercom, evaporator, hot and cold pressure water, mechanical ventilation, refrigeration, deep freeze, automatic washer-dryer, and hi-fi or stereo. The complexity of these systems is balanced very slightly by the pilothouse-controlled and minimum-maintenance main engine, but the whole package would seem as impossibly complicated to the engineer of 1887 as the inside of a computer would to most of us today. An 1880 specification for the mechanics of a vessel of *Nereus*'s size would probably list the power plant as being one vertical, direct-acting engine, 16-inches by 16-inches, propeller 5½ feet in diameter turning 150 revolutions a minute, one high-pressure boiler with two furnaces, flues below and return through tubes, arranged for a working pressure of 100 pounds

per square inch, two iron water tanks, one hand fire pump, one zinc-lined icebox, coal-fired galley range, pump water closets, and manual water pump in the galley and in each toilet room. Steering chains would lead aft to a quadrant or patent screw gear, lamps would be oil, and the principal piece of navigation equipment would be a good compass.

Having cruised on boats of extreme simplicity and on boats of great complexity, I believe that we pay too high a price for the convenience of turning on a faucet rather than the pleasure of operating an easy-acting hand pump. Aside from today's basic mechanical components, the only piece of equipment that I really appreciate is the automatic pilot.

Nereus was designed to be a world cruiser. With sails and lots of wind she can easily and pleasantly make long ocean passages. Without sails, she is a first-class, small motorship. On an over-all length of 85 feet, she is 21 feet in breadth, draws 8 feet 6 inches, and is 75 feet long on the waterline.

The accommodation plan can be followed generally on the drawing. The owner's quarters consist of three double staterooms, with a roomy forecastle forward, a single stateroom for the captain, galley and saloon in the deckhouse, a large pilothouse, and — of particular interest — a roomy hold forward of the mainmast for stowage of motor bikes, skin diving gear, stores, and all the accumulation that ends up on board during a long voyage.

The engineroom is located aft, with ample bench space to work, good elbow room, and easy access to auxiliaries, main engine, and the various components. A flush, semi-permanent, deck hatch is located over the engineroom for access during major repairs, with a trolley rail under the boat deck overhang for hoisting. The engineroom contains a 300-horsepower, turbocharged, Caterpillar diesel, two 15-KW Onan auxiliary generators, batteries, switch panels, evaporator for making fresh water at sea, air conditioning, hot-water tank, air compressors, fresh- and salt-water pumps, and the maze of auxiliary equipment required on a modern vessel of this size. The engineroom leads up through a fidley to the after deck and watertight door, or through an alternate door into the main saloon for use when the vessel is buttoned

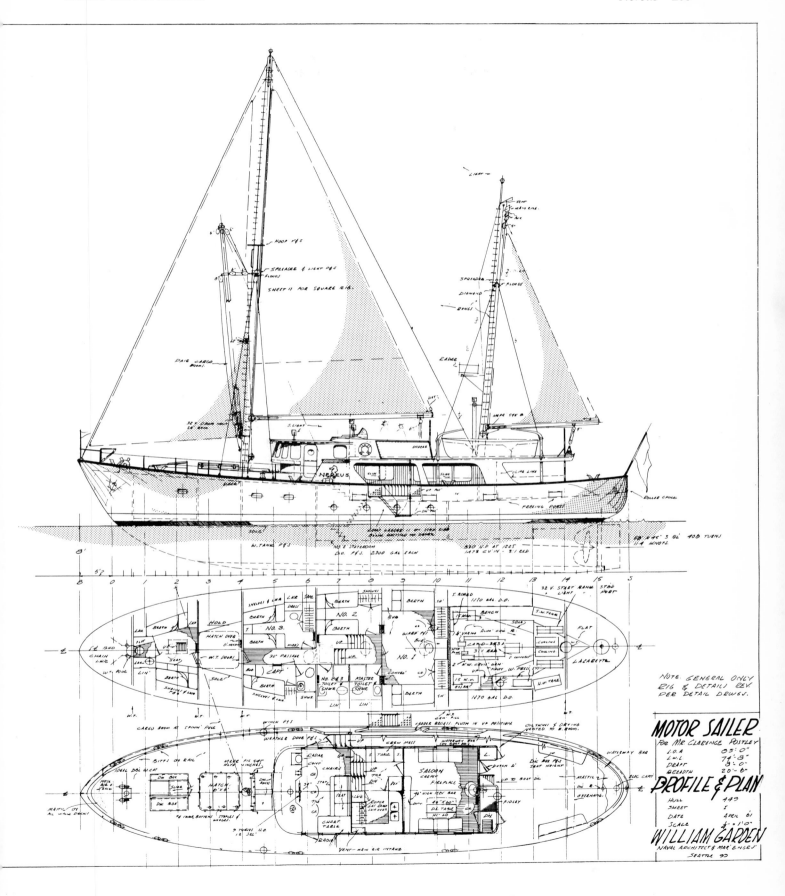

MOTOR SAILER
FOR MR. CLARENCE POSTLEY

L.O.A	85'-0"
L.W.L	74'-8"
DRAFT	9'-0"
BREADTH	20'-6"

PROFILE & PLAN

HULL	449
SHEET	5
DATE	APRIL 61
SCALE	½"=1'-0"

WILLIAM GARDEN
NAVAL ARCHITECT & MAR. ENGR'S
SEATTLE 99

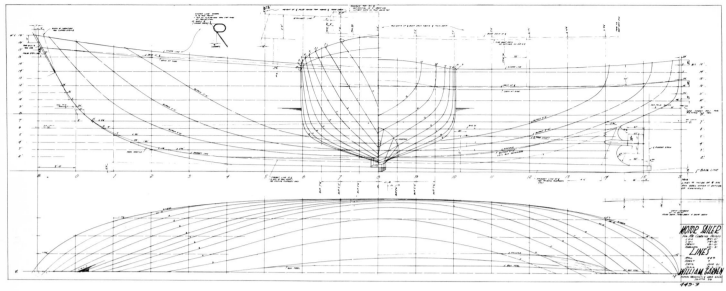

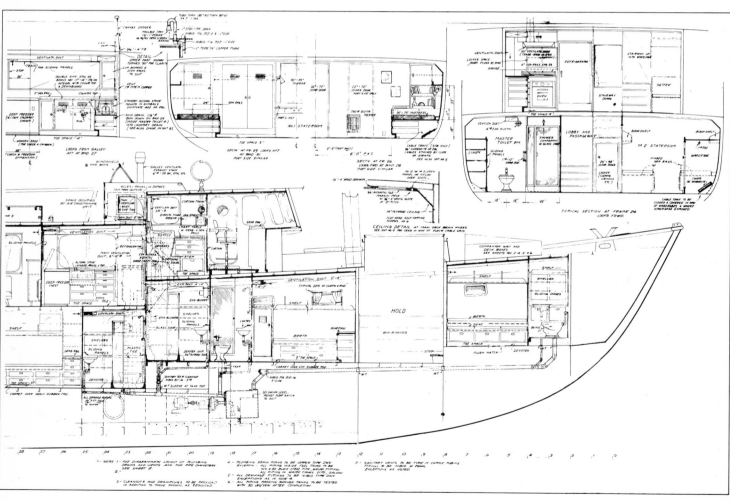

down in heavy weather. The toilet system is through Sloan valve toilets to a central sump tank. Mechanical fittings throughout are massive and of motorship rather than yacht caliber.

Structurally, I believe she is one of the

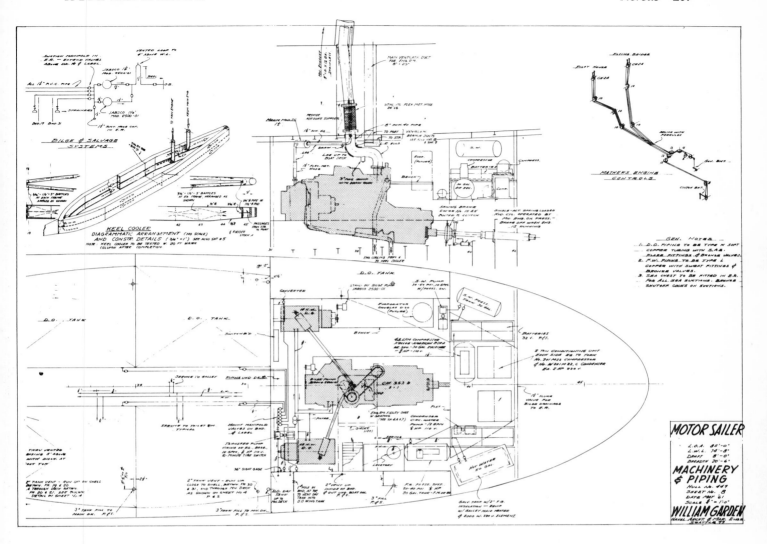

safest yachts of this size built to date, with heavy four-dog watertight doors throughout and watertight compartmentation on a horizontal plane at the double bottoms, which in turn is divided up into three athwartship cells. The deep tanks in the engineroom and double bottom tanks contain 7,000 gallons of diesel oil and 3,000 gallons of fresh water. She is of all-steel construction, with quarter-inch plating, and is transversely framed with T bars. The decks are quarter-inch steel covered with Dexotex mastic and terminate in a flat bar to form a waterway at the bulwarks. All deck fittings taking chafe are hot-dip galvanized before being welded to the structure, and steel elsewhere is treated before painting.

On deck, she gives the feeling of a small motorship with wide passage decks and good elbow and working room throughout. Starting from forward, twin Forfjord safety anchors are located in stainless steel hawse pipes, with a davit worked into the pulpit for anchor handling. The scuttle to the forecastle has deck boxes port and starboard for miscellaneous gear; and directly forward is an Ideal electric anchor windlass leading into a chain locker in the peak. The cargo hatch is located between the forecastle scuttle and the mast. This is a ship-type hatch with high coamings, hatch boards, battens, staples and wedges, and a canvas cover. From the stem to the pilothouse she is flush decked, then a deep break is formed to accommodate the galley, saloon, and sheltered after lounge deck. The steel pilothouse is situated on the forecastle level with stainless steel in the way of the compasses. Trico air swipes are fitted in the wheelhouse with fresh-water valves, and entry is made port and starboard through

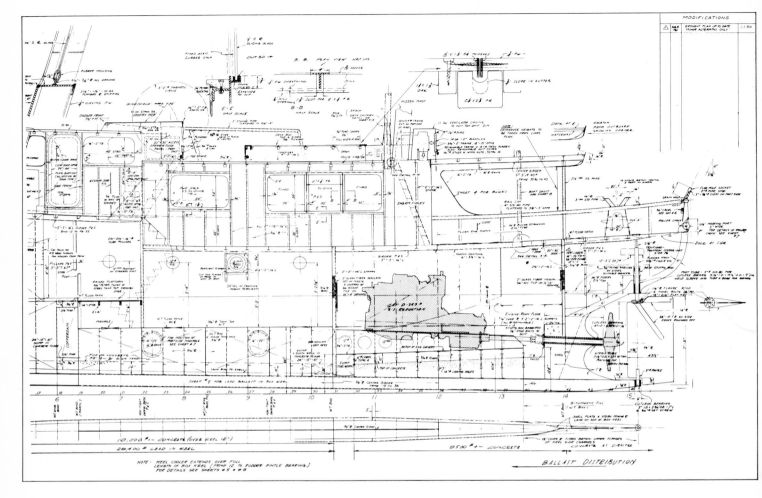

watertight Dutch doors. On the boat deck above is a dual steering station, compass, chart table, and duplicate controls. On the after end of the wheelhouse is the air intake for the air conditioning.

Shore boats are stored port and starboard aft — one 16-foot fiberglass fishing launch, inboard powered, and an outboard-powered fiberglass boat. The davits are electric, housed in lockers in the after end of the boat deck.

The rig will be of interest to the dyed-in-the-wool cruising yachtsman, since, in addition to the fore-and-aft mizzen, main, and jib, she originally carried a course of about 1,000 square feet and a raffee of approximately 600 square feet. The raffee is set from the deck, and the course is furled or set from the deck without going aloft. The brails can be seen in the photo. This is the same method used by many of the small barquentines of 60 years ago and has proven highly successful in this service on the *Nereus*. One man is able to set or take in the course in a fair breeze. A heavy track is secured

under the yard, and the course is set by casting off the brails and setting up on the outhaul. Either port or starboard side may be set, or both. The brails dead-end on the forward side of the sails, run through cringles on the leeches and lead back to the centerline through a block worked into a heavy centerline tabling and down to the pinrail. The brails generally secure the sail, and the man then goes aloft up the mast ladders to pass the gaskets. *Nereus*'s second owner removed the square rig, and she has since been a ketch.

The fore-and-aft rig consists of jib, mainsail, and mizzen of sufficient area to be of some assistance on long ocean passages and act as fair stabilizers under most conditions.

In form, *Nereus* is similar to the small, European, distant-water trawlers. In this case, however, we are operating without cargo, ice, or fish, and have a sailing rig, so she has 30,000 pounds of lead poured into the box keel section. Concrete ballast covers the lead to the top of the floors throughout, making a clean, cement hold